# ANNE BOLEYN

# ANNE BOLEYN

## VERCORS

*Translated from the French*
*by*
*Alexander MacLehose*

The Overlook Press
Woodstock, New York

First published in 1989 by
The Overlook Press
Lewis Hollow Road
Woodstock, New York 12498

Library of Congress Cataloging-in-Publication Data

Vercors, 1902–
Anne Boleyn.

Translation of: Anne Boleyn.

1. Anne Boleyn, Queen, consort of Henry VIII, King
of England, 1507-1536.   2. Henry VIII, King of England,
1491-1547.   3. Great Britain—History—Henry VIII,
1509-1547.   4. Great Britain—Queens—Biography.
I. Title.
DA333.B6V4713   1989        941.05'2'0924   [B]        88-22511
ISBN 0-87951-348-9

# Contents

# Acknowledgements

The author expresses his gratitude to M. André Miquel, administrator-general of the National Library, for the special facilities he so kindly made available to him; to Mme Geneviève Chastenet for the rare quality of the documents which she was able to produce; to Mr Christopher Dean for valuable pieces of information about Anne Boleyn; to Mr Russell Barnes for having enabled him to consult a work not normally accessible; to M. Yves Florenne for the trouble he took to identify anachronisms in the text.

But above all he must render to Caesar what is Caesar's. For the author would have had difficulty in bringing his work to a satisfactory conclusion if Mme Rita Barisse, his wife, had not closely collaborated in it; by selecting and translating significant extracts from the copious works extant on the reign of Henry VIII and on the sixteenth century in England and thus taking on the lion's share of the historical research; in keeping an eye on the often disconcerting spelling of proper names; and finally in rectifying numerous errors in the manuscript.

# Why Anne Boleyn?

*England is an Island*
Charles de Gaulle

Readers who do me the honour of keeping track of my published works have the right to ask why, rather than recount the story of the past twenty years and so bring up to date my *Hundred Years of the History of France*, I have turned aside: turned aside suddenly to concern myself with the life of an obscure queen of times long ago about whom the little that is known in France is that her husband Henry VIII caused her head to be cut off; and in England that she was first a coquette who had made her way up into a level of society where she had no business to be, and then a shocking wife. I used to take this accepted view of her myself.

My decision may therefore surprise, but I had two strong reasons for it.

The first was negative. These twenty years of French history (1962–82) were those of a new republic and one too close to our own time to allow any considered judgement upon it. Moreover, I had for reasons that are understood taken leave of politics, its public declamations, manifestos, controversies, ideologies and utopias. In consequence, I could do no more than watch from a distance the history of this period as it passed me by. Taking no part in it myself, I should have had nothing to say about it that others could not have said better.

The second, positive reason for my choice is that just then my thoughts were being drawn back to the forties, that most vivid period of my life, and I found myself face to face once more with an enigma which has possessed my mind ever since that time. Following the disaster which, in the wake of the surrender first of Austria and then of Czechoslovakia, had

9

overtaken in turn Poland, Norway, Denmark, Holland, Belgium, France; which had made Hitler master of Europe both by land and by sea so that all, Hitler the foremost, felt sure to see Britain crying quits in hopes of saving something from the wreck: a moment when any other people at such a crisis would have sought safety in negotiation – we saw Britain, quite the reverse, steel herself to press on with a war that to all appearance was already lost.

So I asked myself from what well-spring the British people standing solid behind Churchill – and Churchill himself – drew the resilience (if not the madness) to stand out all alone against an irresistible army and I could find only one answer: a robust determination to identify themselves with their island-fortress – an island under siege, isolated, open to attack, its garrison dramatically under strength, but protected by that formidable rampart, the sea: the sense this gave them of being a nation apart, different, a tight-knit unity, and able to make that coherence, that oneness within themselves the sufficient answer to no matter what assault. It was this rock-hard sense of nationhood that caused Hitler, like Napoleon, to falter; he saw in it the beginning of his end: saw it given to the rest of the world, with Europe and with France, to take the measure of him one day.

Even now, after a victory more costly than defeat, after an interminable struggle which left her exhausted, impoverished, stripped of her Empire; even today when she sees herself penned within her own back-yard, Britain remains just as much (if not more) imbued with this sense of being not only a nation but an island; and so a mini-continent on her own set apart from Europe and the rest of the world: with rights equal – or, as George Orwell would have put it, a little more than equal – to those of the nations opposite, *les autres*, her partners in the Common Market.

This consciousness of being in a class by herself, of singularity – superiority – from which in destiny's hour she drew the crazy courage to challenge this threat to her very survival: how did she come by it? In all the long history of England, whether in bad times or in good, nothing marks her off essentially from other nations that like herself have tasted defeat and victory in turn. So I went back into her past to look for the explanation. And it was in the course of this research that I came to realise the unexpected part played by one whose role on the stage of English history would appear at first sight to have been very much a secondary one – yes, Anne Boleyn. It was to this queen in the shadows that I felt I must assign a determining influence on England's evolution into awareness of being a nation apart, with the consequences we have seen. This is what has justified the choice I made.

Let me explain. Measured against 2000 years of history, this feeling of uniqueness and superiority that I speak of is a myth of comparatively recent date. Over a period much longer than these last four hundred years (in that earlier time the question of her island-character never came up) England was not or rather did not feel herself in any way different from other nations on that continent of Europe to which she knew she belonged. Not only because for centuries she had been in no position to identify herself, as in 1940 she did, with her island: an island of which she occupied no more than a third, sharing it with the Welsh and the Scots – the Scots moreover allies of France and never ceasing their warlike endeavours to wipe England off the map.* Not only because she was for a long time under domination by the Danes; nor again because she was long linked under one sceptre with the duchy of Normandy to whom she was like a sister across the Channel. But also and especially because as much as France, Spain, Italy and Central Europe from the Rhine to the Vistula she was a child of the Church of Rome, that immense apostolic community, dominant over the secular States and reigning across frontiers, mountains,

* *Translator's Note.* This puts it too strongly. The Scots never had the power nor (except for a mad moment under Prince Charles Edward) the intention to conquer England. They fought only for their own freedom (except, at another mad moment under James IV at Flodden, in response to an appeal from France).

rivers and even seas. The Pope in those days was sovereign above all kings.

Immersed in this community, how should England have felt herself different from the rest? The words "religion" and "catholic" have rather lost their etymological meaning in our day. Originally "catholic" was the universal, "religion" that which tied or bound together. The binding power of this knot has become much slacker in Europe but in the time of Henry VII and Henry VIII it was still a strong force. Rome was the knot that bound all together; issued all the commands; exercised entire control. In order to become herself England had either to unpick this knot or slash it through. That is what caused the schism. It was the schism with Rome in 1534 which cut the moorings of the good ship "England" and set her free to go out and steer her course over the wide oceans of the world. It was by breaking loose from the authority of the Holy See and founding a church of her own, thus opening the flood-gates to fresh thinking purged of dogma, that Albion made a place for herself on the map, set herself apart from the entire continent; that she made of herself this nation like a reef in the sea upon which the ogre vessel "Nazi" would one day founder. Hence the interest in the reign of Henry VIII, author of the schism, that ever since that tragic summer of 1940 has filled my mind.

Now the mediate, even immediate, cause of that secession which for the first time enabled England to see herself as England was less the will of the king than the will of his second wife, Anne Boleyn. Hence again my curiosity to learn about this queen of a day, a curiosity that was to lead me past one surprise after another to some quite unexpected conclusions.

My first surprise was to find how unconvincing was the portrait of Anne Boleyn, invariably reproduced as freely in the many works on Henry VIII's six wives as in those few devoted only to this lady, his second wife. For it was always the same portrait and bristling with contradictions: to begin with, a frivolous, far from attractive young girl who out of vulgar conceit takes

12

it into her head to oust the king's first wife and so replace her. Now Anne's ancestry was a succession of London haberdashers while the queen she was intending to replace was Catherine of Aragon, daughter of a long line of kings of Spain. At a period when the aristocracy were governed by an unbending pride of caste it must have been clear to any person of sense that the chances of a draper's grand-daughter supplanting a Catherine of Aragon were derisory. At best, long years of struggle would be needed; she would have to sacrifice her whole youth to it and probably for nothing. A girl must have very little brain, let her be as conceited as you will, who would risk herself in a venture so uncompromising.

Now, curiously, all these writers credit Anne not with little brain but with remarkable intelligence. She is the subtlest, most perceptive and penetrating woman at the court of Henry VIII. But this seems not to surprise them; which is why I felt drawn to look closer.

From the moment of the king's first advances Anne makes no bones about it but there and then decides that she is going to marry him. An intelligent woman, as we saw, is not going to risk her whole future on so chancy a gamble if the motive is simply to indulge a childish fantasy. But suppose she is cherishing in secret some great political design involving the future of her country? Suppose she needs political power to bring that purpose to fulfilment? Then her gamble is justified.

If it had been a question of ordinary female ambition Anne would have established herself as favourite much earlier, once the king took notice of her. There was at that period for women or girls of modest extraction, indeed of the lesser nobility, no employment more honourable or more rewarding. Perhaps it might be difficult to hold the position for any length of time, the king having such a roving eye. Even so, while it lasted the lucky woman would be revelling in the utmost splendour. When it ended the king would marry her off to some rich lord of high standing. What commoner of humble fortune would not have chosen this "bird in the hand" rather than two "birds in the bush" and not have relished this swift

13

elevation while she was still young – rather than discard this easy prey and fritter away in obscurity all the years of her youth?

Unless she is cherishing some great design.

And another thing. Anne was a Christian believer and like all the women of her time pious in the sense of inclining to accept what the Church teaches. But intelligent as she was, she was bound to foresee that to undo the sacred ties of marriage between Queen Catherine and King Henry VIII would involve a by-passing of Catholic law and a stand-up fight with the all-powerful Church of Rome. Now, so far from drawing back, Anne was to precipitate things to the point of finding herself excommunicated, at that time a penalty implying tragic consequences. If she walked into this without knowing what she was doing, it would have been an enormous folly. But the choice is understandable if it was made in full awareness and with some great design in view.

Once again: if the volatile King Henry was such a slave to his passions that in order to indulge them he could be led into this sacrilegious divorce and unbelievable marriage, would anyone at all clear-headed not have foreseen that any other woman, singled out by the king in her turn and following Anne's example, would get rid of her with far more ease than Anne had got rid of Catherine, and therefore that such a union as she contemplated stood no chance of any long duration? And this is what in fact came to pass – indeed, four times over.

A stupid woman would not have thought of all this. But Anne was intelligent. Which convinces me that what drove her on was not the contemptible ambition of a crazy girl but the imperious ambition of one who had a policy to impose upon her people of England.

What might seem to invalidate this conclusion are the dark colours in which all her biographers paint Anne's character. They portray her in adolescence as charming, merry, cultured; adult, as obstinate and ambitious; finally as queen, malicious, bitter, vindictive – possibly a murderess. But where do they get the idea for this sinister change? The sources are few. They amount in substance to the letters of Ambassador Chapuis to his master Charles V, Catherine of Aragon's nephew, and to those of the countless other enemies whom Anne in taking the throne away from Catherine was sure to range against herself. Her biographers have accepted this evidence at its face value – not noticing or not giving full weight to an impressive number of improbabilities.

As depicted by her enemies, Anne Boleyn appears incapable of making herself loved except by the king. Now the authors who refer to these enemies and adopt their opinions have shown us Anne as courted first of all by the gentlemen of the court of France (and perhaps by Francis I); later by Henry Percy, the future Earl of Northumberland; by her cousin who became the celebrated poet Thomas Wyatt; by a group of other courtiers in her suite, all of whom were to sacrifice their lives for her; not counting those humble admirers who have left no trace. For a woman without the capacity to make herself loved, this was not a bad record! May we not believe that if she had the capacity to make herself hated as well it was because she wished, though all were against her, to become queen; still more, because after six years of struggle she achieved it; finally because, once crowned, she used her power to put into effect a policy so far-sighted and, for the time, so audacious that it could arouse only resistance and fear? From all this you will understand that I could not be satisfied with an Anne Boleyn intelligent and yet malicious and stupid, without ambition other than to satisfy a woman's vanity.

In trying in this book to show what this great political design might be, I shall make no claim to have proved my case. I shall try simply to sketch in my turn a portrait of Anne Boleyn as I believe she was. I will never falsify events of history (nor invent any to support my case). All actions are capable of more than one interpretation and I will merely suggest my own. In the imaginary dialogues between Anne and the narrator I will introduce nothing that is not directly founded on established facts; my characters will be allowed only to explain these events each after his or her fashion; also, what they themselves events each after his or her fashion; also, what they themselves do and how they behave will have the same relationship to known facts of history. But at the same time I will hold myself free not to accept as gospel of doubtful evidence obviously inspired by hatred. In brief, I am by no means laying claim to give proof of objectivity. Still, if in working out the assumptions I have made I have been able to invest them with a certain probability I will require no more of the reader, once he has finished and shut the book, than to ask himself what after all are the things about which history can claim to be certain.

# A Short History Lesson . . .
## Catherine of Aragon

It was when I got down in good earnest to this critical moment of England's history that I found I had to recognise and correct quite a number of false judgements.

The very short reign of Edward VI, son of Henry VIII and Jane Seymour his third wife (he had six) was followed by that of Mary, the daughter of his first wife Catherine of Aragon. This queen was known as Bloody Mary. She had no business more pressing than to bring England back into the bosom of the persecuting Church of Rome and to cut off Protestant heads. The daughter of Anne Boleyn, Elizabeth Tudor, having been first deprived of her rights, then re-established in them, twice barred from the throne and put in quarantine under Edward, in prison under Mary, finally took charge of the realm and reimposed the schism.

I imagined this policy was Elizabeth's own and that the kingdom she was inheriting was already prosperous. I had to understand first that before her time the future Great Britain was on the contrary an insignificant power, ranking only ninth in Europe; then, as I've said, that Anne Boleyn had been more than just the mother of Elizabeth the Great (too often reckoned as the sum of her contribution to history). In fact it was she who in provoking the schism had well and truly cleared the way for her daughter. This Elizabeth, brought up in the political ideas of her beheaded mother, had only to set herself to implement them through the force of her will-power and her genius. It was the isolation of England resulting from the schism that obliged Elizabeth to develop her country's agriculture, industry and commerce and as a necessary consequence to give it the strong fleet without which it would have remained a power of the ninth order.

I had finally to grasp that whereas Henry VIII was certainly the king who brought about the schism this was not so much of his own free will. The common judgement of historians rightly represents this prince as a bloodthirsty tyrant. Still more are they agreed, but this time quite wrongly, in picturing him as clever, resolute, ingenious, clear-sighted. This portrait derives more from legend than from reality. The truth is that the schism, the decisive act of his reign, came about despite him, almost in defiance of him. It was due not to Henry's will-power but to his weakness and his indecision.

Around the year 1500 England was no longer the kingdom of the Plantagenets, holding rule on both banks of the Channel and incorporating a sizable part of France. She was already huddled back upon her fragment of an island; her internal struggles had split her and taken the heart out of her; and her scanty population, too thinly spread over land neither extensively nor well cultivated, could not form the compact and stable entity to which we give the name of nation. It is easy to forget that the States of Venice had at that time a larger population than England; that Francis I had under his sceptre five times, Charles V twenty times as many subjects as Henry: three million was the total of England's inhabitants in Henry's reign.

We forget too that compared to France, Spain, Italy and Germany Albion was still a mediæval state; that the Renaissance barely brushed her with its wing while Italy was already glowing with all her fires, her cluster of painters of genius, sculptors, architects too many to name; that in France a Fouquet, a Clouet, an Ambroise Paré signalled the coming of Rabelais and Montaigne; that Spain was sending out her great conquistadors Columbus, Cortez, Pizarro to discover the world, while at home El Greco was getting his brush ready.

Flanders, Germany and Poland, between them, produced an Erasmus, a Luther, a Copernicus just when the art of the greatest painters, from the Van Eycks to Breughel and Albrecht

18

Dürer, was in flower. While Europe was thus caught up in whirlwinds of exuberant vitality, a profusion of discoveries and new creations, England – granted she had already Roger Bacon and Chaucer to her credit – could now point to only one name: Thomas More.

When, in 1509, Henry VIII mounted the throne he had no-one to give his reign distinction: no poet with any breadth of vision, no painter – Holbein was a German – no scholar, no explorer. It is not that either curiosity or culture was wanting at his court. Along with the whole of intellectual Europe people in England at that time had eyes only for Italy, as classical Rome had had for Greece. There was no king or emperor who did not dream of enticing to his court – like Florence, Rome, Perugia, Milan – this constellation of inimitable masters to become the jewel of his crown. If Henry VIII dreamt of it less than his two great rivals, Charles V and Francis I, the reason was not so much the extra distance to Italy as the insufficiency of his means.

Means both in men and money. When his father Henry Tudor (Henry VII) had defeated Richard III in 1485 (his despisers taunted him with having "picked up his crown among the bushes of Bosworth") he had found the tills empty, a pitiful revenue, an administration in ruins, a country being systematically bled by the barons. Having by his victory put an end to the Wars of the Roses his first care had been to secure his sceptre and his dynasty by re-establishing order in the kingdom, treating with France and making use of these years of peace to stock up his money-chests. Accordingly his son and successor found in the Treasury a substantial fortune, but still, by continental standards, one that was modest indeed. His revenues – taxes of all kinds, customs duties, rents on royal domains – were by no means negligible. But the corresponding revenues of the King of France were six times higher, of the emperor nine times, of the Sultan twelve times. Even the seigneury of Venice was richer than the King of England.

No money, no Swiss. To put his finances in order Henry VII had had to cut down on the armed forces, with the consequence that at his death his son found only an army deficient in numbers, in equipment and in discipline. Long past and almost legendary were the victories of Crécy and Agincourt, won by Edward III and Henry V. At sea the royal fleet had been reduced to about thirty vessels more or less capable of manoeuvring, the merchant navy to about a hundred. It was little enough, to compete commercially with Venice, politically to cut Spain off from the Netherlands, France from Scotland. Enough all the same to put a check on them. Hence the overtures made to the old Henry by Louis XII of France against the Emperor Maximilian, and by Maximilian against Louis XII. A competition by which Henry profited, to rebuild his finances and strengthen his position. At his death therefore he had left to his heir, Henry VIII, besides money-chests tolerably full, this political novelty – the appearance of England on the international scene. Even so her finances (like her diplomacy) remained strictly dependent on the Continent. Albion was not yet an island except in a geographical sense. It remained for her to become one politically and psychologically.

If Henry VIII was in part responsible for that achievement it was, as I have said, the effect of his bad qualities much more than of his good. It goes without saying that for his period he was very cultured. His father, though a brave fighter, was practically illiterate and he resolved that his son should be given the education he himself had missed. At the age of fifteen the Prince of Wales spoke three languages as well as Latin, a little ancient Greek and some Spanish; he seemed to have a gift for mathematics; he revelled in the lessons Thomas More gave him in astronomy; he corresponded with Erasmus on points of theology; music and dancing he adored – but still more wrestling, tennis, throwing the javelin, archery, hunting and tournaments. It is not surprising that once king this fine and accomplished young lord should have been able to create a false impression of his abilities, of his flair for politics in particular. But reference to his correspondence with his ministers, to the orders and counter-orders that he issued, the dispatches he sent to his ambassadors, reveals him on the contrary as uncertain, hesitant when not a positive coward and at his wits' end to know what to do; brutal rather than determined; more a tyrant than an organiser; not so much a disciplinarian as cruel; and reversing his decisions according to whoever happened to have been the last person giving him advice.

More at home as he was in sports, in the arts and in abstract ideas that in the government of a kingdom, his vacillating will was at the mercy of one stronger than his; and if that other became obstinate he would weakly give way to it. Left to himself, would Henry ever have found the nerve to break with the Vatican? It was his personal weakness when up against a woman bolder than himself that led and indeed forced him into a rupture the idea of which might have tickled him but still more would have put our Henry under the harrow. And this woman, as you will have gathered, was Anne Boleyn. Hence the importance I assign to her in the destiny of England – and by consequence in France's also.

Before coming to her and to her reign it is scarcely necessary to remind the reader that England in those times was still living under a feudal regime though a more centralised system of power was already beginning to take shape. Parliament was consultative only but in fact in the Upper House the nobility made law, while the Commons of the Lower House were advancing in importance. They still could not force the king to adopt any particular measure but they were well placed to forward the economic interests of the towns and villages. Serfs were on their way out. Those of them who had become yeomen ("free men") were winning rights of their own as well as certain exemptions of tax, sometimes gained by force (as in the capture of London in 1381). The merchants held the crown of the causeway, lending money to the king to make war and little by little from a base of wool and textiles were edging their way up into the lesser nobility.

When the sixteenth century began it was the king who governed, surrounded by his ministers and by what was not yet known as the public service. Facing these were the lords, peers of the realm and proprietors of their lands and of their revenues; they were still kinglets and levied their own troops. The days were gone when their ancestors had made and unmade kings but they still dreamt of those days. Plots were a part of their life.

The shrewdly designed administration which the king opposed to the power of the lords was new and the work of Henry VII. Ministers, magistrates and other "civil servants" were chosen exclusively from among citizens of the towns; wholly dependent on the king, they were attached to him body and soul. Prepared for anything that would take them up a rung of the ladder and make them rich, they were game for all the dirty work that had to be done. And since they had to eat humble pie in order to get to the top, the higher they rose the more extortionate they became. Nothing could be got out of them without a bribe. A judge's verdict would depend on the presents he had received. They had many enemies as a result and there was always a pack of ruthless rivals hungry for their jobs. This suited the king very well since their one safeguard against plots by the lords and the anger of the people was the king's protection. Let the sovereign lose ever so little of his authority, and they would be the first to suffer. The king could therefore count on them without the least fear, confident that they would be on guard as eagerly as himself to thwart any plot against him.

Facing, or rather alongside, these two great orders, the nobility and the public service, stood a third, no less powerful: the Church. The top clergy (bishops and cardinals) sat on the right in the Upper Chamber; elected members from the lower clergy sat in the Commons. The clergy as a whole enjoyed a social status that had two sides to it; on the one hand the Church, reputed as sacred, inspired the fear and respect proper to things divine. But against this, it was an age when everyone was expected to defend his property, his honour, his life even, by sword or dagger; when knights and barons, if there were no fighting on hand, had no other resource than the chase, the tournament or amatory pursuits; and so the priests, being in theory unable either to beget children or bear arms, were looked down on as something less than men.

But formidable just the same. A good number of bishops, enjoying enormous revenues and caring less about faith than about their secular interests, held some very high posts in the kingdom and played a major role in politics. Since they were dependent on Rome, the Pope had his hand on all that was going on. This dependence on a foreign power was resented by the common people, who had further ground for complaint against the bishops in their corrupt practices, their financial exactions, the goings on in the ecclesiastical courts and the moral obliquities which the bishops took little trouble to conceal. At Court, the mutual hatred between the three great corporations – the lords, the bishops and the top-ranking civil servants – might hide itself under the traditional courteous manners of the time. But the flame blazed beneath the surface, a flame whose heat penetrated to the threshold of the king's own chamber, if not into his very bed.

That bed, on the day when Anne Boleyn was to come on the scene, Henry VIII had shared for fifteen years with Catherine of Aragon.

At the time of their engagement in 1503 Catherine was six years older than Henry, Prince of Wales. He was twelve, she eighteen. And this engagement itself had not been arrived at without many tribulations.

For Catherine was the daughter of Isabella of Castile, who, in the interest of her strategy against France and with the delighted agreement of Henry VII (it gave England importance in the eyes of Europe), had first married her at the age of sixteen to Arthur Prince of Wales, elder brother to the young Henry. But Arthur had a weak constitution and after only a matter of months he had left her a widow. Isabella wanted straightaway to marry her to this young Henry, who in his turn had become Prince of Wales and was the new heir to the throne. Now it is written:

23

"Thou shalt by no means know the wife of thy brother; for in uncovering her nakedness thou wouldst uncover the nakedness of thy brother". It was therefore desirable that this first marriage should be annulled, and it could be annulled only if it had not been consummated. Unluckily, quite a number of courtiers had heard Arthur on the morrow of the wedding declare with great gusto that he had "passed the night in Spain". This did not stop Catherine for the good of the cause and for the sake of the alliance with Albion from affirming that she was a virgin and her mother affirmed it more emphatically still. Catherine's virginity was in fact crucial, for the French had just launched an attack on Perpignan. To cut the matter short and be on the safe side Isabella decided to obtain a dispensation from the Holy See. Alexander Borgia, a pope half Spanish and half Italian, would certainly not have turned a deaf ear if poison had allowed him the chance. But Julius, his successor, was no less obliging. Virgin or not, Catherine received the dispensation and the engagement could go ahead. Whereupon, in 1504, Isabella died.

Castile passed at once by inheritance to Joanna the Mad, wife of Philip of Habsburg and mother of the Archduke Charles. Catherine was now only the daughter of the King of Aragon and for Henry VII no longer a good bargain. Better in these conditions for his son to marry Margaret of Austria. The engagement with Catherine could easily be quashed, for although Pope Julius had certainly granted the dispensation, he had not denied that Arthur and she had been man and wife. Whether therefore one wished to use the licence or revoke it would be simply a matter of getting one bishop to declare it valid or another to declare it null and void. Thus the king held two cards in his hand. To put the licence still more evenly in balance he made the young Henry, his son, sign before some ecclesiastical authority a protestation against the engagement and this was deposited in the archives along with the dispensation.

Thus, depending on whether or not a better bargain came up, the king could either honour or denounce the engagement with Catherine. Since she became a widow she had been living at the court in London. Henry now put her "in reserve for the Crown", that is to say at a distance from the court, and reduced her from month to month to an ever more pitiable situation. Her father Ferdinand had lost interest in her, too taken up with his plan to marry the beautiful Germaine de Foix from the Nivernais and so strengthen his hold on Naples. Not only did he grumble at having to pay Henry VII the dowry he had promised, but he left his daughter without either means or support. In her distress she contemplated death as a way out.

But two years later Philip of Habsburg died of congestion and once again Henry VII saw Castile glisten before his eyes. Why should he not himself marry Joanna now that she was a widow, and forget her madness? To bring pressure on Ferdinand what better lever than his daughter, Joanna's sister, the exiled Catherine? Suddenly this lady's stock shot up like a flash; she found herself at a day's notice released from quarantine, fêted once more at court and made much of by the king, now once again her father-in-law-to-be. Had he not besides, when his son Arthur died, thought of keeping Catherine for himself? It is true, but only after setting his sights on Joanna of Naples, then on Margaret, daughter of Louise of Savoy . . . But now there was no better bargain than Joanna the Mad with Castile for dowry.

(These matrimonial tergiversations of the old Henry VII may appear comic to us. In that age they scarcely were. Hardly more surprising indeed than the constant reversals of alliance that the kings made between themselves. Thus in 1494 with a view to the conquest of Naples, Charles VIII of France made sure of his rear by forming with Henry VII, Maximilian of Austria, Ferdinand of Aragon and his wife Isabella of Castile, what would nowadays be called pacts of non-aggression. But when Charles VIII established himself in Piedmont, Isabella, Ferdinand and Maximilian were disturbed by this easy conquest and forthwith allied themselves with Venice and the Holy See in order to extrude him. Thereupon from about 1509 the Italian princes made alliance with one side or the other according to their quarrels of the moment. In that year, for example, the Duke of Ferrara and the Count of Mantua formed an alliance against Venice with the Vatican, Ferdinand of Spain and Louis XII of France, known as the League of Cambrai. This combination, having defeated Venice in the battle of Agnadello, divided her lands among themselves and France, as the strongest, took the lion's share. The Pope, finding himself outwitted, switched his allegiance and formed with his late enemy Venice, the Swiss, Henry VIII of England and, naturally, Maximilian and Ferdinand a league against France to drive her once more out of Italy. They achieved this at Ravenna in 1513 – two years before the battle of Marignan opened the door to the French king Francis I to come back . . .)

But it is time we ourselves came back to Henry VII and his plan of marrying Joanna the Mad. He had, as we've seen, pressed Catherine of Aragon to write to Ferdinand to obtain his consent. After taking the advice of her confessor she did this and obtained from her father the answer Henry wanted. Her position at the palace would have been still further improved if a new obstacle had not arisen. Joanna the Mad had brought back to Castile the body of her husband and obstinately refused to part with it. She was perfectly willing to marry Henry VII because her father wished it too; but still more she wanted to be able to have the coffin with the body beside her. This promised to be a long business.

Patience was not Henry's strong point and without waiting a moment he turned to look in another direction for a project that would bear fruit more quickly. Why not rather marry Margaret of Austria, whom he had at first thought of for his son? That would be a link with the Archduke Charles, Philip's heir and the future Charles V. No sooner said than done; a messenger went straight off to Vienna to plead the King of England's cause with the Emperor Maximilian. This messenger was a chaplain of large appetite, recently appointed to the court. He was called Thomas Wolsey and officiated every morning at the private chapel of the king whose confidence he had lost no time in gaining. This mission to Vienna gratified his fiery ambition; he had his foot in the stirrup. More, his success with Maximilian was so rapid that on his return Henry could not believe his ears. In recompense Wolsey was appointed Dean of Lincoln and Chaplain to the King. Better than a stirrup, it was a fine spring-board that was being put under his feet.

Straightaway the unhappy Catherine, once more without market value, found herself back in quarantine. Meanwhile the Prince of Wales had grown: by now he was a tall young man who excelled at sports, at games, at the joust, at hunting, at kissing; in all these domains surpassing the other lords of the court. He mollified them, however, by throwing his money around liberally; charming the ladies by his magnificent physique and his musical accomplishments, playing both lute and organ; and attracting the praises and devotion of his companions, both male and female, all of them entranced by such exuberant vitality.

Nevertheless, it was already possible to distinguish another side to his character. Full of charm when he was given way to, he could not bear to be contradicted, still less to be resisted. Touchy and unstable, from charm he would pass in an instant to brutality and anger. This disposition to take umbrage might have suggested a rebel spirit if his conduct had not demonstrated the reverse. Once back from the chase, from tournament or from amorous adventures he would be infinitely biddable as regards his responsibilities of state and he fulfilled his religious duties with profound contrition. At eighteen years you would say a conservative before his time.

Accordingly he was obedient to his father, Henry VII, in everything. Now in 1509 the king found himself embroiled once again in a quarrel with King Ferdinand. Furious at having to keep Joanna the Mad on his hands, Ferdinand threatened to come at the head of an army and chastise Henry if at least the Prince of Wales did not marry Catherine without further delay. We do not know what answer the old monarch had in mind to send, for this was the moment that he chose for leaving this world.

But on his death-bed, fearing both for his son and for

England, he had advised him to calm things down by marrying the Spanish princess. As always, Henry obeyed him, not concerning himself much over the divided views of a Council of the Throne, some of whose members were a little shocked by the idea of a marriage in which trickery had played so large a part. And since Catherine also wanted the marriage, and the sooner the better, there was nothing for it but to bring them to the altar before the coronation; in this way she would be queen at the moment he became king.

For Catherine of Aragon, it was the fulfilment of hopes that over seven years she had cherished in her affliction day and night. This long-drawn-out ordeal, nonetheless, had embittered her. She needed to savour her revenge. She saw her marriage as one. The crown itself was another. But that did not compensate her for her suffering, and the young king was not slow to become aware of it.

The marriage ceremony had taken place privately first, so that the public wedding should coincide with the coronation. When the great day came Catherine was carried in a litter to Westminster, bedecked in white satin with her hair streaming down to her waist as a sign of virginity. Henry was a dazzling figure, clad in velvet and ermine under a cloak of silk spun with threads of gold. For, breaking with the tradition of parsimony followed by the kings of preceding generations – one wearing woollen rags, one an old felt bonnet, another with his stockings darned, another with sleeves sewn on to his old doublet – Henry, a king of the Renaissance, wished to display luxury and generosity in his palace, and effrontery and daring in the world outside, so long as it was only for a brief moment.

Now the queen's feeling was quite different. Brought up as a strict daughter of Spain, she was used to passing a quarter of her time in prayers; under her royal finery she wore the frock of the religious Order of the Trinitarians; she rose at midnight and again at four in the morning to kneel and say her prayers. Far from sharing in these austere practices, the new king by contrast gave himself freely to all that he did, causing four horses to founder under him in a single tournament, disputing medicine with the doctors, music with the musicians, coats of arms with heraldic experts, theology with the bishops. But in this he was really not so much being original as conforming to the fashion of his time: a fashion come from the East and passing through Italy and France that required a man to shine in all the ways in which it was possible to shine. Henry simply carried this fashion to exuberant excess.

Despite this opposition of tastes and temperament Catherine and he didn't get on too badly at first; and the queen, so far as possible, diverted her ill-humour away from her husband and against the ministers and church dignitaries. Thus from year to year she put them increasingly against her; so much so that by 1513 after four years of this régime they reached the point of complaining to the king about it. Becoming conscious of this hostility, Catherine began quite naturally to put herself under the protection of the lords. And since these never ceased to plot and intrigue, Henry had no choice but to lend a complaisant ear to his ministers. On top of this for some time now the queen, having reached her thirties and become very stout, had had little appeal for him in the marriage bed; he was further irritated by the influence or rather domination under which she had kept him ever since the marriage. Conscious of his ministers' support, he felt free at last to take an independent line with her. Various unfortunate events played their part from year to year in aggravating the disharmony between the two. Three infants stillborn, with a miscarriage to follow; the death of another son at a tender age, and the affliction of the father at finding himself still without an heir, combined to divest the queen more and more of her ascendancy. Whereupon instead of curbing her Spanish pride to humour the king and win him back, she committed the mistake of deeply wounding his vanity in the course of a double campaign in which Henry rather lost his way.

By what aberration could this young king of four-and-twenty years, relying on the insufficient forces at his command, have supposed that he could embark on the conquest of the

29

kingdom of France? It had always been his Golden Fleece;* or rather he was the frog in the fable of the frog and the ox†. In short, it was a mad adventure, doomed from the start. A minor success at the outset encouraged the king in his illusions. Certainly after a brief siege Thérouanne opened its gates to him; but this little city had no strategic value and the main consequence of its fall was to irritate the Archduke Charles, who found himself threatened on his Flemish frontier. Henry had one further success. He captured Tournai, but there his wild-goose chase of a campaign had to end. As compared with what he had hoped for, it was a paltry result, even a little ridiculous, and Henry's pride was hurt.

This pride was to take a much worse bruising still. While Henry was overseas, the King of Scotland, France's ally, had responded to her call to seize the opportunity and create a diversion. He launched his troops across the Border and invaded the north of England. The battle of Flodden, won on *English* soil by *English* soldiers under command of an *English* nobleman, the Earl of Surrey, excited far more enthusiasm among the English people than the distant and only moderate success in Flanders of an army made up for the most part of German mercenaries.

If upon the king's return the queen had had the native wit to withdraw again into his shadow, Henry would have been grateful to her. As it was, her pride in the victory at Flodden, intensified by the old resentment, led Catherine to expect the king to acknowledge his wife's glory. Worse still, she made the unforgivable error of taunting him before the whole court; it was no great credit to him, she said, to have captured one French duke (M. de Longueville) when, in his absence, three had been brought back from Scotland. Those words were her downfall.

Stung to the quick and jealous for his prestige, Henry swore to re-establish his standing in the country, with his authority

* Jason and his Argonauts landed on the coast of Colchis and came away with the golden fleece.
† Fable by Jean de La Fontaine.

over the queen and his supremacy over the lords. But to do this he had to overcome one great obstacle of which he was well aware: the indecision of character which was his weakness. There was only one way to make up for this defect; he had to find some strong arm to lean upon, the arm of a man who would know how to uphold and enforce the king's will.

The problem was to find him. To look for him among the lords would be to bring the wolf into the sheepfold. Then among his ministers or his high officials? Imprudent. Their hostility towards the queen might push them too far and produce disastrous consequences in Europe. So there was no alternative but to find the man in the third group: the Church.

No need now for any further search; the man was there. It was Thomas Wolsey, lately the favourite envoy of the old Henry and currently chaplain to the young one. That appointment was not merely honorary. On the contrary, Wolsey had the handling of much secular business; he was in touch with all that was going on both in the kingdom and abroad. Henry found him agreeable, resolute, inventive, devoted, always ready to keep him amused by fresh distractions. When the chaplain understood what his sovereign expected of him he knew that his hour had come at last. And he prepared to become first minister.

To attach Wolsey to himself, the king began by making him a grant of the bishopric of Tournai and of the archbishopric of York. And he put out feelers to the Pope to obtain a cardinal's hat for him. Finally, in the sixth year of his reign he appointed Wolsey Lord Chancellor.

It did not take the king long to regret this decision as keenly as he had at first been pleased with it. Wolsey had a character far stronger than Henry's. From day to day the chancellor took more and more of the government of the kingdom into his own hands and to allow himself a free rein he troubled less and less, as time went on, to ask the king's opinion before acting. This naturally caused Henry acute vexation. But being hesitant and weak he put up tamely at first with the cardinal's dominance as he had with the queen's and did not venture to adopt any effective measures of control against him. Wolsey also had been clever enough to gratify the king by ceding to the Crown his fine palace of Hampton Court while ostentatiously retaining for himself a much more modest property. On the other hand he had drawn the king into a disastrous project called the Amicable Loan, an expression intended to disguise what was in fact a formidable supplementary tax. There were hardly any voluntary contributors for this and it raised for the king a harvest not of money but of intense unpopularity. So Henry's feelings against his chancellor became daily more sour and he waited for some occasion which would enable him to strike down this troublesome priest and take back the governance of the realm.

One thing after another now made the king sway first this way and then that. For Wolsey had succeeded in what Henry had most wanted of him; he had promptly brought the queen to heel, a service for which Henry continued to be grateful to him for several months. With less now to fear from Catherine he forgot some of his resentment and after receiving a sumptuous present from King Ferdinand he even fancied that a little of his old tenderness for her had come back. Unluckily, the next year the queen gave birth with difficulty to a daughter – Mary – instead of the male heir whom, after the deaths of his other sons, he so desperately desired. For Henry, the disappointment was too bitter. Moreover, after this birth it appeared that the queen would never again be able to conceive, still less bring into the world an heir.

It was just at the moment when the king despaired of ever having a son that a young maid of honour appeared at Court. Her name was Anne Boleyn.

# PART I ⬡ ANNE

I
(150?–1515)

## *Early Years*

So long as Queen Elizabeth remains alive I shall not be able to tell you my name, which in any case is of no distinction or renown. And since I am already old and she still young it is likely I shall die without having disclosed it. At least she has not forbidden me to write this Life of the Queen Anne who was her mother, subject to its not being published until after she has died. If by ill chance the manuscript were to fall into the hands of her enemies during her life-time my name would compromise her and give them ammunition.

The family connections that linked me to her mother would also give me away, so I shall not say what they were. But it is these links, above all of affection, that will not permit me any longer to hold back. I am conscious that I have no right to allow the detestable reputation that still clouds the memory of Anne Boleyn to continue. All the more since the queen her daughter who owes everything to her – and I am well placed to know it – will neither do her justice nor even so much as pronounce her name in public. Reasons of state, I know. Is it possible for *me*, then, to leave her memory to be buried ever deeper and deeper under these calumnies? Too well did I love and admire the young girl, then the maid of honour, then the queen of a thousand and one days, not to rise up with all the force that is in me against the odious lies that a cruel king, servile judges, timid ministers and a court crammed with venom have poured out even over her dead body.

For readers in fifty, a hundred years' time or perhaps still further ahead it ought to be set down in writing what Queen Anne really was, with her good qualities and her bad – but the first far outnumbering the second! – in the course of a short life that took her from humble origins to the throne, from the throne to the Tower of London and from the Tower to the scaffold.

Ah! dear Anne, my dear Anne, to think back to that wan morning when the executioner cut off that little white neck in that ghastly courtyard of Tower Green, near the very turret and its bloodstained chamber where the abominable Richard had his nephews' throats cut! To think of all the blood that has been spilt in that Tower of London by a succession of heartless, barbarious, hypocritical kings! And Henry, eighth of the name, you the worst hypocrite of them all, "out of regard for the queen" substituting the sharp-edged sword for the "degrading" axe!

But it is not to ease my own heart's anguish that I write. I write to set back in its proper place a truth that has been ridiculed, to give Anne Boleyn the portrait she deserves instead of one that from base motives was deliberately blackened. I am not blinded by my feelings for her. I shall tell the story of her life with its ways and by-ways. But I will do it with the feelings of a sister. Like a sister I loved and supported her, lived with her and shared her good hours and her bad; now like a sister I open this notebook today to wash her memory clean.

It would be true to say that we had known one another since we were born. I saw the light soon after she did, not quite two years, and we grew up together. I shall not reveal – it would expose me – the post my father held first at Blickley Hall where my little Anne was born, then later at Hever Castle where we were brought up. She was at four years old a ravishing little girl whom, as you can well believe, I admired, envied and adored. My mother found her chin too heavy (my elder sister's had been minute) but to me by contrast it gave her an air of determination which I found captivating.

But the devil take my feelings! I am not writing to talk about myself – how hard it is to keep the self out altogether . . . so let us return to the calm impartial outlook proper to a writer of history. I shall advance no propositions touching the king, the kingdom or Europe which I cannot wholly guarantee. The basic knowledge I had on all these subjects I acquired from Queen Anne, who herself was kept well informed by the host of agents she maintained in every court on the Continent and by the spies first of Wolsey and then of Cromwell in England. The king could not rise in the morning, go to bed at night, come and go, eat, hunt, speak, receive an audience without a bevy of courtiers around him to attend to his wants. Every word therefore that falls from his lips or that his followers repeat is heard on the spot or next day by a swarm of informers who pass it on at once to their masters. Apart from what is whispered in the secrecy of the king's closet, everything flies abroad, everything becomes public knowledge. You will not expect me, then, to quote my source for each particular event – except where it concerns Anne personally. So without holding up my story I will start with a few bare facts regarding this Boleyn family about whom so much has been said and its opposite said as well.

I hope I may be excused if my memory sometimes lets me down. For example, to find the exact date of Anne's birth I must take a line on it from my own birthday and even about that I can't be too sure. I suppose it was entered (though it was not the invariable practice) in the registers of the church where I was baptised. But that church had become Anglican, and in the reign of Bloody Mary had been burnt down, together with all its contents, including the registers. Now my mother had always told me that she brought me into the world on the day of the feast of St Blaise in the fourth year of the century, the year of the Great Floods. After she died I discovered the priest. He had escaped the flames and was deputy to the Archbishop of York. It was he who had held me over the font and he told me he remembered very well that the floods had afflicted England not in the fourth but in the sixth year of the century and it was on the day of Epiphany that he had baptised me. It is too late to confront my mother with this priest and since it was in the same church, now burnt out, that Anne Boleyn had also been baptised two years before me I have no means of verifying whether that was for her in the second or the fourth year of the century. Anyway, it matters little. Of one thing I am, however, certain. The date 1507 which appears in the marriage register in Westminster Abbey is wrong. Anne pretended to it so as to seem younger than she was (what woman does not do the same?). But let's get on.

My family has always – at least as far back as my great-grandfather – had links with the Boleyns. The name Boleyn itself calls for some remarks. William Boleyn, Anne's grandfather, claimed as his far-off ancestor a great Norman nobleman called Boullant who after taking part in the battle of Hastings would seem not to have gone back to Normandy but to have established himself in Kent. William's son Thomas made a different claim according to which he was descended from a Vautier de Boulan, baron of Picardy and related to Baudoin de Biaunoir, Lord of Avesnes. Neither ancestor is therefore quite certain and at the court there was much mockery of these attempts by ex-drapers to work themselves into the aristocracy. For what is certain is that William Boleyn's father, the grandfather of Thomas and great-grandfather of Anne, Geoffrey by name, was a merchant in London dealing in textiles. He was for a time on the City Council and did his work so well that in the year of the Great Frosts he acquired the dignity of Lord Mayor.

This male obsession, even among the richest, for acquiring dubious titles or ones to which they had clearly no right, was something that Anne and I had often joked about. At the game of Peers and Paupers we sided, as all children do, with the Paupers. We mocked at those who wanted to be Peers and played on them all the tricks we could. It is true that later when she was adolescent I saw her put out by the gibes she overheard from behind a door about the rights of the Boleyns to their noble lineage. Perhaps it was at one of these moments that there was born in her the need to obtain for herself a more secure title.

Thomas Boleyn (my father's closest friend) had a fortune in no way corresponding to his ambitions. But Geoffrey, his paternal grandfather, had bequeathed to him his keen intelligence and acumen: perhaps also his hardness of heart. Arrived in London to seek his fortune, Thomas found a way to please a lord who had been stripped of his possessions after the battle of Bosworth. This was Howard, Earl of Surrey and future Duke of Norfolk, the highest title in the kingdom. Perceiving in Thomas the gentlemanly qualities necessary for success in life, he gave him his daughter Elizabeth Howard in marriage. The young couple lived at first in modest style at Blickley Hall. The lands of the property supplied them with a small but regular income and there Thomas patiently awaited the inheritance from his father which, when Anne was two (or three?), brought him in fact the fortune in wool made by his grandfather Geoffrey. To this there was later added the residence of Hever Castle. James Howard, Boleyn's brother-in-law, had in the meantime married a Plantagenet, connected on the female side with the old Henry, seventh of the name. Thomas considered that through his wife, James's sister, he was now by marriage one of the royal family and he set out to get himself admitted.

Now his father-in-law, Surrey, after years of disgrace had won back the esteem of King Henry little by little and he was as eager as his son-in-law to assure for Elizabeth the rank which was her due. Quite soon this came about and he had the pleasure of seeing the beauty, the charm, the wit and gaiety of his daughter make a sensation at court. Thomas became a king's councillor and it was not long before he received the Order of the Garter.

When the old Henry died there were uncertainties. Thomas had reached his fortieth year; the young Henry had just turned eighteen. Would he not get rid of "yesterday's men" and surround himself with advisers nearer his own age? Thomas was a little apprehensive but Henry treated him with elegance; he disposed of him by sending him as ambassador to the Netherlands, ruled by Margaret of Austria. This meant that

Thomas's revenues became still more comfortable, allowing him to think of a privileged education for his children. They were not many; of the dozen children that Elizabeth had given him in twelve years before being carried off at last by fever following childbirth, most had died at a tender age, of croup, thrush or green diarrhoea. Only three had survived: Anne, George and Mary.

It was George, naturally, who was given the most finished education so as to develop in him the qualities of a gentleman. But neither Anne nor I – for we were practically brought up together – had cause to complain. We were given everything we could want in the way of governesses, private tutors, professors of literature, languages and mathematics, not to mention singing, riding and etiquette. But Anne, as not only the elder but the more gifted and industrious of the two of us, soon left me far behind. She took full advantage of all our lessons while I often found it difficult to pay attention. She preferred French to Italian; I liked Italian better as the less difficult. It is true French became familiar to me, but this was because everyone around us spoke it as often as they spoke English. Our teacher was a young woman born in Calais; she was called (I can't remember now) Simonin or Simonnet: she was ugly and she beat us when we stumbled over the accents. At least we have to thank her for a solid grounding in the language.

Very soon my friend Anne was dreaming of leaving for France, land of elegance and splendour. When we played at rounders, table-tennis or tail of the wolf we had to say the nursery rhymes in French. Sometimes in the early morning we would take breakfast together. Shame on me if I asked her to pass me "the beef" and not *"l'entrecôte"*, "the beans" and not *"les haricots"*, "the ale" and not *"la bière"*. She would scold me, reminding me that perhaps one day we would find ourselves at Court and would be taken, if we could not speak good French, for country cousins. Her appetite, from the moment she got up, filled me with wonder. At the midday meal, out of the twenty courses we were served each day, she missed none and helped herself generously to several. She could eat six plovers one after the other. This insatiable appetite was a joy to behold.

She did not put on weight as a result. It all went into muscle, while she remained willowy and proved herself unusually robust in the games we played. She was troubled a little – her elder sister Mary was a beauty – by a complexion that was dull if not sallow; by the colour of her hair, deep black when the fashion was for auburn; and by a little deformity of her index finger whose nail spread out as though it were on two fingers joined together. She took pains to hide this minor defect under long sleeves, and to conceal under high collars a mole awkwardly visible on her neck. In compensation she had, besides a very straight nose and well-formed lips, a superb presence with immense eyes in which glowed and glistened two marbles of purest ebony. She was proud of only one thing: the richness of her hair, which streamed down behind her to below her knees.

I played the harp, Anne the lute and the spinet. Her brother George composed for us pieces grave and gay; he aspired also to poetry, translating Dante and Plutarch into French or English verses as the mood took him. Besides knowing Latin and Greek he was familiar with Italian, Spanish, rhetoric, mathematics, astronomy and theology. He was a splendid rider and at the age of sixteen already a star in tournaments. He adored his younger sister and she him. As for my own feelings for him this is not the place to speak.

From all this you will have gathered that our life at Hever Castle was not unpleasant. It is true it was an ancient castle, two hundred years old or more; but generations of successive owners, down to Thomas Boleyn himself who had lately inherited the property, had kept it up, enlarged, improved, beautified and furnished it with taste. How often, as children, did Anne, George, Mary and I play on the more or less cracked ramparts, raising and lowering the drawbridge, now out of use, to keep the chains from becoming too rusty! Despite having only a modest staff – barely fifty, all told – the Boleyn family's life style, though falling short of luxury, was not wanting in comfort. In winter time the floors in all the rooms were covered, as in the king's palace, with a good layer of dry straw renewed every two months. Anne slept, as the queen did, on a feather bed; the water-jug was protected by a covering of fur so that she could wash her face without having to break the ice. Amusements there were in plenty. I have spoken of our own, the children's. Those of Thomas and his neighbours consisted essentially in hunting the stag, the wild boar and the fox, and in falconry. It was rare if there was not a haunch of venison or of young boar at the five o'clock supper, not to mention thrush, woodcock or wood-pigeon in season. The forests around abounded with game.

This life of the well-to-do lord of the manor lasted until Thomas left as ambassador to The Hague. My friend Anne was at that time eleven or twelve. She had reached puberty, while I had not yet, and though it did not keep us apart, this sudden difference between us nevertheless put a certain distance between her caprices and my games. But it only made me all the more her "little sister" and her fond admirer.

It was in the year of the drought, four years before that of the epidemic, that an exceptional opportunity came Anne's way. Queen Catherine had just presented the king with a little girl. The infant had as godmother Mary Tudor, the king's sister, and was given the same name as her aunt. And despite the disappointment of the father, who would have preferred a male heir, the court was nonetheless celebrating this fortunate issue of the royal bed with a thousand festivities when the impending marriage was announced to us of this same Mary, the king's sister, to Louis of France, twelfth of the name. In advance of her going to meet up with him beyond the Channel the marriage was consummated by proxy (by a ritual in which the bare calf of the royal envoy was brought close, under a sheet, to the bare calf of the bride). But Anne and I were horrified by this marriage. The King of France was an old man of fifty-two, thirty-four years older than she. To think of this adolescent in the arms of that crippled, poxy old ass! Neither Anne nor I had at that time much understanding of high policy of state and the necessities it imposes. We were still only a pair of sentimental little girls.

This ill-assorted union was the work of King Henry, the bride's elder brother, who had just turned twenty-three. But everyone knew that its originator was above all Thomas Wolsey, the head chaplain, Canon of Windsor and the king's chancellor. It was common knowledge that the real power lay in the hands of this future cardinal and that he was making use of it with full ecclesiastical vigour. So Mary Tudor, become Queen of France, would very shortly be going to join her old and royal husband. What had now to be done was to make up her retinue – a large one, to include four-and-twenty maids of honour; these were to be chosen officially by Queen Catherine, from girls between the ages of ten and twenty. I said to myself straightaway that Anne was sure to be one of them. That must have also been in the mind of her aunt and namesake Anne Boleyn, the wife of Uncle Edward; and since this lady was Catherine's favourite companion she had no difficulty in obtaining an interview. As it turned out, the younger Anne pleased the queen; the girl's naive and musical French amused her and touched her heart. Catherine personally recommended her to her sister-in-law, Mary, who, no less touched and amused by Anne, gladly accepted her into her retinue. Anne had found her in very low spirits, so she told me.

It remained, however, to convince Thomas and obtain his authorisation. In great excitement Anne wrote him in French a letter whose handwriting was still a little childish. Thomas, in the Netherlands, was surprised by the maturity of her thinking while her whimsical orthography made him laugh. So he was easily convinced; the maturity of her mind was proof that she would know how to uphold her rank; the handwriting, that she could find no better instructor than the court of France. Two reasons, then, for letting her go and live there for a time. In France, Anne would pick up those graces and refinements whose renown at the court of England made the women dream and the men jealous.

I think today that Thomas Boleyn needed no convincing, and

41

that in fact he jumped at the opportunity. He had already taken his daughter Mary to the court of the Habsburgs at Brussels in the service of the Archduchess Margaret in the hope that there her beauty would attract a fiancé with a large fortune before she reached marriageable age. Granted, her sister Anne with her doubled finger, the mole on her neck, her too-black hair and her dull complexion had not a corresponding beauty to attract some rich gentleman, he counted on the grace, the charm, the elegance she would acquire in France to make up for these defects. I am afraid that in desiring these good matches for his daughters Thomas was thinking less for them than for himself. English fathers do not enjoy a good reputation abroad. Cynical egoists is the name they have as regards their children. This is untrue; I can vouch for it because my father and I . . . but hush! I must admit I could not say so much for Thomas Boleyn, whose conduct as the years passed was by no means a brilliant exhibition of caring. After killing his good and beautiful Elizabeth through constant pregnancies and losing no time in remarrying, he was concerned for his children only so far as they could help him in his personal ambitions. In sending first Mary to Brussels, then Anne to Paris, he was really thinking only of himself.

Thanks to my father, Anne had obtained permission for me to be included in the party for France. Not of course as a maid of honour (I was still too young for that) but as an attendant with functions not clearly defined, serving as a sort of lady companion. The almost panic fear that had seized Anne at the last moment – of being considered as low-bred and awkward in France – was thereby much relieved. She would have me beside her and I would lend her the support of my affection.

Mary Tudor and her innumerable suite – including among a thousand others, besides Anne and myself, Anne's father Thomas and his father-in-law Surrey, now Duke of Norfolk – left to catch the boat on the eve of St Nicholas. King Henry, Queen Catherine and all the great of the kingdom accompanied us as far as Dover. But we were kept waiting there by contrary winds before we could put to sea and when at last we were able

42

to leave port we were again overtaken by stormy weather and all, naturally, fell victims to sea-sickness. Or rather, all of us women; for the men pretended to be good sailors and if it came their way to be sick, as no doubt it did, they took care not to be seen. But Mary Tudor, her four-and-twenty maids of honour, my friend Anne and myself could none of us find the courage, throughout the crossing, to get up. For during seventeen days there was no end of making tacks in the Channel without our little fleet being able to get across. There was breakage of all kinds, sails torn off, masts split, hulls adrift. Some of us women, I do believe, actually died. The rest of us, one night, came near to perishing also. Worst of all was the arrival. With no hope of being able to make the port of Boulogne the flotilla sought refuge in the estuary of the Somme. But there Mary, her whole suite, Anne and I had to be carried in the arms of sailors from the ships into little boats and from the boats on to dry land.

For us young ones all this was more a joke than anything. "We almost capsized!" we repeated proudly to one another in the excitement of childish ignorance. But it was far otherwise for Mary Tudor. And most unfortunate. For King Louis was waiting for her at Amiens while the queen, worn out and bruised, all her finery still wet and mouldy, refused to leave Abbeville. On top of this it was raining cats and dogs. As a result, with Mary so young and yet in so wretched a state and the elderly king by contrast so sprightly, the difference in their ages seemed to be obliterated, if not reversed.

This meant that there was very little spirit in the merry-making, though there could be other reasons for that too. For I am almost sure that Mary exaggerated her physical exhaustion so as to justify the sad figure she cut. Anne and I were still too young to be aware of it but all the world knew that she was in love with another and that this marriage was breaking her heart; she had promised to marry the very handsome Lord Brandon, Charles Duke of Suffolk; and King Henry had wrecked his sister's happiness by marrying her to Louis of France, with his gout and his varicose veins. When I say that all the world knew, I have to admit that what they knew was only rumour.

But the event soon showed that the rumours had been right.

These dismal celebrations were the prelude to more sorrow yet. For fearing the effect on the new Queen of France of a retinue exclusively English, Louis made all of us women re-embark – and briskly too. It filled me with despair to see myself thus separated from Anne. For Anne, having won the affection of Princess Claude – wife to the Francis of Angoulême who was heir presumptive to Louis – was being retained in the princess's service. Anne's one companion was her young cousin Elizabeth Grey, grand-daughter of the late King Henry VII; long afterwards it was this Elizabeth's niece, Jane, who was to occupy the throne of England before being beheaded by Bloody Mary.

The vessel was already on the point of weighing anchor and there was I, weeping at the stern, when at the last moment someone came to make me go below. It was Anne, dear child, who despairingly had brought such pressure on Princess Claude as to persuade her to have me sent for. The tears of parting gave way to the laughter of reunion and soon Anne at the court and I as her shadow shared from month to month in the enchantment and magnificence of the royal household. Claude was like a mother to Anne and we might perhaps have been captivated by the engaging Francis, full of wit and always scheming after young girls, if his long sensual nose and his roguish little eyes had not frightened us off – and not without reason.

But I anticipate. We were not there yet. Anne was twelve and I was ten. Though Anne was fully adolescent her breasts had not developed and she did not yet attract the interest of men. So let us return to Mary Tudor; it had been to no purpose her brother's wrecking of her happiness for the sake of a connection with the King of France. Eighty-six days after the marriage Louis died of gangrene, carrying the high hopes of Henry with him to the grave.

Mary was now a widow and I had the idea that there and then she would be sent back to London and we with her. But Francis having become King of France, first of his name, had no wish to inaugurate his reign by such a piece of brutality. Claude for her part, now queen, had become so fond of Anne as to ask Thomas Boleyn, who had come over for the funeral, to allow her to keep his daughter. Thomas was indeed only too happy to agree. Let us make no mistake: Anne was not the only young woman in whom Claude took an interest; this queen had a marked propensity for the education of girls and her attentions were widely distributed. Between Anne Boleyn, her cousin Bessie Grey and a cluster of young Frenchwomen she divided her concern impartially within an institution that she had lately founded for young ladies of quality. There they all received a very strict training, in line with the character of this austere queen. The plan was to develop their gifts in singing, music, drawing, but above all in good manners, manners decent and restrained, to fit them for their entry into society. Although officially Anne's position was as maid of honour to Mary Tudor, Claude had withdrawn her from that service as soon as the king fell ill. Did she foresee the scandal that would supervene immediately upon the mourning and, foreseeing it, wish to spare the young girl? The fact is that when Brandon, Duke of Suffolk, arrived from London to present the condolences of the king and the court the widow, her face bathed in tears, threw herself into his arms and persuaded him to marry her within the hour; she knew that her brother would not hold her quit: failing the King of France, he would want to propose her to the Archduke Charles. A fine blaze of fire-works this set off on either side of the Channel.

But the first to get a laugh out of it was the king, Francis. I have just told you the poor opinion I had of him in the matter of morals. He flew from mistress to mistress – rare was the woman who resisted him – as drunkards flit from ale-house to ale-house. If this made the queen suffer she hardly showed it, barely manifesting a prudish disapproval, far less any humiliation as a wife, and less still any pain at heart. There had never been love between them and the marriage bed seemed to her a hell without any compensating pleasure. As for the king, he followed his desires without troubling himself about what she

45

thought. One even heard it whispered that his preferred mistress was his own sister, Margaret of Angoulême. I rather doubt it, though it was quite possible. They both had the same frivolous outlook in these matters, the same want either of restraint or of contrition. The very unconcern with which they carried on their misdemeanours helped to make these forgotten.

I ought by the way to say that Margaret impressed me a lot. She had married, six years earlier, Charles Duke of Alençon; but this was (as the saying goes) a marriage of convenience. Francis and she had for their tutor the first valet of King Louis, John Marot, the father of Clement. This gave the three children – Francis, Margaret and Clement Marot – a strong taste for poetry. Francis was not very gifted, but Margaret and the young Clement were rivals in the composition of excellent verses, rather in the manner of Boccaccio.

You will be surprised perhaps that I had stayed on at Court – where by the way there was open gossiping about all these things – since there was nothing any longer to justify my being there; I was not a maid of honour nor even from now on a lady companion for Anne in her college. So I was without employment. If the queen still kept me at court it was from pure kindness – more to Anne than to me – so that during the Christmas and Candlemas holidays, those of Holy Week and Ascension, Pentecost and Corpus Christi, of the Assumption of the Blessed Virgin Mary and the Ember Days, and above all during those longer holidays in the hot months of summer, Anne would not find herself without a friend to entertain her. But those holidays were times to remember. There were frequent festivities and together we disported ourselves with a little coterie of young ladies and pages who loved to laugh, to dance and to whisper sweet nothings to one another.

Anne was coming on now to thirteen and she adored dancing, giving herself to it body and soul. The liveliness of her mind made the boys love her and this put the girls against her. But at the age we were then feelings were fickle; the one who felt jealous of her today would be madly in love with her tomorrow. Between us all there was perpetual to-ing and fro-ing. One affection alone remained immutable: that which bound Anne and me.

Thus the weeks, the months, went by, divided between formal education, instruction of various kinds and our amusements. We were not yet allowed to join hunting parties, which vexed us a good deal; we thought it unfair because we were both by now very respectable riders. On the other hand, we had the best seats at tournaments, at tennis and at greyhound races. And since Anne was not one to keep her eyes lowered (no more was I, by the way) she was quick to spot the preferences of the ladies for this knight or that. Or to have the sense of amorous intrigues building up behind the scenes. These two schools, one of an education edifying and strict, the other of a court plentiful in wit and fun: one of a severe morality, the other of manners more emancipated, soon had a liberating influence upon her. She understood perfectly how to accommodate in her mind these two opposing outlooks and prepare to adapt herself accordingly. Here let me say that in this balancing Anne leaned rather to the grave than to the gay – in which, naturally, I as the younger followed her. But she had learnt that in the world around us we must know how to reckon with the one as with the other.

In growing up she had advanced as much in fineness of perception as in intelligence and charm. Her company was sought by young men a good deal older than herself. I believe that those relationships, which continued up to the time of her return to London, had a great influence on her thinking. Gentlemen all of Margaret's circle, and like her emancipated, like her profoundly given to thinking for themselves, discussed with Anne (whose precocity astonished them) God and the Church, men and nations. They did not conceal from her their dislike of dogma, of the stifling hold of the Church upon men's minds and upon nation-states. They made her read – it goes without saying – the works of Erasmus and of his English friends Colet and Grocyn but also those of older writers – Maricourt, Nicholas of Cusa, Lefèvre of Etaples – and of our compatriots Roger Bacon and his master, Grosseteste. Though

Anne was very devout she enthused over these open minds and would talk to me for hours about them before going to bed. I was too young – only ten – to follow her easily but her reflections were for the most part intended for herself. This seriousness beyond her years had not the least effect, I ought to add, on her childish delight in balls and fancy-dress. Often at the close of one of these deep discussions she would put on her beautiful brand-new shoes to whirl around in a galliard or circle in a slow sarabande, throwing herself into it with all her heart. Or she would saddle her mare and go out and compete in trick-riding with riders twice her age.

She had nearly completed her twelfth year when the whole court of France rang with King Francis's victories in Italy.

## II

## (1515–1522)

# *The Field of the Cloth of Gold*

To speak impartially today of King Henry will require of me great self-control. Ever since his hateful legal murder of Queen Anne I cannot help loathing the man. He is dead and although by now his corpse must be as rotted as his soul I would still, if I could, tear his eyes out. But this is how I feel about him now. I must in good faith admit that these were not always my sentiments. My idea of him when I was young was very different.

In those days Henry displayed himself in all his brilliance. He was tall, willowy, radiant, a splendid figure. Stored with knowledge of all kinds, his mind blazed with a thousand fires. Mountjoy, chamberlain to Catherine of Aragon, would delight in recalling that Henry had once said to him when he was still only Prince of Wales: "Without science life would have no meaning". In argument with Thomas More on metaphysics Henry could hold his ground at every point; and the great philosopher had greeted his accession to the throne with a poem inscribed on parchment, illuminated with miniatures adorned with precious stones. Beside the king the highest-ranking nobles appeared as ignorant brutes. To say truth, at the time when we were in France people in general seemed not much further advanced. The taste for letters and the arts that had come from Italy had penetrated only into the palace and those around King Francis. On either side of the Channel military glory was the one thing that counted for the majority of nobles. Daring and strength, victories on the battlefield and in tournament were all that they admired. Poetry, music and painting seemed to them pastimes for women and impotent men. They took it as an insult to be mixed up with clerks.

49

Perhaps, by the way, if Anne and I had never left England, had had no better education than that of these semi-barbarians, had known only these rough manners, this male boorishness, we might never have noticed it. We had to live long enough at the court of France to discover its refinements. For there King Francis was making an effort to escape from those Dark Ages, to make the arts more glorious than arms and return scorn for scorn to these dull-witted fighting men.

I shall not pretend to have come to consciousness of this all at once. When something is changing from day to day under your eyes, you take it in as a matter of course and do not notice any movement. Then one day you wake up with a taste for the refinement which has flowered in you unawares. I have to go back to my memory to be able to measure, between our arrival in France and our departure seven years later, how swift this development was. At the time of our first year in France the king had still, if he wished to win esteem, to give proof not of a lively mind but of manly valour. This last had shone out in good earnest in the Italian campaign when, at the head of his troops and on the morrow of his twenty-first birthday, Francis had defeated at Marignan the forces of the Duke of Milan. On his return to Paris crowned with glory he now had the authority to impose upon his court a new set of values, no longer setting in the front rank great feats of arms but rather great works of art and their creators. It was the start of a new world.

Anne and I had naturally been swept into this movement. We fully shared Francis's irony over the rumours coming from London where the echo of this warrior-glory had stunned the court. Henry could afford to sleep no longer. He saw his rival eclipsing his own prestige and we asked ourselves in smiling wonder how he would set about restoring it. Not long before Marignan, so the story went, he was receiving with great pomp and ceremony an embassy of lords from Venice who had passed through France. He had interrupted their compliments impatiently to ask about Francis: "Is he as tall as I am?"

"Yes, Your Grace, just about."

50

"And as broad across the shoulders?"

"Not quite."

"Ah! and his legs?"

"Rather thin, Your Majesty."

"Look at mine!" And the king had opened the folds of his tunic to display his thighs: "And my calves too are every bit as beautiful!" Then, after relishing their stupefaction, he had added with a condescending smile: "I am very fond of the King of France".

Unwisely he had told these Venetians that Francis would never cross the Alps except with his permission. Consequently, when a little later he learnt that the hardy fellow had indeed just crossed them, followed by twenty thousand men to fall upon the backs of the Swiss and cut them in pieces, he was beside himself. In reporting this news to us our games-companions at the French court had the fun of teasing us: would we, as good Englishwomen, be upset with Henry or, like the Frenchwomen we had almost become, rejoice with Francis? Truly, within our circle these tales of fighting men, of victories or defeats, of losses or annexations seemed as far away as they were unimportant. At our age what fascinated us much more was the news that Henry was consoling himself for Francis's success by a great sentimental adventure, his first after six years of marriage. The object of his attentions was a girl of seventeen, Elizabeth Blount, who had shown herself quite forward in relation to the king; and with whom he had taken refuge in his lands of Abingdon to escape the pestilence which was ravaging London. Bessie Blount's father meanwhile had been rewarded for his understanding by being promptly raised to the dignity of Equerry of the Palace. We asked ourselves what would happen if Queen Catherine took umbrage. Did it astonish us to hear that this romantic idyll had in no way envenomed relations between the royal wife and husband? So far from that, to win pardon Henry was redoubling his attentions to the queen and to his little daughter Mary, whom until then he had neglected.

This was also the moment when Martin Luther set in hand

51

the reform of the Church in Germany. It was not too clear what he expected to come out of it nor what would be its consequence in a land where every novelty is at risk of spreading like a bush-fire. Francis seemed not to fear the contagion for the "eldest daughter of the Church"; taught by her friends, Anne saw in the movement rather a prospect of liberation. But the Most Christian King of England viewed it with grave disquiet; there were in the kingdom certain spirits too much inclined already to these new ideas and he felt a great need to draw close to Rome and to France. To win the goodwill of Francis he began by proposing to sell Tournai back to him at half the price its conquest had cost him. This affair once settled, Wolsey followed it up by broaching an engagement between Princess Mary of England, then aged two, and the scarcely older Dauphin of France. It was Catherine of Aragon whom this news troubled more than any. As the aunt of the King of Spain, the Archduke Charles, she saw in it the germ of something she had always dreaded: a reversal of alliance in France's favour. On the other hand, as a fervent Catholic she was no less alarmed by the progress Luther was making in Germany. There are situations where it is not easy to know what it is one really wants.

All this we learnt in confidence from certain English gentlemen who had come to the court of France in the ambassador's suite. King Francis took a fancy to them and we watched with great amusement how they lent themselves to his extravagances with the ardour of novices. They accompanied him on horseback through the streets of Paris, disguised and masked like him, and found delight in showering on passers-by such stupid projectiles as doughnuts stuffed with honey or soft-boiled eggs. The court, though far from prudish, considered that this conduct went beyond the proprieties; out loud it blamed the impertinence of the young Englishmen but secretly laid the blame on the levity of the French king. But to Anne and me, remembering the affectation of starchiness with which gentlemen at the court of England mask their private misdemeanours, this upsurge of joyous emancipation was refreshing.

*

In the January after the pestilence Maximilian of Austria died of a stroke, leaving the throne of the Empire vacant. Election of a new emperor was to take place in the month of June.

From them on we lived as in a whirlwind. Each royal candidate tried to outdo his rivals by a display of his riches and splendour. Francis's hat was in the ring, along with those of Henry and Charles of Spain, and there were rival and sumptuous receptions at all three courts the whole time; those of Paris or of Amboise led us in our little coterie into endless discussions, disputes and forecasts as to who would be the likely winner. Anne bet on Francis, I on Henry; we did not know much about the King of Spain, who was hardly any older than ourselves. How could we suspect that the issue was already decided, over the heads of the candidates? What determined the election was the ingenuity of Margaret of Austria, governor of the Netherlands. Quite simply, she pawned the port of Antwerp with all its ships to the great German bankers, the Fuggers of Augsburg, and with the money so borrowed bought at one stroke the votes of the Great Elector princes. A smart trick! So it was Charles, fifth of the name, who won the day; Anne found him very ugly, with his protruding chin – to me his air of melancholy was touching. Spain, Austria, Germany, the Netherlands and Southern Italy were now united under his sceptre and he became, at nineteen years old, the absolute master of half Europe; until the day, that is, when Luther would challenge his authority on the soil of Germany.

Anne and I had lost our bets. We could well imagine Henry's bitter disappointment and in some anxiety for our fun and games we watched to see how Francis would react. And in fact for several days Francis hardly appeared and there was an air of gloom at Court. But not for nothing was he known as the "Champagne-King". His light and bubbly spirit soon got the better of his grief. And after the failure of his candidature, with the same whirlwind enthusiasm that he had put into it, he now set about putting the failure out of his mind. Accompanied by fifteen hundred squires and pages and as many ladies and young maids, including Anne and me, the king set off to ride from town to town and from castle to castle to enjoy this whirl of pageantry. I could not give you the names of all the cities where we followed him, for I can't remember them myself. Nor describe these entertainments in detail, which besides would be boring. But I can picture in my mind Abbeville, Boulogne, St Quentin, Ecouen and especially Rouen where our reception was more sumptuous and dazzling than at any other town in the kingdom.

There was a profusing of tapestries; there were altars of repose; *tableaux vivants*; allegories, nymphs, goddesses and that strange marriage of Mount Olympus and Paradise at which Minerva claimed from Jupiter a place at his right hand for Francis: all under the Blessed Virgin's watchful eye while in her arms she cuddled a lamb, symbol of the city which was giving itself to its king. Throughout these festivities Anne delighted me by her eagerness to take part. As for the King of France, none of his political projects was ever so bold and inventive as the ones he thought up in the course of these joyous merry-makings. When at last we found ourselves back at Amboise he had made up his mind to drive Charles V out of Naples and made ready for armed conflict.

This put my friend Anne in great danger. Up till then Francis had hardly taken notice of this young damsel of fifteen years. But if he were now to oust the emperor from the peninsula the warmer relationship with England which Wolsey had embarked upon had become urgent. With this in view, seeking a contact with Thomas Boleyn, England's ambassador to the Netherlands, Francis remembered that this man's daughter was at his court. He sent for her and found her charming. She herself cherished for the French king one of those adolescent infatuations which come to nothing. Even so, I trembled for her virtue. What perhaps preserved her virginity was the fear and horror that physical love inspired in both of us. Francis, fortunately, was too frivolous to waste his time in forcing the defences of so tender a creature. Besides, his first concern was that she should be a link for him with her father. Perhaps he also relished this naive resistance. Or else – it is quite possible – he feared to draw on himself the ire of Anne's protectress, his own Queen Claude. At all events, from that day Anne enjoyed the protection of the King of France as well.

Thomas, not being able to quit his post in the Netherlands, despatched to France his right arm – who was, as you will have gathered already, my father. Thus it was that Anne and I came to see for ourselves that an understanding between France and England was on the stocks. Back in London, my father informed Wolsey of the King of France's friendly dispositions. Thomas let my father know that at the same moment Wolsey had received similar overtures from the Emperor Charles, concerned as he was to put down a strong movement of opposition in Spain. So my father, unintentionally, found himself in possession of the trumps in the diplomatic game on which Wolsey was engaged. But his heart, like Anne's and mine, inclined to France. Naturally I do not know how far Wolsey was still hesitating between Charles and Francis and in my ignorance I would not dare to venture an opinion. It was, however, in favour of the second that the balance inclined and in this my father – at least I like to think so – played his part.

A meeting between King Henry and Francis was accordingly arranged. It could have taken place quite simply. But Henry loved splendour, a taste in which Francis was his equal. Each counted on a magnificent display to upstage his rival. Nor did Wolsey lag behind in this sort of competition. His wealth, acquired in the king's service, the revenues of the numerous bishoprics and abbeys that were in his charge, left him small need to envy even the king's own fortune. In his extensive palace at York Place in London, which housed some thousand of his servants and dependants, Wolsey had amassed carpets from the East, tapestries from Aubusson, vessels of gold, et cetera, which he was by no means loath to display. With this taste for ostentation on the part of the two kings and the cardinal the encounter was sure to be of triple magnificence, so Anne and I, whom Francis invited to the ceremonies, could reckon on a gorgeous spectacle. In the event its splendour far surpassed even the wildest imagination.

All the same we ought to have expected it. Francis's enthusiasm for art in all its forms, together with his appetite for festivities and ceremonial, had driven him to attach to himself in his residence at Amboise two or three Italian painters around the elderly Leonardo da Vinci. I do not know whether anyone has ever made so strong an impression on us as Leonardo. When Anne and I passed him in the gallery it was as if we were passing Moses as Moses is depicted in the Bible. The day when by a gesture he made Anne stop so that pensively he could lift her chin towards him she felt, she told me, as though the earth were opening under her feet. The blood drummed even in my ears. While thus, head on one side, he studied her, there appeared to me on his face so profound and melancholy a sadness that pity for him took possession of me. I could see him slowly shaking his majestic beard and verily I thought I heard him murmur, "Too late". Not long after, he died, in Francis's arms.

Meantime it had been this Leonardo who had organised the most dazzling entertainments, each time with a little more luxury infused into the beauty, as he had done earlier for the Sforzas in Milan. At the time when Francis went to meet Henry, Leonardo had been dead a year. But the king had learnt from him now to find room for ever more gold, ever more diamonds, within the pompous setting of a royal ceremony. Henry and Wolsey were aware of it. So as not to be outdone, they inquired from my father, who inquired from us, what was preparing in the workshops of Blois. That is how Anne and I came to have a share as involuntary artisans in the unprecedented spectacle which at this moment was dazzling our eyes and took the name of the Field of the Cloth of Gold.

Never have political discussions opened, and perhaps never will again, in so extravagant an overflow of luxury. Never also, no doubt, in a parallel uncertainty. For longer than four hundred years the two countries had been at war. Up to the last moment everyone kept asking whether the friendly meeting might not turn into a pitched battle from the outset. Henry had sent ahead of him an army of carpenters and glaziers from London who had erected a fabulous palace of glass for him on the frontier crossing the plain south of Calais (between Guines on English territory and Ardres on French). More than three thousand tents of white satin starred with gold surrounded this grandiose construction where the morning sun could look himself in the face.

Opposite, on the French side, an equal number of tents sparkling in gold waved in the breath of the breeze. At an equal distance from the two camps towered a pavilion of such prodigious height and spellbinding opulence that you would have thought it purloined from some legendary sultan. A statue of St Michael trampling the dragon crowned it. Some way away a colossal triumphal arch arose and behind it a vast enclosure intended for tournaments and encircled with platforms. These were draped in velvet and silk in the colours alternately of the two kings. The organisers on the English side had been Thomas Boleyn (recalled for that purpose from Brussels) and particularly my father, his right arm; so that Anne and I had been at the centre of the whole affair and in consequence were given the best seats. All that I shall now have to tell of the spectacle passed under our eyes.

The prelude to the meeting is worth relating because it was so comical. Henry had announced that from that moment he would let his beard grow and not cut it. Francis sent word in reply that he would do the same; it would be a symbol of their pact of friendship. But this came very near to turning sour. For Catherine, put out and irritated by this getting-together with France, had never ceased badgering the king and making a mock of him, so that eventually he gave way and shaved himself. It did not take long for the French queen mother Louise of Savoy to hear of this. She sent for Thomas Boleyn and warned him that if this were meant as a breach of promise she would tell her son, let the consequences be what they might. I can see us now, all four of us, Anne and me and our two fathers, discussing what would be the answer

57

most likely to placate Louise. Diplomacy had become second nature to Thomas Boleyn and he inclined to some formula which could be interpreted any way you liked and would commit no-one to anything. My father worked himself almost to death in trying to draft something that would answer the purpose but it was so delicate a business that hours passed and we got nowhere. To the surprise of us all it was Anne who in the end proved the most sensible. Why not keep to the simplest explanation? "Henry had cut off his beard out of love for the queen"; it was answer enough. My father said she was right. Thomas followed his guidance, reassured the queen mother and obtained her promise to say nothing. But he let Henry understand what a danger his gesture had created. Henry took his point, stopped shaving and when he embarked on the "Henry Grace of God" to go to the Field of the Cloth of Gold he was as well-bearded as Francis.

There was nothing for it but to await a meeting which remained as big with menace as with hope. The general public had been forbidden access to the Field. But how to hold back an inquisitive, excited crowd! The archers had the greatest difficulty in keeping them out of the enclosure, which was guarded only by frail barriers. When Henry who had disembarked at Calais appeared on the hill-top with his retinue of armed knights the tension rose to a climax. A crowd that had been garrulous, cheerful, astir and boisterous fell suddenly silent and rooted to the spot. On the hill opposite, Francis stood with his armed gentlemen. Under the sun, breast-plates glittered in both parties. My father, who was present on the English side, confided to us later the very real fears he had experienced during that time of waiting which had seemed to us interminable. For around King Henry opinions remained divided up to the last moment.

"Sire," Lord Shrewsbury had urged, "we are the stronger in numbers. Go boldly on and Francis falls into our hands."

"Stop," Lord Abergavenny entreated. "It's the other way round. I have been in the French camp. They are twice our numbers."

"I also," retorted Shrewsbury, "am just come from there and I can assure you that their soldiers are more afraid of us than we are of them."

The king swayed between the two counsels, each equally supported among his suite. Between the word for war and the word for peace Henry's irresolute character chose the middle way: the one which destiny would choose. On a sign to his officers the trumpets sounded, the horns of the French replied and the two companies, each the pride of its nation, hurtled downhill at top speed face to face. For one minute Anne and I, in the front row of that breathless assembly, trembled in anticipation of the two squadrons running one another through. But with a motion of his arm Francis brought his lancers to a halt; and leaving them where they were he went on alone, at the trot, upon his mount. It was a sight to see. Whether Henry was in two minds or whether it was Francis's gallantry which decided Henry's mind for him I do not know; at any rate he likewise brought his knights to a halt. And the two kings galloped at full tilt directly towards one another. They drew bridle at the same moment, set foot to ground and then, opening their arms wide, held one another in a long embrace to the sound of applause and ovations from an audience both exuberant and relieved. Then, side by side, they made their way to the colossal pavilion while their respective escorts, since the word was not to tear each other's guts out, made high holiday as brothers and went off to drink together.

No one knows what was said under the superb curtains of the pavilion but the two monarchs seemed to be on excellent terms with one another when they came out. Games came next, then tournaments, in the course of which Henry who wanted to impress Frenchmen (and Frenchwomen) spent the afternoon in discomfiting one adversary after another and foundered eight horses under him.

In fact the French gentlemen around us were so astounded that Anne and I gained in prestige from Henry's performance; our companions spoke to us with a respect tinged with admiration. This would have been very gratifying if we had not

59

observed in them at the same time a certain tension. It was becoming evident after the effusions of the first day that mistrust subsisted. Security measures to protect the king in either camp, far from being relaxed, tended to be stepped up.

An invisible but seemingly impassable barrier kept the two sovereigns apart. It was this barrier that the King of France – to the wonder and astonishment of all – resolved to break down.

He did it with his habitual fantasy – and smiling audacity. As soon as he woke in the morning he dressed, mounted his horse and with a single squire for escort presented himself before the dozen or so watchmen on guard before the tent of the King of England. So astonished were they to see Francis that they did not dare to stop him; a single bugle only rang out in haste to sound the reveille; it was this that woke Henry at the same instant as Francis lifted the fold of the tent. Jumping from his bed and quite flabbergasted, he found himself presented at the hands of the King of France ("I am your valet") with his shirt and doublet. "I am your prisoner" was Henry's prompt retort, as he slipped off a necklace to put it over Francis's head. He received in exchange a bracelet and thereafter the two kings were "tu" and "toi" to each other.

This stunning occurrence was at once reported by Henry's squire to Thomas Boleyn, by Thomas to my father, finally by Anne and me to our games-companions and from there it spread like wildfire. As a result the festivities became infinitely joyous. At dinner Anne found herself seated so that she was practically face to face with the King of England. She had thus full scope to study him. But when I asked her afterwards how she had found him she made a bit of a face and said, "Not so handsome as the King of France". It is true, as I've mentioned, that she felt a certain fascination for Francis. Some make out that it was Francis who with a smile drew Henry's attention to the young girl. What is certain is that while Henry was looking at her I noticed him saying a word or two to Wolsey beside him. But this one look, according to my own observation, was not followed by others. Anne at that moment simply blushed a little.

The two sovereigns met daily over a period of two weeks. On the night of St John a sudden tempest carried off the tents, well lashed down though they had been. It took three days to set them up again. At the time this seemed to us a bad omen (and so it proved). But the conference results were reassuring. In sum, in pledge of lasting peace Henry solemnly renounced by treaty his rights of inheritance to the territories in dispute. As a set-off, in exchange for the matrimonial agreement which should unite the Dauphin to Princess Mary, Henry was to receive, up to the celebration of the marriage, an annual payment of a hundred thousand gold crowns. My father learnt later that Wolsey had not been forgotten and that to reward him for his good offices he requested and obtained from Francis a comfortable pension. It was the wealth of France that made this liberality possible.

All seemed settled, then, for the best. There followed new tournaments and fabulous celebrations. My father had been present at the talks and he laughed to tell us of the disconcerted look on Henry's face when in the throes of discussing matters of substance, Francis would put on a fantastic, frivolous, facetious expression; then, next moment, on a minor issue, suddenly appear imperturbably serious. These switches of mood disconcerted the English king. Thomas Boleyn was no less put out, I might add, at finding himself one evening taken by the arm: "The day you see me as emperor", Francis had said in his ear; "give me a few months and I will have advanced right up to Constantinople or I will have perished on the way". Did Henry, to whom this remark was of course passed on, see this ambition as a challenge? Anyhow, after the archery at which Henry had excelled in front of the ladies, he suddenly grasped the King of France by the neck, shouting: "Let's fight!" and immediately seized him in his powerful arms.

"Oh! He'll make mincemeat of him," Anne whispered to me in distress. I, who did not share her tender sentiments for Francis, had no objection to the idea of an English victory, which indeed seemed more than likely. The Englishman was tall, broad, massive and weighed half as much again as the

Frenchman, whose slimness in the other's arms made him seem as flimsy as a wisp of straw. In fact, in no time Francis was thrown to the ground, one shoulder touching. But, nimble as an eel, he slipped to one side and was on his feet, laughing good-humouredly. He was thrown to the ground a second time and Henry, pressing him down with all his great bulk, saw himself as already the victor when Francis, by an adroit pass which Henry had not foreseen, making him fall over on his thigh, came back on him and taking him by surprise had him touching with both shoulders. Anne refrained from applauding. I could see at once that when Henry got up he was livid with rage. He called out loud for a return match but Catherine, taking Queen Claude and her suite outside, had the wisdom to put an end to a dangerously tense situation.

Throughout the rest of the evening I noticed that Anne remained pensive. Already in the matter of the beards she had surprised us by a sureness of judgement rare in an adolescent. In days to come she was due to surprise me far more by her insight and political acumen.

"The king," she said to me after dinner with an air of anxiety, "is not one to digest his humiliation. Not able to take his revenge on the sports ground, he will try to take it on a field far wider. And you and I will very soon be recalled to England."

"Recalled?" I said, astonished. "And why? What field? What revenge?"

"If I can imagine myself in his place, I can guess very well what Henry is going to do. In humiliating him by his victory Francis has given him mortal offence. I would stake my life that the first care of this shifty devil will be to meet the emperor."

"Oh no!" I protested in alarm. "That would be to destroy everything."

"It is in fact what I fear. Let us hope I am wrong."

In the days that followed we heard nothing. It was not till much later that Anne and I learnt that the king had lost no time in proving her right. And even sooner than she had supposed.

For first of all the unexpected presence of the emperor in

Flanders had come to Henry's ears. Charles had been anxious about this interview with Francis and was already thinking of levying his troops. Henry sent him word that before re-embarking at Calais he would meet him at Gravelines should his well-loved nephew so wish. To which Charles was quick to agree, and a few days later they met. On parting they seemed to be well satisfied. Knowing that Francis would soon hear of it, Henry took the initiative and with an appearance of frankness and honesty sent him word that all he had done was to pay a visit of courtesy to his nephew by marriage; if the emperor, as one might expect, had pressed for some agreement, Henry had given nothing away: he had kept his faith with Francis intact.

But Francis was no more of an innocent than Henry. Just as capable himself of similar underhand procedures when the occasion called for it, he realised without any great surprise that he had been fooled and must lose no time in taking his dispositions accordingly.

In fact it was not long before the court at Amboise learnt that the English seemed to be preparing for war; that Henry had just put ships into his yards for fitting out; that, if rumour could be trusted, he had contingents ready to march; that he was sending ammunition to the Netherlands for the emperor's troops and was dispatching volunteers to fight in their ranks. So Francis felt he must get a start on him as early as possible.

Perhaps, as things turned out, his response was a little too hasty. He had sent a regiment to help Henry of Albret to win back Navarre for Margaret but the expedition failed. In the north, certainly, the emperor's men had been forced by Bayard and Montmorency to abandon the siege of Mézières but they took prompt revenge by occupying Tournai. In Italy Sforza was returning to Milan. Lautrec was losing Parma and Piacenza, and then went on to die of cholera before Naples. Whereupon Francis's agents informed him that Henry, seeing him in this sad plight, had signed the treaty of alliance with the emperor; while from the Vatican came news that the Pope, Leo X, had joined with them, taking sides against France.

Back in London, my father and Thomas Boleyn realised that Francis could not put up with such a series of reverses without losing face; that between France and the House of Austria some game of immense proportions was about to be played out; and that England would find herself fatally involved in it. As Anne had foreseen, they gave us orders to leave Paris as a matter of urgency and cross the Channel as soon as we could.

Anne had been glad of Francis's victory in the wrestling match against Henry; she blamed Henry openly for having allied himself with Charles; she would have liked to believe that Francis would keep her with him. He did nothing of the sort and even speeded up our departure. Between our French friends and ourselves the farewells were heartrending. But the tears Anne shed were not only of regret; they were much more of resentment and vexation. She had thought that France was adopting her and now it appeared that she was no longer in demand. Her mind underwent a sort of revolution. She had felt she had become almost a Frenchwoman; now she discovered she was English again. Between one day and the next she found her strength of character once more; she would look reality in the face. The future she had hoped to construct for herself in France had been refused to her? Very well! It would be in England, then, that she would carve out her destiny.

III

(1523–1526)

# Thomas Wolsey

Return to the court of England was a severe ordeal. Coming back from Paris or Amboise where certainly there was great freedom of manners, but with refinement and elegance to soften it, we had forgotten the uncouthness of the court of London. It struck us now as coarser than ever. What was done discreetly in France was performed here in all its crudity. Ladies showed off their legs. They kissed the men as they would a lady being presented to them. They went out to dinner unchaperoned with their husbands' friends (or enemies), and the husbands did full as much on their side. Gentlemen, not caring (as they do in France) about the "point of honour", would be at daggers drawn for a mere word, striking their enemy even in the back; then they would go off to some tavern together to get themselves drunk and forget their wounds.

There was the same tendency to excess in the magnificence of their receptions, as at the Field of the Cloth of Gold. Anne arrived just at the right moment to find herself included in one of the most spectacular. Against her return her father had kept a place warm for her as a maid of honour to Queen Catherine. Following the interview at Gravelines Charles had sent ambassadors to London to negotiate the basis of an understanding. Wolsey welcomed them at York Place with a sumptuousness that beggars all description. Hundreds of torches lighted the approach, illuminating the stained glass of the windows and the tapestries on the walls. At the far end of the apartment the cardinal had had a delicate construction run up at short notice – an emerald castle with turrets and machicolations, the whole coated in cloth of emerald colour, while over a fire a decoction of vinegar and verdigris floated upwards in clouds of the same hue. It was a fairy vision. On the ramparts the Vices and the Virtues were represented by eight young girls on the one side and eight in white on the other. Anne was there in the middle of the Virtues.

Whereupon, when the cannon had sounded to welcome the plenipotentiaries, the action commenced. It was an attack on the fortress led by Edward Neville, the king's cousin who was as like him as a brother, tall, broad and similarly dressed; so that Henry, watching from the wings, could see himself leading the assault. The battle was fought out with blows from flowers and bits of sponge steeped in rose oil. When this artillery was exhausted the lady defenders capitulated, well and truly perfumed, and the king's "double" made prisoners of them. Then to the vast delight of the German ambassadors and their suite he handed the ladies to them as their dancing partners.

I have shown you already how precocious Anne was in her mind, though still so young, while this in no way diminished her zest for games and dancing. I found her that evening in a state of high excitement. Without mistaking the identity of the pretended king she had enjoyed dancing with him. But when I spoke to her of the king himself she dropped her light-hearted manner and looked very stern.

In France to win the good will of Francis and that refined court Henry had kept his own rude manners in check, to the point that it was possible to be mistaken about his real nature. Whereas here in London he was giving that nature free rein. He was a mature man now, in his thirties, and his athletic build had given way to a certain stoutness; at the same time his ardent character had turned to an impatience that was brutal, loud, impudent and conceited. Anne's perspicacity had seen the mischief and the danger this could lead to. Perhaps her judgement of Henry had been given a still sharper edge when she learnt on her return from France that her elder sister Mary was the king's mistress.

She loved her sister and her father, but what had added pain to her indignation was the way things had been managed.

What Thomas Boleyn had earlier hoped for his daughter in sending her to Flanders had been realised according to his wishes. A gentleman of the king's chamber, come on a visit to Brussels, had singled her out immediately. His name was William Carey, he was not without fortune and a marriage was soon concluded. Back in London with him and thus every day under Henry's eye, Mary had dazzled the monarch by her beauty. Reckoning a royal adultery as in no way comparable to ordinary infidelity, the husband had eagerly pushed his wife into the sovereign's arms. It was Thomas Boleyn himself who had become the intermediary in this liaison which was to bring them as a family such big advantages. For the complaisant husband, I might add, this proved a bitter disappointment; the king found his presence at Court more of a hindrance than a help and got rid of him without much in the way of compensation. But it was otherwise for Boleyn, the father. Henry valued his sound judgement, his skill as a diplomat and above all his eagerness to please the king. He rewarded him for his trouble in this affair by a succession of lucrative appointments – first, Treasurer of the Royal Household, then Steward of Tonbridge and of Swaffham, Collector of the Royal Revenue at Bransted, Warden of Thunderley and of Westwood Park – all of which gave him the means, if not the right, to hold his head high in the aristocracy. Accordingly the king conferred on him the title of Lord Rochford, which had just fallen vacant.

From this time on Thomas, and necessarily Anne with him, were no longer absent from the court where Mary was queen in all but name. Boleyn established himself luxuriously, quite close to the royal palace, in a three-storied house built of brick and half-timber. Over the kitchens, the ground floor, richly furnished by the king, was reserved for Mary. A door giving out discreetly on to an alley enabled Henry to visit her at any hour without being seen. Anne's apartments were on the second floor where she was installed according to her tastes and, in order to have me with her, had reserved for me two rooms on the side with a spiral staircase which left me independent. Anne's father shared the first storey with George, lately married to Jane Parker; the king had enriched its furnishing with gold ornaments, crystalware, mirrors, tapestries, etc., and it was this that put Anne into constant agitation. Certainly at the court of France she had seen this kind of thing and worse. But not with this cynicism bordering on boorishness. Like any other daughter she had loved her father and admired him; she was still firmly attached to him but it revolted her that he should coldly treat his daughter as a piece of merchandise. At the same time she could not help being happy for her sister's sake, whose future seemed now to be well assured. She fought in her mind between these contrary sentiments, not knowing how to disentangle the good from the bad, until finally her one idea was to leave the house where everything reminded her of a shameless transaction. But where to go and how to live? She could see only one way and that was to find a husband as soon as possible.

She could perhaps have done this in France if only her father had left her the time. One of those lettered young men (in the circle of Margaret and William Budé) who had taught her so much during her adolescence had fallen in love with Anne when she was grown up; another sent her verses in the style of Clement Marot – clumsy verses enough, to say truth. Anne had felt flattered but her heart had not spoken. She was inclining to a third suitor at just the moment when Thomas had recalled her to the fold: which he did not only because he saw the tension rising with France but also because for the past two years he had been preparing for his younger daughter, naturally without consulting her, a husband whom he thought would suit her.

Between the English branch of the Butlers, to which the stepmother of Thomas Boleyn belonged, and that of the Irish chieftain, Piers Butler, lord-deputy to the viceroy of Ireland it was war to the knife. Both parties laid claim to the same county of Ormond, whose lands Piers had taken possession of by a provisional judgement. But the title had remained in suspense for many years. The English branch had the ear of Wolsey and the Irish that of the king, so the matter was stuck without hope of resolution. Now Piers had an illegitimate son James, who could make – so her uncle Norfolk had said – an excellent match for the great-granddaughter of a draper. It would be the way to unite the two branches of the Butlers, to establish their joint right to the county of Ormond and put an end to their quarrel. Cardinal Wolsey had pronounced himself in favour of a marriage which would make an amicable settlement of this tiresome business; the king on his side looked forward to having the lord-deputy's support to strengthen his hold on an Ireland which was continuously in turmoil. Everyone, then, was satisfied until Piers, on thinking it over, became afraid of losing his hold on his son after the marriage and so put in an impossible claim for compensation by way of dowry. For a whole year Norfolk and Thomas Boleyn had tried to work out a compromise. To no purpose; Butler was inflexible. The project had had to be shelved indefinitely.

In France we had known nothing of this move and it was only on her return that Anne heard of its breakdown. She shuddered to think what a fate she had escaped! To see herself a prisoner for life in that far-off country, damp, uncultured, violent and for good measure surrounded on all sides by the sea; in that castle of Kilkenny, sure to be half in ruins and open to the winds: cloistered with what she pictured as a lout with red hair. She would have died there of boredom and despair.

It was soon after her return to London and when she had shaken off this emotional upheaval that she made the acquaintance of a handsome and ardent young man with rosy cheeks, fair hair and broad shoulders, named Henry Percy. His father the Earl of Northumberland had placed him with Cardinal Wolsey to learn the ways of public life, etiquette and diplomacy. In attendance on the cardinal Percy was thus almost daily at Court where he met Anne Boleyn often. He lost no time in singling her out from the other maids of honour, whom she surpassed with her French elegance and the liveliness of her mind. He was soon madly in love with her and Anne herself was not indifferent to his attentions.

Unluckily, Northumberland had betrothed him in infancy

to the heiress of a great family with whom the Percys were in alliance; Mary Talbot was her name, daughter of the Earl of Shrewsbury, and the date of the marriage was already decided. Percy had never seen the girl, but hated her from a distance and was resolved to marry Anne. Certainly he had no lack of physical courage but, as often happens, under this martial vigour was hidden a spineless character. He would willingly have confronted a squad of armed men with only a sword but he trembled in fear before his father. Rather than have the pluck to tell him that he wished to break the engagement, he fell back on the solution which, though the bolder, made less demand on courage – to fly with Anne Boleyn and marry her secretly in Scotland.

But meanwhile people had got wind of the romance and Wolsey had been informed. On the very day that Percy was preparing his flight he was summoned to appear before the Cardinal and all the gentlemen of his suite. It was one of them, Thomas Wyatt, who told me later how Wolsey made the young man confess his matrimonial purposes. Wolsey represented to him that they were impossible: his rank, his fortune, the extent of his lands constituted an obligation. They destined him to marry the young lady of high rank whom his father had chosen for him and not the impertinent young commoner who had wanted to seduce him.

Percy wept and threw himself at the cardinal's feet. He swore by all the gods that Anne had made no advances to him; the whole fault was his own. The Boleyns, he pointed out, were related to the Norfolks and Thomas had just been made a lord. He implored Wolsey to break off the engagement made in infancy which reduced him to despair and exert his influence in favour of the union marked out by love and his high esteem for Anne's character.

But all this only irritated his protector. He was bluntly dismissed and Wolsey lost no time in warning the Earl of Northumberland that he ought to remove his rebel son as soon as possible. The earl impressed upon Percy that he must obey him if he did not want to be thoroughly beaten, and receive his father's curse into the bargain. The young man made an effort to hold out but his resistance weakened and finally collapsed. Without any further struggle his father carried him off to his lands on the Scottish border where the marriage promptly took place.

If I had not already had occasion to measure the strength of Anne's character, her gallantry now would have surprised me. She sobbed for an hour, wept for two days, moaned for a week and was sad for three months. Then one day when she seemed in a sombre mood and I tried again to comfort her, she put up a hand to stop me, saying almost with a smile: "No good; it's over. I've buried my grief and this whole business. More even than his deserting me, it's this traitor's cowardice that I resent. That he should give way as he did disgusts me."

"We don't all have your strength of character."

"So much the worse. I don't want to think of him again and I'm even going to tell you: I've come round to being thankful for this break-up. Yes, it saves me from having to discover too late that I'm married to a piece of old rag. But there is no ordeal which has not its good side. From now on I know very well what it is that I want."

The piece of old rag wrote to her from the north letter upon letter. She tore them up without reading them. She was informed he was dying of despair. She merely shrugged her shoulders.

"But there is another person," she told me, "whom I shall never forgive, and that's Cardinal Wolsey. I shall pay him back in his own coin and one day he will know it." This hostility, by the way, was mutual, as the cardinal was quick to show. He told Thomas Boleyn to shut up the "seductress" in Hever Castle, before sending her away overseas. He had no difficulty in persuading Catherine to give up her maid of honour and recommend her instead to Margaret of Austria like her sister Mary before her. And very soon Anne was embarked for Antwerp.

During her stay in the Netherlands I had no means of knowing what passed through her mind beyond what she was kind enough to tell me in her letters. And since Wolsey had established a first-rate system of censorship she had to write and I to read between the lines. Two years went by in this way, and sad and lonely years they were for me. Hever Castle with my friend not there seemed to me a gloomy place. As a young lady of leisure I lacked her resilience to escape from boredom. Anne waited on in the Netherlands until after the battle of Pavia where for Francis "all was lost except honour"; and when at last she could return to Hever Castle long months had still to pass before she was readmitted to court.

Meanwhile near Hever she met up again with a friend of her childhood – her first cousin, Thomas Wyatt, the same who had reported to me the frightful scene of Wolsey's humiliation of Percy. In him Anne found an affection that sustained her. They had tender memories between them of their childhood years and their intimacy was quickly re-established. He was already a fine poet. As an ardent reader he had acquired a thorough knowledge on all subjects. He was passionately taken up with public affairs and always delving into the old chronicles and parchments of long ago He never tired of the history of England and would discuss it with Anne for days on end. Sometimes I saw her contradict him, become warm, protest; at others she would listen attentively and say no word.

In the course of those years the ideas of Luther, which had burst like a bomb upon Germany, were beginning to find their way into England under the name of "new knowledge". Having made a stir originally in Cambridge, they were spreading from there into the city of London and from the city into the great houses. I should explain that at that stage this was rather matter for discussion than for taking up sides; the Church of Rome still reigned supreme. On these themes – England, the Church, Reform – I would watch Anne of an evening fill entire pages with notes and comments. I did not ask to be allowed to read them, for I was still at eighteen only a feather-head; these tales of kings and barons, civil wars and campaigns abroad bored me more than I can say. Whereas my friend Anne, who already in France had been a glutton for books, was becoming, with her cousin, a glutton also for archives and old documents. When Wyatt was not there to take up the argument she would talk to me sometimes of her ideas on the future of the kingdom, to which I found it very hard to make any reply. And when I heard her come out with strange axioms like "England is an island but she is not aware of it" or ask "Why the devil should we have to ship all our merchandise abroad in foreign bottoms?" I had to stay mum.

I must admit that too often her conversation wearied me. I found that her interest in public affairs went beyond her age – and beyond mine. She had lately reached her twenty-first birthday and could form a clear judgement of herself. She would no doubt have wished to be more beautiful, with a whiter skin, a nose not so long and hair less black, but she was conscious of possessing charm enough and refinement to make up for it. Timid by temperament but daring by force of will-power, she had gradually developed in herself a second nature, with self-confidence overcoming fear. She could even know how to be insolent, when there was a need for it. But all the same I had never known her play the coquette with men. She had not responded to those squires in France who had courted her and whispered sweet nothings in her ear. Had she, in those two years spent out of my sight, had romantic relations with Flemish or Dutch gentlemen? She said nothing of it to me and I would not have dared to ask her. If it ever came my way to put an indiscreet question to her on this point or another she answered me only with a mute smile that forbade my pressing any further. But her relationship with the nice Thomas, who wrote verses for her, took place almost under my eyes.

"Could you be turning into a coquette?" I asked her. It was easy to see that she was attaching Wyatt to herself by links that had gone beyond the purely intellectual. Yet a love affair between them could lead nowhere. Wyatt was separated from his wife whose scandalous conduct had been the talk of the court; but he could not divorce her, still less have the marriage annulled, for she had borne him a son.

"Coquette, no. This is something different," she said with the smile that I have described. "Don't meddle in it."

I would have taken her word for it if I had not seen the poor lad falling more and more deeply in love with her. "Take care at least not to fall in love with him yourself. Where do you think that would lead you?"

"Nowhere, certainly. But don't worry. I'm practising, that's all."

And when I opened my eyes wide: "At getting myself madly loved," she said. "I must be sure of my methods." I still looked at her without understanding: "It's a harsh world, you see, and one thing I've learnt. Women in public affairs are without weapons. Men treat them as children so as to keep all power in their own hands. Therefore if a woman wants to acquire any authority there is only one way she can do it; by gaining an ascendancy over one of those men. And to gain it she must make him love her without loving him."

"But your poet holds no authority!"

"Therefore it is not of him that I'm thinking."

"Why, you have him at your feet!"

"I told you: just practice."

"This is not the you that I know. Is your heart made of stone? You'll drive the poor lad to despair!"

"No, no. I know what I'm doing. I'm simply making him lose his head a little. He will get it back when it suits me."

"You frighten me. You're playing with fire."

I felt pretty well at sea. I went back over her strange words. "To grasp, you say, some authority! But heavens alive, for what purpose?"

"To realise certain aspirations."

"There is only one aspiration a proper young girl can have, and that's to get herself a good husband."

"Say rather, to have one imposed upon her by her father. There again is a thing I've learnt: only among the common people here is it possible to marry for love. In our great houses gold marries gold, estates marry estates. As children we are just instruments to serve a purpose; our hearts are an encum-

74

brance. First, they wanted to unite me to a brute with red hair; then they tore my heart to pieces over Percy. I have suffered from it more than you think, because I do not wear my heart on my sleeve. I have not battered you to death with my complaints. But it's over. I shall never marry, nor shall I love another man. Besides, a proper young girl can have other marriages in view than with a good husband."

"Well then, what other?"

"With Christ, for example."

"Don't tell me that you're getting ready to shut yourself up in a convent!"

"After a fashion, yes. I am a good Christian and if I had had pride enough I would no doubt have called upon Jesus to welcome me in my sorrow. I shall pronounce my vows, but it will be in the name of a more earthly incarnation."

"Which is?"

"The kingdom of England."

As I was obviously waiting for her to explain, she said that if she had not been able to fall in love with Thomas Wyatt she had, in listening to him, fallen well and truly in love with her native land. And she cherished particular ambitions for Albion, thanks also to those Frenchmen who had opened her mind to the relationships between the Church and the nation-states.

"And since these ambitions," she went on to tell me, "seem to be in no way shared by the kingdom's authorities I shall devote my life to making them prevail. By means that only I can operate. Ah! this time you smile, you're laughing at me. You think me still a little goose who deludes herself with absurd ambitions and powers that exist only in her imagination. But believe me, dear one, you are wrong. I have been planning it for years. I know what I'm doing. In all innocence, I made Percy love me. In the Netherlands I was naughty and made myself loved by men who were nothing to me. All that is past. But now to win Thomas's love was a challenge. He is married, father of a family – a man of learning and judgement, a man not likely to be carried away . . ."

"But a poet . . ."

"True, and therefore profound, inaccessible. Well, you see, I've won the challenge. He desires me, even if only superficially. I have trusty weapons; I have the measure of them and will know how best to make them serve me. I shall be able to bring to my feet men who think they are strong because they have in their grasp a morsel of power – barons, ministers, bishops, cardinals, but who are often just poor devils, anxious and vulnerable like anyone else. The king? He is never sure what he wants. Wolsey? His thoughts are only for himself. He wants to wear the tiara. To become Pope he will be prepared to sell his father and mother. But he will find me in his way."

She had said all this in a voice so quiet, so entirely devoid of exaltation, that I had to believe she meant it. But I was none the less flabbergasted.

"And your nice poet, where does he come into all this?"

"I have told you; he will recover. To set out deliberately to captivate does not lead to lasting attachments." She seemed, looking into the future, to be turning this over in her mind. She pursed her lips, then parted them: "I must admit, it's the weak point in my plan . . ."

She had murmured these words rather to herself than to me. Without saying any more, she waited thus a moment, with a faraway look in her eyes; then with a shrug of her shoulders broke off her thoughts, as though to say: "We shall see".

On what she had in mind and evidently had slowly conceived and matured over the years she shed no further light that day. Besides, did she know herself precisely what it was? I believe she was simply making ready to grasp any opportunity that might come her way. When that opportunity did actually present itself, one that must have far exceeded anything she had imagined, I was to see her take hold of it with a recklessness, a skill and a determination that I was never to meet again in any woman – unless, much later, in her own daughter, in Queen Elizabeth the Great.

IV

(1526–1528)

# Mary Boleyn

Bessie Blount had given Henry a bastard, Henry Fitzroy. Despair at having no legitimate offspring except daughters, allied to his repugnance at the idea of a woman on the throne, caused the king in years to come to consider making this Henry Fitzroy his heir. Mary Boleyn, who had succeeded Bessie, gave him a son in her turn. But one bastard was enough for the king and this one was sent without further ado to the monastery of Syon. Mary was still his favourite nonetheless although, as his appetite grew with eating, he did not refrain from being nearly as unfaithful to her as to the queen. Cheerfully he cast his line into the fishpond of young girls who made up Catherine's suite and most were eager to rise to the bait. Meanwhile Anne Boleyn had taken her place again among the young maids of honour but without at first attracting the king's attention more than any of her companions. Naturally the court was in a buzz, expecting to see one or another supplant Mary as favourite, just as she had supplanted Bessie. The bets were fast and furious: after Bessie, Mary; but after Mary, who? Names succeeded one another as did the brief adventures of the king. But so far no-one had thought of betting on Anne Boleyn.

The fact is that she took care to escape notice. Far from putting herself forward like the other girls, she tended to stay in the background. It was not timidity; it was a prudent reserve. Perhaps in the long run this was what intrigued the king: why should the sister of his favourite remain so aloof when she had in her single person as much charm as this whole battalion of girls? Or perhaps the idea of being the lover of both sisters at once excited Henry to a gluttony more titillating even than it was perverted? At all events he sent for Anne.

I cannot say that I saw her excessively surprised. Conscious of possessing the finest manners, the most graceful figure to watch on the dance floor, the sweetest voice to hear singing; of being the subtlest in conversation whether in listening or responding: in a word, of being the most "French" of all these young Englishwomen, she expected (as did I) that one day notice would be taken of her.

I would not swear that she had not brought her discretion adroitly into play in this design of hers; the honour of passing a night with the king was a bait to which, unlike her companions, she had no inclination to rise. What she wanted was that Henry should like her company well enough to introduce her into that upper crust of men who took decisions. This happened, in fact, quite naturally; several, of whom some were unmarried, had been quick to show their interest in her. Often she and I put questions to one another about the social and political weight each might carry, and the chance she would have, by marrying this one rather than that, of exercising an influence through him. While I listened to her I said nothing of what I could plainly see and she apparently did not yet realise, that the one most assiduous in his attentions to her had become the king himself.

I think I saw this growing sentiment in the king's mind take full flight at one of those festivities, those *masques* of which Henry was so fond. It was his opportunity to display himself in garments even richer than those, already sumptuous enough, that he wore on ordinary occasions. He loved to disguise himself as Doge, Sultan, Hospodar, Maharajah; to array himself in multicoloured silks, in gold, jewels, bracelets and chains. He did not expressly forbid the lords of his court to rival him in opulence but a healthy prudence prevailed and so the king, spared all competition, found each time that he was also "king of the fête".

It was after one of those *masques* at which pastorals were succeeded by *tableaux vivants* that in the course of the ball,

Henry was struck by the charm and grace of one veiled young girl. Though she was wearing an entirely new costume that evening it cannot have been long before he recognised her because, on his recommendation, the organisers of the festivities had repeatedly made her – when she did not deliberately slip away – the fascinating centrepiece of some spectacular scene, one from old mythology, where she might play the part of Armida or the huntress Diana.

Mary at that time, however, still ruled the king's heart and he would do no more than applaud. But on this particular evening, Anne's gracefulness enhanced by a dress entirely of velvet and brocade which I had sewn for her myself (I had got the idea from an outfit worn by Margaret of Angoulême), so far excelled that of the other young girls – boorish as they seemed by comparison, rigged out in their finery cut in the English style – that the king could not help being dazzled by her. Over the past few months, his attachment to Mary had little by little lost its zest, and in the course of this ball everyone could see that he was neglecting her for this young masked dancer who moved around with the suppleness of a sylph. He never took his eyes off her. Then, when the band struck up for one of our country dances, the king wanted to take her for his partner. But she pretended not to recognise him under his disguise as Hospodar and at every fresh turn in the dance she would choose some other partner, anonymous under his mask. To make up for it, every time she passed the king she would throw him mocking glances through the slits of her mask from the black diamond pupils of her eyes. Until Henry, unable to stand it any longer, seized her by the arm; thereafter, forcing her to remain as his partner, he kept her to himself, not allowing her to dance with any other the *pavane*, the *volte*, the *duchesse* or the *guimbarde*.

Was it at that moment that Anne first conceived the idea that she could aim higher than with her customary good sense she had originally thought possible? Naturally, she said nothing of it to me, after the ball or later. And had she made me her confidante must I not have had great fears for her

79

reason? Who would not have supposed her struck with illusions of grandeur? Only in fairy tales do kings marry shepherdesses.

When I think back to that evening I still find myself stunned. What extraordinary mental audacity the young girl must have needed first to grasp the long-term chances that Henry's amorous passion opened up; then to calculate her ways and means to exploit them; finally to devise out of this an un-deviating line of conduct, when any other than herself would have been only too impatient to fall without more ado into the king's arms! In any case it was from that day, that night, and through nine years, that I was to watch with wonder the most astounding tournament of love-in-politics to which any obscure young woman could have dared to challenge her sovereign.

At that moment, however, watching them dance together, one did not have the impression of a well-matched couple. He at thirty-five had grown heavy and fat; she was still a slender one-and-twenty. No-one would have thought that under that fragile frame was concealed a will-power that nothing could shake, firmer by far than Henry's wavering resolution – despite his sturdy back and broad but deceptive chest – could ever be. An observer shrewder than I who watched them that evening twirling around together perhaps might have foreseen this.


Rumours of course began to circulate at once. The king was going to have a new favourite; tired of Mary Boleyn, he was about to put her sister in her place. People were envious already of Rochford, their father, who must surely see himself raised to new honours and new possessions. Thomas himself was not so sure; what you have is one thing, what you are going to have is another. He had no anxieties about Mary, always calm, docile, not asking for much; with Anne by contrast he could never feel at ease. He did not understand her character and was always afraid she would break out, there was no telling in what direction.

But the girl's behaviour surprised everyone, myself included. On me the effect was happy. I may be a bit of a prude but I would not have cared to see her in the role of favourite or worse still as deputy-mistress. As it turned out, far from exploiting her success with the king she became from the very next day more aloof than ever; instead of appearing more often at Court she stayed away from it whenever she could. When the queen insisted on her attendance she remained obstinately in the background behind her. Catherine, who on the night of the ball had missed nothing of her husband's assiduous attentions to Anne, appreciated this reserve. Having at first felt trepidation in view of Mary's outstanding beauty, she had soon ceased to worry about it; therefore Catherine must dread any new favourite who might aim to rise higher. Because she was so discreet, Anne caused the queen not the slightest anxiety. King Henry on the other hand found this self-restraint which kept him at arm's length at once astonishing and inflaming.

For the first time since his coronation the absolute master of England was finding himself frustrated in his desires. To his surprise this intimidated him. His search for every possible opportunity to come near to Anne often made him follow her right into the queen's apartments and wait there a long time before saying good night. Catherine smiled – she was no dupe – but allowed herself to find great comfort in this apparent return of tenderness. It made her feel a kind of gratitude to this haughty young girl who knew so well how to behave and who was the cause of these visits.

In this independence of Anne's Catherine recognised again the energy of the Boleyns; the pride and daring of the Howards which must have come to Anne through her mother from Grandfather Surrey: the one with whom Catherine had long ago won the battle of Flodden – he was still at the age of eighty straight as a ramrod and fighting fit. So quite soon Catherine had made of Anne her favourite companion in that intimate circle. There was not only friendship in it but design. For shapeless as she was, fat and ageing, it was not in her power to give a brother to her daughter Mary, to her husband a male heir. More and more, though he consulted her often and showed her the most marked respect, she felt this husband becoming a stranger to her. She was not displeased, then, to see this reserved young girl take the place in Henry's heart of a favourite who was beginning to weary him. If it was absolutely necessary that he have a reigning mistress, better this one than another more dangerous. Like everyone else she supposed the new liaison would be a matter of weeks only or of months at most. Hitherto no woman had resisted the sovereign beyond a day or a few hours.

But season followed season and still Anne did not surrender. This came as a surprise to everyone, was even in a sense a scandal. One cannot take a line much different from that of the group – in this case the court ladies – to which one belongs. For the fair sex winter is a time of endless boredom. Men, missing their tournaments, still have their private business, as well as intrigues and rivalries among themselves. For the ladies, apart from the rare days when there is no fog, rain or snow and it might just be possible to get up a boar-hunt, there is nothing to fill their leisure hours. One cannot spend five months out of the twelve, sixteen hours of the twenty-four at embroidery or plucking at a guitar, playing tarot or the new craze, faro. When all these distractions are exhausted there is only the one resource: love-making. Such being the case, no-one can think he or she is doing wrong in forming a liaison. It's not a thing that lasts and so one changes partners as readily as one would change a shirt. No-one would dream either of being surprised, still less shocked, if some bastard came into the world. The scenes that would sometimes ensue between husband and wife even though both had been unfaithful, were a subject rather for laughter than for any deep emotion.

Let me be excused from saying anything of my personal joys and sorrows in these matters, because that would reveal who I was. I like only to think that I have not been the most frivolous of my sex. But this chastity of Anne's from one year's end to another was held to be excessive.

Among the ladies it was a good subject for talk and for

calumny. They judged Anne's conduct as not modest but prudish, the product not of virtue but of pride. Another subject of controversy was Henry's attitude towards the queen. As the years went by, rumours multiplied that Henry, in his bitterness at no longer being able to expect from her a legitimate son, was thinking of repudiating her so as to be free to take a younger wife, chosen of course from among the great families of Europe. There were many rival speculations about the princesses available, Madeleine of France, Maria Christine of Saxony and two or three others. One jester who pretended to bet on Anne Boleyn got a good laugh from the gallery. It seemed pure joking to me too; though I did bet on early disgrace for Catherine of Aragon, if not tomorrow, then the day after: not only because she was no longer capable of giving the king an heir but because she was the emperor's aunt. Ever since Charles's victory at Pavia Henry had not been able to stomach the insulting lack of regard that the victor now paid to his royal person – in particular, the scant notice he had taken of Henry's proposal that they should divide between them the spoils of France. It was his pride above all that was hurt and again and again he complained to the queen about her nephew and made it a grievance that she took that nephew's side. Catherine became irritated, anger flared between them and at the court there was fresh talk of an impending divorce. Some were already saying that it must come.

"It will be a long time," Anne said to me one day.

"What will be a long time?"

"The divorce. But it will happen, let's hope. It's a question of patience."

"Why should we hope for it? *You*'ve not got much to complain of in the queen, I would think!"

"It's true, and I like her; so it was not of myself I was thinking but of the fact that so long as she remains queen she will be a danger to England."

"How so?"

"Because she is not English. Her country of origin is Spain; her family is that of Charles, her views are the same as her nephew's. She thinks that this crumb lost in the sea has nothing better to wish for than to be merged into the Holy Empire. The influence she exerts upon the king is damnable."

"There is nothing to prove that anyone else would have a better."

"Pre-cisely," she said, drawing the word out and accompanying it besides with a smile so strange, with a light so brilliant in her eyes that there was no mistaking what it meant. Nevertheless it was a meaning too incredible for me consciously to subscribe to. I had the premonition only of some vast design not yet fully formulated, the resolve to make it succeed – and perhaps the ability to do so.

Besides, was the interest the king was taking in her much more than a caprice? It seemed to me foolish on Anne's part to wait till the opportunity had passed her by. While I listened to her telling me of things that went beyond my understanding, it was at least clear to me that she wished to forge a great destiny for herself. For a young girl of her social standing would it not be such a destiny – and one of the most financially rewarding – to become the king's favourite? Certainly the prospect of finding herself married off thereafter to some rich lord in the provinces was not very inviting. The horror she had shown at seeing herself buried away in far-off Ireland spoke loud enough for me to understand the little taste she had for becoming next in line to Bessie and Mary. But can one stand out for long against an all-powerful king with his various means of putting pressure on you, including blackmail, and, if you are finally recalcitrant, shutting you up in the Tower of London? Curiously, however, there was nothing to show that giving him the cold shoulder was having the effect of making the king angry. It seemed rather to pique him. He had never in the seventeen years of his reign encountered a similar resistance and he had a taste for novelty. Looked at in this way, you could say that Anne thrilled him.

But if Henry had a taste for novelty, he had a greater one for tradition. As to that, Anne had no illusions.

"People think," she told me, "that Henry's one idea is to

repudiate Catherine. But, believe me, he is less eager than anyone to have to contemplate it. Granted, he is only thirty-four; she is in her forties, old, overweight and faded; the hair that she coils around her neck is going grey and thinning out. It is also true that she is an austere daughter of Spain, never laughs, never jokes with him; that she bores him to death and, still more, irritates him. But I well know the deference that even now she inspires in him. If you could see how in front of her he behaves just like a little boy! What he reveres in Catherine is the Princess Royal of Aragon. And what he appreciates is her pride, her sense of responsibility, her competence in important matters. He still depends on her for everything. I feel much esteem and affection myself for her. Such a pity that she remains so fundamentally committed to Rome and to the emperor! If I could bring my influence to bear upon her and persuade her I would need no other intercessor to forward my ideas. Through her I would make them triumph. But this woman is a rock. Nothing will ever wear down her profound convictions. That is why I have to fight her."

"And you hope to bring the king to share your views?"

"I have told you; it is a question of patience."

"Listen, Anne dear, you're fooling yourself. It's true, he desires you; to gain his affections you're using the ways and means I've watched you trying out on your nice cousin. But he is the king and Catherine is the queen. To seek to supplant her in the influence she has over him can only be a wild dream. Don't you see that all he, Henry, is waiting for out of these games of gallantry is that you should end up by sacrificing your virtue to him?"

"He will have to wait a long time."

I had no doubt of it, knowing as I did her constancy and strength of will. But like everyone else, I believed the king would soon tire. I was wrong. The more she left him on the rack, the more he sought her company. When she was in London with Catherine he kept on organising festivities so as to have her near him. When she was staying at Hever Castle he went stag-hunting in the forest nearby so as to be invited in. His efforts were in vain. At the end of a whole year of this regime he had not yet obtained from her one caress, not a single kiss.

Nonetheless he persevered in his pursuit, but he continued to hesitate to use his power despite the violence of his desire. For as time went on there came a change in this desire. Through seeing so much of Anne, his lust for the beauty of her eyes and the suppleness of her hips had slowly given place to a less sensual appetite. She had conquered him by the vivacity of her mind, the refinement of her taste, the soundness of her judgement, the force of her character. He could no longer do without her. And little by little, giving the lie to my doubts and fears, Anne's influence with him came to equal Catherine's and she often made hers prevail.

At the same time there were successive impulses working on Henry to repudiate the queen when she irritated him too much, when she disappointed him and when the idea tickled him of a younger spouse who could give him a son. In Catherine's favour was the ascendancy she still exerted over him. But against her was the influence which Anne now brought to bear and which the chancellor appeared to support. Wolsey was hostile to the emperor and wished the King of France well – partly for financial reasons: the pension Francis was paying him – and saw his plans thwarted by the single circumstance that Charles's aunt was Queen of England. Besides, the cardinal had in mind the advantages he would earn after the divorce by his intervention in favour of a new marriage between Henry and some royal heiress. So he pushed his sovereign that way. At times the king would listen to him, at others the idea scared him. Nonetheless he thought about it more and more.

But the first difficulty was that a breach of the sacred bonds of marriage would be possible only with the consent of Rome, a consent obtainable without a struggle only if the union with Catherine could be made null. This appeared out of the question unless it could be established that Henry had contracted an illegitimate marriage in marrying his brother's widow.

If the king still hesitated, Wolsey did not and in his search for support it struck him that Anne Boleyn's could be invaluable. If he had known what she had in view, he would beyond a doubt have recoiled from such an enterprise. But how could the thought have occurred to him any more than it did to me?

Anne for her part saw Wolsey's offer of alliance as something more than she could have hoped for. Alone now against both, Henry appeared to give way. With the Archbishop of Canterbury the cardinal set up a secret tribunal at Westminster for charging Henry Tudor with incestuous marriage. The king duly presented himself and whether he was pretending in the defence he made or whether after all he was sincere I do not know. Unsure, as always, I would willingly believe that he did not know himself. Perhaps he both wished for this divorce and dreaded it. Or, at the bottom of his heart, had he come to the point of desiring to possess Anne, whatever the price? Or was he so infatuated by Anne that he was resolved to bind her to him by bonds that nothing could break? Even today, naturally I could not give an answer. But whether for this latter reason or for others more involved the cardinal was authorised to employ all the resources of theology to bring the matter to the desired conclusion.

But meanwhile Wolsey had come to see that the authority of a couple of archbishops would not be enough to satisfy public opinion, which in general favoured Queen Catherine. So he arranged for a synod to have it decreed by the Bench of Bishops that any marriage with the wife of a deceased brother was forbidden as being a mortal sin. They were willing enough to admit that on principle such a marriage was to be avoided but still they concluded that it remained valid on condition of a dispensation by the Pope. Now this dispensation existed of course; it had been deposited in the archives. Ferdinand and the old King Henry had obtained it from Pope Julius when Henry, then Prince of Wales, was twelve. It seemed difficult to go back on that.

All this had taken place behind closed doors and in secret. But a secret held by more than one person does not take long to become noised abroad. The queen soon had a warning of what the king and the chancellor were plotting against her. Catherine summoned Henry and made him understand that if he went ahead she would appeal to the judgement of the Pope.

Moreover, like the prudent woman she was, she lost no time in sending word to her nephew Charles in Spain. The problem was how to do it without the king's knowledge. So she sent to Henry her Spanish tailor, Felipez, who pretended to complain that the queen was being difficult and would not give him leave to take a month or two off and go to Spain to visit his old mother who was ill. But Henry sensed it was a trick and thought up another to match it. He pretended in his turn to authorise the man's departure and even be ready to pay his ransom if by ill chance he should fall into some dangerous ambuscade on his way across France. At the same time he gave orders to have the Spaniard intercepted at Calais and removed from sight. But the Spaniard was never seen to come ashore. The queen, anticipating some such interference with her plan, had instructed her messenger to avoid France and travel to Spain by way of the Atlantic. And shortly afterwards Charles had word of Henry's intentions.

He received the message at the moment when his troops, driving from the field those aligned against them by Venice, France and the Vatican, took possession of Rome and sacked the city. The Spaniards especially were appalling. Perhaps it was their jealousy of the splendour in which the Roman clergy lived that directed their rage against monks and priests most of all. Abbots, vicars, bishops were pursued into the churches, right up to the altar itself and there they were slaughtered. Every nun, no matter what her age, was raped before being disembowelled. Bodies strewed the streets or floated on the Tiber while the soldiers set fire to everything, yelling "Flesh and blood! Flesh and blood!" The Pope just managed to escape by flying for refuge to the fortress known as the Castle of Sant' Angelo, where he barricaded himself in. The emperor feared that if the sack of the Holy City were to be followed by murder of the Pope the Catholic faith in all parts might suffer its death-blow, and would not allow the fortress to be carried by assault. Instead he authorised it to be besieged and in consequence the Pope found himself imprisoned there for a long time.

Remote from the tumult, Henry calculated what this captivity would mean for him. It suited him insofar as Catherine could not now appeal to the Pope; against this, he could no longer count on Clement's hostility to the nephew leading him to take sides against the aunt. A little naively, Henry then had the idea of getting the queen herself to share his views. He represented to her the state of mortal sin in which the two of them had been living since their marriage; how in the interest of her salvation she ought to put an end to her sinful condition, live apart from him and retire into a convent. But Catherine's answer to his exhortations was that she would turn nun when he turned monk. Tearfully and obstinately, she refused all his entreaties.

When Henry was thwarted in his wishes he had to find some scapegoat. He chose his chancellor, Wolsey, overwhelming him with reproaches for not having been able to convince even his bishops. At the same time all these setbacks brought him closer still to this unapproachable Anne Boleyn who always held to the same argument – "You are married" – which threw him into a frenzy. One day she would allow him just to kiss her fingers, the next to hold her to his breast; the day after, she would allow him nothing at all: like the skilful fisherman who holds the salmon at the end of his line, reeling it in or letting it out according to whether the fish is tired or is fighting back. There was one point only on which Anne showed herself perfectly amenable, and that was to go at once each time the king sent for her. This he did more and more often, Neglecting the business of the kingdom, he would sometimes devote the whole afternoon to the young girl, or an entire evening. Everyone was agreed that she was already his favourite; whether she was his mistress remained open to discussion. I alone, and I was well placed to know, was certain that she granted him nothing. But how many of us would have dared to entertain her incredible project?

"Do you love him, at least?" I asked her, observing that she submitted to all the king's wishes except one.

"Me? What an idea! If I loved him I would have given myself to him long ago."

"Then why do you encourage him?" I repeated for the tenth time. "What do you expect from him at the end of the day? Where on earth do you expect that this will finally get you?"

"Why, of course – to marrying him."

I realised then that if all this time I had refused consciously to admit such an answer it was solely because of incredulity and dread.

"What madness!" I cried. "Even supposing, against all likelihood, that the king ever comes to the point of divorce, how can you imagine for a moment, little girl from nowhere that you are, that he would do it in order to choose you? There is no shortage in the world of princesses of the blood, and more beautiful than you!"

"No doubt," she said with a smile. "All the same, it is me whom he will marry."

This self-assurance took my breath away. I trembled for the consequences. With good reason – for when this extravagant ambition came to be understood by the whole court, when the king himself no longer concealed his intention to satisfy it, his motives for the divorce and the scruples he paraded about his "incestuous marriage" were shown up publicly for the false pretext they were. The mere plan for a divorce had shocked public feeling; it had the air of a vile plot. All minds turned in favour of the victim and the reputation of the "seductress" took a hard knock. It was as I had feared. But Anne accepted this hostility philosophically.

"Whatever you go out for, you must be willing to pay the price. The conquest of power is sure to give offence. People are attached to what is there already and hate to see it overturned. Do you suppose they love Catherine? They don't even know her. But she has been on the throne fifteen years; the idea of a change distresses them and all of a sudden they imagine that they love her. Of course the repercussions fall on me. That had

90

to be. But what counts is not me nor is it Catherine; it is our country's future. And for the sake of England's future the queen has got to be repudiated."

"But does it follow that the king must marry you? It's a wild idea. Moreover, it isn't necessary; he already does nothing except as you advise."

"But since Catherine is there he takes her advice as well. And it is the opposite of mine. Then he vacillates, cannot decide what to do and finally leaves it to Wolsey. And that man, what does he want? To become Pope. If to achieve that he has to sell England for thirty pieces of silver he will do it. And that is why I, and none but I, must be the king's partner on the throne."

"But you, then, what are you hoping to make of England?"

There was a hint of irony in the question.

Anne said nothing at first and she looked so deep in thought that I wondered if she herself really knew. Then in the kindest way she began to explain to me. I am not sure if I understood it all at the time and it is only by looking back over a quarter of a century and seeing how things have worked out that her answer has become intelligible to me. Let me be forgiven, then, if my memory is incapable of rendering here the exact words she spoke. All I can attempt is to give the gist of them.

She said there was only one country in Europe which was a real nation and it was France. All the others, England among them, were no more than pawns on the chessboard of kings and were more or less interchangeable. Catherine would like to offer our kingdom to her nephew to become a province of the empire. If Henry had had the luck to be chosen by the Electoral Princes in place of Charles, it is what he himself would assuredly have done. "Look," she said, "at one of these maps which come to us from Genoa. Italy may have the shape of a boot but in fact she is just a loose collection of provinces and duchies perpetually at war and falling into the hands now of Maximilian, now of Charles, now of Francis. Germany is no better; between the Elbe and the Rhine she is just as fragmented. Come, do you know why I so admire that girl whom we burnt alive at Rouen? Not for her high deeds nor yet for her saintly conduct at the stake. I admire her because, until her time, France did not exist; France under that name was nothing but a land-area between three seas, nothing but a land-area like the Italian boot, like the Iberian peninsula itself made up of competing kingdoms. I admire her because before her time the King of France was only the first among dukes and like them reigned only over a province. I admire and envy her finally because it was only after her time that every Frenchman came to recognise himself under those two words: *la France*."

"I do not follow you very well."

"It is because you were born and grew up and are living in these present conditions, so you take them for granted and have no conception of any other. Yet you can see well enough that – till they find their Joan – a Florentine feels nothing in common with a Calabrian, a Catalan with an Andalusian, a Bavarian with a Prussian."

"It isn't like that in England."

"But it is, it is. A Marquis of Durham, who thinks of marrying the daughter of the Duke of Normandy, feels closer to him than he does to his neighbour the Duke of Cumberland, whose lands he covets. We need not speak of Scotland, our declared enemy. That is why I told you one day that we are an island but do not know it. What I want to do is precisely that: to make Englishmen, Scotsmen, Welshmen understand that they are only one country – this island on which they all live."

She went on to say that she would lay a wager on France against the Holy Roman Empire because Charles was satisfied to reign over a sprinkling of states without appearing to see how fragile was this structure that had no mortar to hold it together: "The one who, like Joan of Arc, is perhaps going to reveal Germany to itself – though I say it with regret – is Luther."

"You sound as though it's what you wish."

"No, but what I wish for us is some event of the same order. One that reveals England to herself in a similar way. Without that, she will never become other than she is."

"Well, and that's not too bad!"

"You only say that because you lack ambition. My wish is for Albion to become the first power in Europe instead of remaining – as she will, if nothing happens – the last."

"That's what the king also wishes. He doesn't need you for that."

"That's where you're wrong. No doubt he would like it to come about; but without me he'll never achieve it."

"God forgive me! And why so?"

"Because he sees no further than the end of his nose. He commands, he is rich, and he thinks that with that he can conquer the world. But he can do nothing at all."

"Whereas *you* can!"

"Whereas I know what changes are required before England can even think about making herself felt."

"I must admit that I'm another who doesn't care much for changes. Which ones are you thinking of?"

"For a start, one that will mark her off from the hundred other counties, duchies and petty kingdoms of the Continent, separated by their frontiers from one another but huddled together in the same powerful hand – or call it the same casserole: the Church of Rome. So long as we are all shut in there together none of us, not England herself, will be free to move hand or foot."

"Why move? I'm a good Catholic."

"Because in this casserole England can only simmer. Till she has found some Luther to get her out of it she will go on simmering there with the others. And that's why I shall use all my strength to unearth another Luther."

"What!" I cried in alarm. "You'd turn us all into heretics!"

"That's a thing I'm not yet quite clear about," she acknowledged. "For these teachings have some way yet to go. Certainly both Oxford and Cambridge are teeming with new ideas. But Henry still thinks only in terms of Pope and cardinals. It's not that he's a pillar of piety; often it's I who with Catherine have to drive him to chapel. But despite his air of 'I can cut my way through mountains', he of all men has the profoundest respect for authority."

"I find that very much in order for a Catholic king."

In doubting as she did Henry's religious enthusiasm, Anne underestimated his devoutness. Yet she knew better than me that in opposition to Luther he was writing a pamphlet of uncommon virulence on the Seven Sacraments – with which the Pope when he came to read it would be so pleased that he would confer on its author the hereditary title of "Defender of the Faith". Henry had no need of church authorities to prompt him to stand out against heresy. And I was much afraid that Anne might be starting off on a very dangerous path.

# V
## (1528–1529)

# *Clement VII*

It must be clear from the way I as a patriotic Englishwoman felt, how far ahead Anne was of public opinion and of the king's thinking in particular. It is a fact that, increasingly frustrated by the resistance Anne was putting up against his infatuation, and obsessed by the single means he had of overcoming it, Henry was giving less and less attention to the business of the kingdom.

For several months not a day had passed on which Anne and he had not met. He took her out everywhere, to his hunts, his tournaments, all the receptions that were given for him or those he gave for others. It was practically only to the Council meetings (at which his continual absent-mindedness was the despair of Wolsey) that he did not yet dare to take her with him. And his own resistance was weakening. That she was of a mind to give herself to him he did not doubt but what was more and more clearly understood between them (though never expressly formulated) was that this must be within the marriage relationship; in response to his pleadings to her to accept his caresses she would excuse herself, saying, "But you are married". Little by little the notion of marrying Anne, which a year earlier would still have seemed only a joke, had become so pressing a reality that after passing as the months went by from a state of day-dreaming to idle wishes, then from irresolution to acceptance and finally determination he had now reached a state of utter impatience. Once Henry came to the boil his impatience was apt to take a violent form. So Wolsey was given orders to speed up procedures for the divorce and for this purpose get together (or if necessary, create) all means necessary for it to be pronounced without delay.

The cardinal had failed the first time, it will be recalled, at his attempt with the synod. That certainly had annoyed the king but Henry himself had not at that time been too sure of the strength of his wishes and so his resentment had been short-lived. Now it was different. Now he experienced an overwhelming desire for the divorce and Wolsey understood that this time there could be no question of failure. So he looked for a more effective plan whose success would re-establish his credit. Never doubting that he had made himself indispensable to the king, he was still entirely confident of his power over him. In this he underestimated the new powers of Anne, whose keen intelligence and sureness both of apprehension and of judgement made her the adviser to whom Henry most inclined to listen.

Anne told me that to make her views on England prevail she had to get the better not only of Catherine but of Wolsey first. Not because the cardinal was unwilling to hurry on the divorce, but because if the divorce were obtained and the king were then still under the chancellor's influence what we should soon see emerging would be an engagement with some royal princess. And though Anne was sure that Henry only wanted the divorce so as to be free to marry her, there would nonetheless be rivalry in the air with many hold-ups and complications yet to be faced. Perhaps after the marriage of Wolsey's cleverness and great abilities might once more make him a useful chancellor. But if she were to be led to the altar she must first have Wolsey excluded from all public business.

"Besides, you want to pay him back in his own coin," I reminded her with a smile (it had been an expression of her own).

"Yes, and my memory is not a short one. But the good of my country must come before revenge."

In fact at that time Wolsey had no idea of setting himself up in opposition to Anne to bar her accession to the throne; for the sufficient reason that the king had taken good care not to let the cardinal know of his new intentions. There could be no doubt in the king's mind that if the cardinal were aware of what these were (with the consequent lapse of his plans for a remarriage with royalty) his ardour for the divorce would have gone into reverse. Fortunately Wolsey had no suspicions and he therefore set about working out a new plan with an inventiveness fired by his will to succeed. He believed himself to be the one best placed to set his scheme in motion, which if it came off would have the added advantage of raising him in the church hierarchy – promoting him indeed, as we shall see, to the rank of cardinal *papabile*.

He was due to embark for Calais very shortly with a substantial suite, and from there make for Amiens where he was to meet the French king. Since Francis, confronted by the emperor, wanted an alliance with England – even, should the divorce go through, a marriage of Henry with Renée of France, the French queen's sister – Wolsey promised himself that with Francis so minded, he would have small difficulty in rallying that sovereign to his plan. This was to instruct the French cardinals to summon to Avignon those of their Italian brethren who were not detained in Rome. Once the conclave was assembled, he felt confident of getting them to agree that while the papacy was in abeyance the powers should be delegated to a college of limited number. And Cardinal Wolsey would be at the head of this college and would take in hand the government of the Church. As interim Pope he would then have the sole power to annul the incestuous marriage, authorise the divorce, promote the union of Henry with a royal bride and receive his reward from the two parties.

But when Henry informed Anne of the chancellor's intentions she made him see what a long and risky course this must necessarily prove. To persuade twenty or thirty cardinals – Italians, what's more – to agree on a step so serious, nothing less than to elect an interim Pope, was an enterprise that if not lost in advance would certainly be time-consuming. This was a severe blow to Henry's patience. Anne on her side had the time-factor to consider too. She was in a hurry, as we saw, to put her ideas into practice but she could do it only as Queen of England and her one chance of becoming queen depended on

Henry's not being forced to mark time so long that he would grow tired of waiting – and of loving her. Wolsey's plan was therefore rejected but another had to be found at once to take its place. We noticed in the matter of the beards Anne's genius for simple solutions. It was the same now.

Wolsey should be left to try to carry out his plan but the king, by-passing him, would promptly send direct to Rome a trusted emissary who should obtain an audience of Pope Clement. He would offer the King of England's help and support to the captive, in return for which the Pope would delegate his powers to Cardinal Wolsey during the period of his detention.

This would produce the same result but in a much shorter time. And since meanwhile the chancellor would most likely have failed in his impracticable scheme, would a second time have lost face with the king, and would on becoming surrogate to the Holy Father owe this elevation not to his own cleverness but to the intervention of Anne Boleyn, he would thereafter find it difficult to bar the road to her marriage.

This, then, was the procedure they decided to adopt. It remained only to choose a messenger for this mission to Rome. He must be one on whose fidelity to the king there could be absolute reliance. This was true of one of the king's secretaries, a Dr William Knight, a man of very upright mind, of a simple, military way of thinking and honest, straightforward character, beyond the reach of any dangerous ideas. Anne had noted this quality in him; the king had him sent for; they both liked him and so the choice fell on him – and a bad choice it turned out to be.

For if in the course of his mission he proved to be indeed of an unshakable fidelity he gave evidence still more of a crude and naive openness that bordered on the asinine. He had been told to cross France without a stop. But on his way through Amiens he judged it his duty to go and pay his respects to the French king. Naturally he tumbled upon Wolsey and in no time at all he had his story wormed out of him. The anger that possessed the cardinal was the more violent because, as Anne had foreseen, his own plan had proved to be a fiasco from the start. And there'd even been something of an uproar, for the cardinals one and all had declined to go to Avignon. Now his own king was deceiving him, working behind his back and proposing to marry Anne! He must have felt the earth quaking under his feet and he at once set about retrieving the situation. First, he charged the too-candid Knight with a personal message to the Pope in such terms that if all went well the credit would redound to him. Next he wrote to Henry to assure him that the king's marriage to Mistress Anne was what he, Wolsey, desired above all things. His final thought was to quit Amiens at the earliest, so that he could return to England and re-establish himself in Henry's confidence.

Fortunately for him, he had excellent news to report of his negotiations with Francis. But unhappily, on returning, he found he was already too late.


When he arrived the court was at Richmond. It was the evening of a day of festivities. Wolsey wanted to solicit a private interview with the king at once and with this purpose he sent one of his officers to obtain an audience in whatever room His Majesty might appoint. But the messenger came back with a report which left the cardinal distraught. For the officer had found the king in the great hall of the castle full of people, with his favourite at his side. Delight at the entertainments still glowed in both their faces. The king was dressed according to his custom in brocade and gold; she was covered with the latest jewels, pearls and precious stones given her by the sovereign for this occasion. Together they had heard the emissary present his request. But when he inquired in what room the king would meet the chancellor, with an air of authority Anne replied, before Henry could open his mouth: "In what room would the chancellor propose to be received if not in whatever room the king himself is in?" Far from overruling her, Henry had kissed her hand with a smile. In earlier days the chancellor would have returned the snub and kept the king waiting several days. But now, uncertain of his own position, he did not dare. He was very soon conducted into the great hall buzzing with all the bees of the court. Continually interrupted by the babble of the courtiers and ironic observations by Anne, he could not discuss anything serious with his sovereign.

When he withdrew, Wolsey knew already that he was in semi-disgrace. Anne on the other hand had had proof of her influence with the king and pre-eminence over the cardinal. But she took care to avoid any display of triumph.

"For I know only too well," she said to me when we were back in our apartments, "both the chancellor's cunning and the king's lack of resolution in everything, not to be aware that it will still be a long struggle between the chancellor and me. I will have to show myself as patient as he, and no less devious."

"If I were in your place, I would press my advantage at once."

"No, no. I don't yet feel able to tackle Henry head-on. I haven't got complete power over him yet; he can still elude me. And the cardinal, believe me, knows how to handle him and has more than one card up his sleeve."

In fact the cardinal knew so well how to hide his anger at the outrage, to get the better of his wounded pride and affect to serve his master as though nothing had happened that in the course of the following days and of several private audiences he had once more convinced the king that no-one would be better able than his chancellor to get the divorce moving. Anne on her side put no obstacles in the way of Wolsey's efforts to come back into favour. She showed herself friendly and, as she had foreseen, having measured up the forces on the ground, the chancellor offered openly to serve her.

Though for Anne it was a first victory she did not forget that it was no more than a single precarious success. Between rivals there must often be understandings; but such can only be alliances of expediency and it is prudent not to lower one's guard. But it looked to me as if Anne were beating a retreat before the cardinal. I told her so and she outlined her view of the situation.

"Wolsey has renounced nothing: I mean, of his projects for a royal marriage for the king once the divorce has taken place – with all the profit he hopes to make out of it. At the moment he is lying low, that's all, pending the time when the king gets tired of me, as he did of Bessie and my sister. Because, you see, like so many he thinks I am Henry's mistress. He cannot imagine we would pass so many hours in *tête-à-tête* and not be physically intimate too. And I take good care not to undeceive him. For if he knew that I have so far yielded nothing he would be afraid of my power over Henry and would block the divorce instead of working to obtain it. Let him obtain it for us first, and he can leave the rest to me."

"You are very sure of yourself," I said in some anxiety.

"Why should I not be?"

"Because I see you acting out of character. It is not like you to have so hard a heart."

"No, but in matters of state one has to have a heart of iron. Between the cardinal and me it's a question of power. You have not yet fully accepted the woman I have grown to be."

"True; but there are times when you frighten me."

I did not know, when I said this, whether the thing I feared was to see her falter and give way, or stifle in herself all gentleness and tenderness of heart. That she still had these feelings for me was clear enough. She hid nothing from me, she confided in me as one sister to another and when I became over-anxious on her account she kissed me and made much of me. We had as in old days mad fits of laughter, of almost childish fun; and at those moments I discovered again in her that double nature which during her adolescence had sometimes revealed an almost frightening maturity, at others a youthfulness eager for pleasure. She had hardly changed at all, and after spending the whole day battling against the chancellor, if there was a ball in the evening she would joyfully throw herself into all the dances.

The truce between Anne and the cardinal had been tacitly concluded after Wolsey had represented to the king how dangerous had been the mission of the over-naive Dr Knight.

With his inability ever to keep a secret, Knight would not be long in revealing to the Pope the real motives of his journey. The Holy Father would see that the scruples the king was parading about his incestuous marriage were born out of his new infatuation and would never agree to what he was being asked. Instead of being furthered, the divorce would be compromised.

Far from opposing the chancellor, Anne, though it was she who had originated the scheme, gave him her vigorous support: "We were wrong about Knight, we must accept the consequences." These arguments seemed to shake the king and under the joint pressure of Anne and the cardinal he sent an order to Knight not to proceed to Rome but to wait at Lyons for fresh instructions.

Anne and Wolsey were, however, agreed on the need for an initiative of another kind. With no mention this time of either Wolsey or the divorce another messenger should solicit from Clement a simple bull to the effect that while the Pope was out of action responsibility for judging in canon law any business relating to the Church in England should be devolved to an English ecclesiastical tribunal.

I discovered all this one evening when Anne came into my room in great agitation: the king had done the stupidest thing.

"What a baby he is, what a baby!" she said. "Just think of it! Too impatient to wait and, like a son hiding some escapade from his father, not letting his chancellor know, he has himself written to Knight instructing him to go on at once to Rome to complete the mission with which he was charged. No question but at the Roman Curia he will be made to come out with it all, and more than all – and I dare not think what the consequences will be."

Her fears might yet have proved groundless, had not a piece of bad luck intervened. The situation in Italy had altered dramatically. The emperor was no longer in control there, for his mercenaries had met with a succession of reverses and the whole land was in a state of anarchy, overrun by armed bands no longer obedient to anyone. Travelling in those conditions

involved such risks that Anne was optimistic of seeing Knight
return across the Alps. But the very reasons that had made her
choose this messenger now rebounded against her; a man of
honour and of his word, incapable of giving way to circumstances, and, once engaged on the path that had been traced
out for him, Knight was one to follow it to the end if he had to
cut his passage through an army of tigers. I cannot relate here
all the ins and outs of this journey to Rome. Ten times he was
arrested, ransomed, set free and then, three leagues further on,
recaptured. At Viterbo he thought his adventures and his life
would end between the damp walls of an unlit dungeon. Then
the prison was set on fire, and he found himself outside. By a
miracle he arrived safe and sound at the foot of the Castle of
Sant' Angelo.

But the Pope was no longer there. After six months of
captivity Clement had made use of the prevailing disorder to
decamp, and had taken refuge in the town of Orvieto where the
emperor's mercenaries were not in occupation. But before proceeding there to meet the Pope, Knight had had time to rattle
out his whole story to the papal dignitaries, including the
marriage project and the name of Anne Boleyn. The Pope was
informed, and in his irritation he inclined at first to refuse to
receive the messenger. But because the King of England could
be a recourse to him against the Emperor Charles, he did not
dare to reject outright the request of a delegation of powers to
Cardinal Wolsey. So through intermediaries there began between the diligent cardinal and the most cunning of popes the
subtlest display of covert fencing, which would have been a
most amusing spectacle if I could have forgotten that Anne's
whole future depended on the outcome.

Clement might want to seem to be giving Henry all he could
wish but he had no intention of abandoning one whit of papal
authority. Therefore while he befooled Knight with honeyed
words he made a few slight alterations, without of course letting
Knight know, to the terms of the bull he was being asked to
sign. Knight did not notice this trickery, sent off the document
by special courier and awaited congratulations.

When the bull reached Henry, he at once realised his messenger's imcompetence. What he held in his hand was just a worthless scrap of paper. Certainly the Pope was nominating the cardinal as his legate in England but he was reserving all ultimate authority for himself.

Wolsey could scarcely conceal his exultation. Was this not the proof that no-one but himself was competent to bring these delicate negotiations to a successful conclusion? The king contritely gave way without Anne having the chance to protest. Once more the chancellor was in command.

For a new mission to Orvieto he chose men of his own. One was a clerk, Edward Fox; the other his own archdeacon, Stephen Gardiner. The latter was a scheming, ambitious man and far abler than the unfortunate Knight who, to his utter dismay, had been ordered to go back to Lyons and remain there. The cardinal counted on Gardiner to convince the Pope that never would he, Wolsey, have ventured to put forward or even give his backing to a project that would cause annoyance. His good faith had been abused. Gardiner was to go on to stress the need to support Henry against the emperor and so in the first place against Catherine his aunt, who as Queen of England was having the most detestable influence on the ministers and peers of the realm, urging them towards an alliance with her nephew. As for the king, he had declared himself quite ready to strengthen his hand against the emperor by marrying Madame Renée, the King of France's sister-in-law, if only the Holy Father would grant him a dispensation to remarry.

On the return of Gardiner and his associate the chancellor could well believe that he had won his point. Gardiner related to him proudly the arguments he had used until he had obtained all the concessions asked for. The bull he brought back authorised, beyond dispute, Cardinal Wolsey, conjointly with the cardinal in charge for England, Lorenzo Campeggio, to hear any cause relating to King Henry and thereafter give their ruling.

Anne saw the way ahead becoming clearer, Henry the

realisation of his wishes. But Wolsey, after studying the bull minutely, took good care not to let them see it. The crafty Gardiner, a man cleverer than Knight but less wily than Clement, had equally let himself be fooled. The dispensation had indeed been granted but it was to apply not *after* the marriage with Catherine had been annulled but *if* the said marriage had been adjudged unlawful. This word *if* changed everything. The terms used might be more complicated but the effect was still to reserve the final decision to the Holy Father.

For the cardinal to let the king know that things had gone wrong would involve him in a serious loss of face. If he were to let Anne know, it would seem equivalent to a confession that he had been playing a double game. So he said nothing and made pretence of being satisfied. But thinking that Gardiner, on the principle "once bitten, twice shy", would be the likeliest to avoid being deceived a third time he sent him back in secret to draw out of Clement a pronouncement free of all ambiguity. To make doubly sure, the Pope was to deliver it into the hands of Campeggio in person so that there should no longer be suspicion of duplicity on one side or the other. All the cardinal-chancellor could now do was to hope that this latest move would prove successful.

After a long wait Gardiner came back bringing the good news that under Gardiner's own eyes the Pope had signed the decree which decided, this time without equivocation, in favour of the king. Nothing remained but to send Campeggio to take it to England and bring it back to the Pope. Two months later when Campeggio arrived with the document he communicated its terms both to the king and to Wolsey but refused absolutely to part with it. Clement had entrusted it to him on that condition.

Wolsey and Gardiner had been fooled a third time. For Clement, by retaining control over the decree, reserved to himself the power either to withdraw or release it, depending on whether events should dispose him to placate Charles or Henry.

It was evident to Anne that the Holy Father was only wanting to gain time – the time, as he clearly hoped, for Henry to tire of her and drop the divorce. Not long before, Anne would have been so sure of the king's infatuation that she would have smiled at this new and transparent exhibition of papal wiliness. But meantime an unexpected occurrence had caused her to wonder whether the king's passion was burning so hotly as she supposed.

Every year in London a lot of people died at the end of winter. But this spring the toll kept rising from day to day until there had been nothing to compare with it since the plague. It was clear that a grave epidemic was in the process of ravaging the town. It was not the plague but was almost as bad. For after pains in the head and kidneys the victim was subject to a cold fit and shivering, followed by a fever so high as to make him perspire through every pore until his sheets were drenched. Hence the name "sweat" that is applied to this illness, which kills within hours two out of every three who catch it.

During June one of Anne's housemaids died. Anne told the king, so that they might flee the epidemic together. But instead he instantly left London by himself, leaving her there for fear that if in her turn she caught the disease she might pass it on to him.

"You see," she said sadly to me later, "there is a limit to the king's love. He certainly wants to share my life, but not my coffin."

Anne took refuge at Hever, where in fact the scourge struck her, and her father Rochford also. Henry took good care not to come near but instead fled further still to Hunsdon, for the people in attendance on him had become feverish. All he did was to send to his dying friend his own physician, Dr Butts. Luckily, Anne recovered. While she was ill I never left her side for a minute. God took care of me and I escaped the infection. Thomas Boleyn got better too.

106

"Do you know," Anne said to me when she was convalescent, "who came to see me at Hever? Not a coward like my royal lover, yet not a man who cares much for me. Cardinal Wolsey!"

"Well, it shows he's more sympathetic to you than you think."

"Possibly, yes; and I'm touched. But more likely, his true motive was to disarm me."

"Why always see things in black?"

"Because they are rarely rose-coloured in politics. Anyway, his sympathy, whether genuine or not, will get him nowhere. Wolsey, like Catherine, will have to leave the court."

It was at this time, when Anne was convalescent, that Campeggio had come back from Rome. From whom did Anne learn of the instructions he had been given by the Pope? Perhaps after all from the crafty Lorenzo himself – prudently ensuring that, while faithfully executing his mandate, he should not jeopardise his relations with a queen-in-bud. Or else was it Gardiner who from his post of observation in Rome and as Campeggio's friend might wish, with an eye to his personal future, to keep in with Anne? She told me nothing, well knowing how to be discreet about her sources. Anyway, someone certainly alerted her to the Holy Father's calculations – that all that was needed was patience to wait until the favourite were dismissed. Clement flattered himself that he could persuade the emperor that this disgrace of Anne's was his own doing, and it would be to him, the Pope, that Catherine owed the retention of her title. Beyond a doubt Charles would repay the Pope for this by ceasing to persecute him, nay rather by becoming friends with him again. All the same, until this actually came about he must take care not to aggravate the King of England and perhaps at the same time set the King of France against him. So to put Henry off the scent he had instructed Campeggio to pretend to persuade Catherine, as Henry wanted, to retire into a convent. But thereafter he must use every possible device to stop the proceedings from getting under way or, if they did, from reaching a conclusion. Such were the instructions which Lorenzo was to try to carry out to the letter.

He accordingly put gentle pressure on Catherine to withdraw into some cloister but was not surprised to hear her reply, as she had already to Henry: "I will turn nun when the king turns monk". Meantime, events abroad were making things yet more difficult for Wolsey. The situation in Italy had altered once more; the French forces there had been routed, the Swiss mercenaries of the emperor driving them out of Lombardy; while to the south, before Naples, Lautrec's army had been overcome, less by force of arms than by privation and sickness. Many, Lautrec among them, were dead and the rest falling into the enemy's hands.

Thus better placed in Italy, the Emperor Charles felt better disposed towards Clement. Finding himself all of a sudden under less pressure to satisfy Henry, the Pope declared that he "had decided to change his cassock and to live and die an imperialist". In the belief that the Pope was still anxious to gain England's goodwill, Henry had requested him, via his agent Casale, to authorise Campeggio to hand over the document to him, but he now met with a categoric refusal. He had hardly recovered from this snub when a warning reached him from Casale that "there was now no longer anything to be hoped for from the Holy Father, not even kind words or friendly bits of paper."

Destiny seemed truly bent on foiling him, for a little later Catherine informed her husband that she had just been given an old brief of Pope Julius, found in Spain, which removed all objection to their marriage. By quashing the king's pretended scruples, this left the divorce without a motive. As though to complicate the whole, Clement fell so ill that his life was feared for and until he recovered the powers delegated to Campeggio and Wolsey were suspended. When at last the Pope did recover Campeggio could no longer postpone convoking the tribunal but he demanded and obtained its presidency. By thus stealing a march on Wolsey, he was able to make the proceedings drag on. Catherine challenged her judges, declining to accept that they should sit elsewhere than in Rome and declaring that she would appeal to the Pope to that effect. Soon afterwards, when the judges in the diocese of Rome were sent on leave, Campeggio went with them, adjourning the judicial action and effectively putting it off until doomsday.

Anne could not close her eyes to the fact that the whole thing was threatening to go on for ever. Though she refused to lose heart she felt less sure of herself. She had now passed her quarter-century, had lost something of her freshness and was watching her face for the first appearance of wrinkles. She had none yet but she was becoming more and more impatient. All the same I did not expect to see her abruptly leave the court to go and shut herself up in Hever Castle.

As soon as I could I joined her there and found her in an uncertain mood, a little strange. Instead of replying to my questions she made a gesture with her hand which begged me quite simply to leave her in peace. I took no offence, for more than once on earlier occasions this touchiness had been the prelude to a quite different mood, and led, when she had pulled herself together again, to a new confiding intimacy accompanied often by revelations, if not confessions.

I knew from experience that the best thing to do meanwhile was to keep out of her way. So I withdrew into the wing of the castle where my father and I had our apartments and waited several days. This worked so well that it was Anne who sent for me.

When I entered her room she was sitting by the window, her back to me, her chin in her hands, deep in thought. Away from the court she always dressed unassumingly. She was wearing a simple frock of homespun with large folds. Her slender neck seemed still whiter under the coil of her black hair. She had heard me come in.

"Ah, it's you," she said without turning round.

"Yes, and I would like . . ."

"I know. Listen, rather, and give me your advice."

"You frighten me."

"I am also not without fear, and I ask myself if I have done right or not." She sighed, turned her head, looked out of the window at the trees and the sky; finally she turned round to face me and looking me straight in the eye she said: "I have crossed the Rubicon."

"You mean . . ."

"No, not yet. If I gave myself I should lose everything. But I thought I sensed in the king a something, a nothing, a hint of boredom, of lassitude . . ."

"And so?"

"I let him open my bodice."

"That was all?"

My question made her laugh, but the laugh was mirthless.

"That was all, as you say. But it was nonetheless a first step. And dangerous. After that there will have to be others. How long shall I be able to hold out?"

"So that is why you've run away?"

"Of course. I must make him think that I'm hiding my shame. And that's not so far from the truth, when all's told. But what do you think? Ought I to leave him to champ the bit, at the risk of wearing out his patience? Or go back to him as a penitent?"

"You're not afraid, that being so big and strong and brutal, he might take you by force?"

"No. He won't – he knows too well what the result would be. I would seek refuge with my cousins in Ireland and would be lost to him. I am only at Hever, but it's a warning."

We were of one mind that she must hold firm and not leave the castle until Henry's desire for her had taken full possession of him again. She had played her hand well; her gamble had paid off. Poor Henry, poor king! He had thought himself so close to possessing his fair one and now there he was, fretting in desperation that he might lose her. So worked up as he had been, passionate, powerful, a sheer tyrant, this separation from Anne was turning him into a lamb. He wrote to her at Hever letter upon letter, all full of burning passion, laced now with threats, now with entreaties. He named her his "sweet-and-bitter", his own mad creature, his little serpent, his savage charmer, his daily torturess, his disease, his sovereign . . . Sometimes he would end his letters on a tender note: "Happier than me, this will be going tonight where I cannot go", and would speak to her with exultation and nostalgia of her "charming breasts". Sometimes there would be the suggestion of a warning: "If it is of your own will that you have fled I can only lament my ill-fortune and must try little by little to master my infatuation". But sometimes he could not contain the cry of a heart in agony: "I cannot live apart from the woman I most value in the world".

To all these letters Anne sent friendly answers, assuring him of her attachment but of her virtue also; telling him that when the evening star rises she thinks of her king and asking him to think of her at the same hour. He would retort that to think of her robs him of his sleep – not being able to sleep where he wants, which is in her arms. And she would answer: "When you will", meaning "Just as soon as we are married".

Her long solitude over this period gave her time to reflect. And these reflections all came out in the end against Cardinal Wolsey. For she now had the added suspicion that he had made himself Campeggio's accomplice in order to win the favour of the Holy Father. Could she still simply go on waiting? Time was pressing. She made up her mind to obtain the chancellor's disgrace at all costs.

The chancellor did not want for enemies within the king's own circle – the whole Boleyn clan, for a start. But a man is more vulnerable through his friends than through his enemies. The chancellor's loyal secretary, Archdeacon Gardiner, was just back from Rome. News had arrived that in contravention of his earlier promises the Pope had gone so far as to cancel the mandate given to Wolsey and Campeggio. This caused Anne little indignation or disappointment, for she expected no good from any ecclesiastical tribunal. But she knew Henry was beside himself with rage; it was the moment to strike. She left Hever and returned to the court. So overjoyed was Henry to see her again that he asked nothing more than to listen to all she would advise. They went together to shoot grouse in Northamptonshire and at the dinner which followed Anne brought home to him Wolsey's duplicity: "Is it not wonderful," she said, "to think how the cardinal has put you in debt and danger with your subjects?" Then, as the king displayed astonishment: "There is no-one in the kingdom worth five pounds who through Wolsey's fault has not a claim on you". It was her way of recalling to him that painful memory of the "amicable loan".

By contrast, all the way back to London she never tired of praising Gardiner and the excellent work he had done in Rome. So much so that the archdeacon, given a hint by Anne and feeling the wind in his sails, saw a prospect opening up of the highest responsibilities and hastened to betray his master. While laying on the king's desk some state papers prepared by Wolsey, he slipped in among them a detailed list of the cardinal's immense possessions and fabulous resources. Thanks to these Wolsey had become a prince of the Church in all countries – such as we may be sure will never occur again in England – and had multiplied his endowments of schools and colleges. All this appeared, in the inventory, with figures to back it up.

Henry was at first dumbfounded, then leapt up in fury. He discovered that during all those years while he had been showering money and presents on him his chancellor had never ceased despoiling the kingdom; squeezing his dioceses; plundering his abbeys; selling the king's favours; receiving payments from foreign princes in the form of pensions and life annuities in exchange for his political support; in brief, making money out of everything and everyone. But what put the seal on Henry's fury was the discovery that his own fortune made so poor a showing beside the cardinal's.

Straightaway the king resolved on his downfall. Everything Wolsey had done in the course of his reign was held against him as a crime. One day as proof of the bad books Anne was reading he had brought to Henry *The Obedience of a Christian* by Tyndale, which his spies had found in her rooms. But the passages which Anne thereupon made Henry read gave him no displeasure at all: "The king", it was written, "is responsible for the soul of his subjects as much as for their material well-being". Well then, it followed that the Pope was usurping the royal authority over the souls of Englishmen! Justification enough for Henry to do without the Pope in his own exercise of spiritual power! By consequence, and better still, to do without Wolsey.

From that time on, to all the chancellor's requests for an audience the king opposed an implacable silence. Or else he was leaving for a game of tennis. Or he was going on a stag-hunt. Or to discuss theology with Thomas More. The prelate became worried. He saw himself threatened by the gravest menaces and told his friends: "When the Crown accuses, the jury will make sure to find Abel guilty of the murder of Cain". He now felt both tired and old; he was afraid, if he were prosecuted, he might no longer have the strength to make a fight.

Meanwhile Campeggio, his powers having been withdrawn, set out to return to Rome. Arriving by gentle stages at Dover, he observed with stupefaction the customs officers there seize hold of his luggage and, in violation of his immunity as legate, break straps, force padlocks, open his chests and search everything from top to bottom.

But they did not find what against all hope Wolsey had hoped to seize, namely the document which Campeggio naturally had long since taken care to destroy. If the chancellor could have secured it, then the king in his joy and in the strength of the bull signed by the Pope would have charged Wolsey to sit alone in his quality as legate. Wolsey would have condemned the marriage as incestuous and the storm-clouds would have been dispersed.

In his game of heads or tails the cardinal had lost. Henry was informed the same day of the affair and its pitiful conclusion. Still under the shock of reading the inventory he gave free rein to anger mixed with his old grudges. He had always found it hard to stomach the sight of Wolsey so often managing public business in his place and generally doing it better than him. He no longer had the least motive for sparing him and assembled the materials for a public action at law. The king's prosecutor brought a bill of indictment against the chancellor. Two days later, Wolsey was no longer Keeper of the Seal.

In a last effort to avert the worst the cardinal, like the Burghers of Calais, made an unqualified submission to the king. He abandoned to the Treasury all the revenues of his dioceses, of his abbeys, of his colleges at Oxford and Ipswich, even down to the pension which the King of France was paying him. However, when the king ordered him in addition to surrender York Place at Westminster Wolsey tried to protest; it was not his personal property but that of the Archbishops of York: "How could I give up what does not belong to me?" But, under harassment and threat, he gave way and handed over the keys of the sumptuous palace with its furnishings, vessels, tapestries and jewels. Was the king troubled in mind by the cardinal's final and humble message, calling on him to remember that "there is Heaven as well as Hell"? Or did he simply feel that he had taken vengeance enough? However that might be, he was sufficiently magnanimous as to call off the impeachment and allow the penitent to retire to Esher and pass his days there in peace. But fallen, never to rise again; solitary; a broken man.

# VI

# Thomas Cromwell

Having thus got rid of Chancellor Wolsey with scarcely the need for any personal intervention, Anne thought of nominating to this post her *protégé* Stephen Gardiner, who had brought about the cardinal's fall. She might count on his gratitude and devotion, and be able to put her policies into practice through him. But the archdeacon proved to be not much more loyal to her than to the old prelate. Caring less for power than for titles and possessions, he had no great wish to aspire to a perilous chancellorship which would depend on the king's good pleasure and had proved so suddenly fatal to its last holder. He therefore aimed less high but for a more secure goal, preferring nomination to the bishopric of Winchester with its rich diocese which old Wolsey had left vacant when he gave up all his posts.

Deprived of this support, Anne looked for others. Her uncle Norfolk would make a good president of the king's Council; and so in fact he became. To succeed the cardinal she advised the king to confer the Great Seal and the chancellorship on Thomas More. With the exercise of power thus shared between an aristocrat and a philosopher it would now be the king – and thus the favourite – who would decide what should be done.

It is true that More had made no bid for this employment. He had never taken sides for or against the divorce. To induce him to accept, Henry had to promise never to "trouble his conscience" with matters beyond the government of the kingdom. What Anne appreciated in him, besides his literary works which she admired, was that he saw himself as a thinker rather than a man of action. After Wolsey's excessive presumption and cleverness she had no distaste for seeing a sage instead of a man of ambition in his place.

Anne also arranged for her father to be given charge of the Little Seal; Suffolk was made vice-president of the Council; Fitzwilliam took the Treasury. Between these five – Norfolk, More, Rochford, Suffolk, Fitzwilliam – there was one thing at least in common; all received pensions from the King of France. We may be sure it was not chance that determined this choice if we bear in mind the tender recollections Anne cherished of her stay in France when she was young and in the service of Queen Claude. Those sweet nostalgic memories played their part in her wishing for ties of friendship between England and France.

Meanwhile with Henry she had visited York Place, Wolsey's abandoned palace with all its marvels. The king had some idea of making it his town house when he was not either at Greenwich or at Hampton Court and of installing Anne there. She had noticed straightaway that at York Place it would not be possible to arrange apartments for Catherine and so she urged this proposal vigorously upon the king.

She saw in it a double advantage: the divorce from the queen would be carried a stage further, and thereby her own advance to power. She knew that the German painter Holbein had just arrived in London to make a portrait of the king, and she set him to draw up plans for the alterations that would be required. Her own apartments would be next to those of Henry and their two rooms close to one another. And for still greater amenity the new royal property – Whitehall, as it would be called from now on – would be carried down to the Thames by gardens descending to the water's edge.

Meanwhile, continuing to put new pawns on her chessboard, Anne had had her brother George sent on an embassy to France; Rochford her father, alias Boleyn, was raised to the rank of Earl of Wiltshire, whereby she herself became Lady Anne Rochford. I was surprised and indeed amused, as I recalled how in old days she had shown contempt for titles and honours of this sort.

"You may smile," she said to me, smiling in her turn, "but my feelings are in no way changed. Personally I attach no more importance than *that*" – and she clicked her fingers – "to these grandiose trifles. All the same, just think how much more easily the crown will fit a Lady Anne Rochford, the Earl of Wiltshire's daughter, than it would a poor Miss Anne Boleyn, the draper's granddaughter. And then, wait till tomorrow – the banquet that's to be given in honour of my father and his new elevation. True, he struts like a peacock to find himself called Earl; that's the reverse of the medal. But the obverse is what's going to happen when we're at table. Keep your eyes open."

I did, and it was a sight to see. No banquet since the Field of the Cloth of Gold had equalled this in magnificence. On an immense cloth of white damask sprinkled with lace from Maubeuge gold vied with vermilion, vermilion with silver. Crystal sparkled everywhere under the light of a thousand chandeliers. Into vast bowls of china porcelain there flowed cascades of fruits, among them a sort of apple still extremely rare, golden in colour and marvellously juicy, these *naranjas* that reach us from Persia across Italy and Spain.

In the centre a couple of young wild boars flanked a young fawn, all three spit-roasted and smoking, waiting to be carved. Some hundreds of hares, geese and wild duck also smoked on all sides and there were even fowl from India and of that other kind, dotted with pearls, that we have hardly yet begun to rear in England. A cloud of waiters in blue velvet livery handed around the dishes while behind each guest stood three servants, one of whom lit up the place with his flaming torch, the second held a silver jug and the third a crystal cup so that between courses we could wash our fingers. A gentleman arrived from Lyons had indeed told us of a new invention for carrying the mouthfuls to one's lips: a little instrument, he said, shaped like a pitch-fork. But the king had exclaimed that a pitch-fork was all right in the stable for clearing away the dung, not at table for spearing buntings; and he would never use one. In fact, I also consider it more delicate to wash my hands in perfumed water than to have to handle this barbarous instrument. I would be surprised if that polished court of France were ever to adopt it.

All through the meal while singers, dancers, conjurers and jugglers of every kind performed in turn, an orchestra of twenty-two musicians, hidden behind a sumptuous piece of tapestry, regaled us with light music. Sometimes indeed it was a little too modern for my taste, so discordant are these new counterpoints. To crown the banquet, a huge construction made chiefly of biscuit, oil-cake with nut, and whipped cream was carried in by four servants and set before the king. Out of it sprang a little winged girl disguised as an angel, who, accompanying herself upon a lute, sang a song in honour of the king very prettily: one, by the way, that Henry had himself composed.

But it was not for this great array of splendour that Anne had wanted to prepare me when she had bidden me "Keep your eyes open" – even though so much unaccustomed luxury conveyed its own meaning. For what really struck me, as it struck the whole court, was the astonished realisation, shared by all but spoken by none, that Catherine of Aragon was not there. In her place on the king's right sat the quite new Lady Anne Rochford! Henry had given her precedence over the duchesses of Norfolk and of Suffolk, over all the marquesses, countesses and baronesses. Seeing this, no-one could any longer doubt that the great-granddaughter of the draper Geoffrey Boleyn was not just the favourite: that before long she would be queen.

Throughout the banquet I hardly took my eyes off her. But she, who had invited me to keep my eyes open, seemed by her bearing to want to play down the importance of the place that she was occupying. Far from affecting the appearance of a sovereign, she kept her eyes down as though to make herself forgotten. Even her dress was on the modest side for such an occasion. It was a long time since I had stopped making her clothes; the king had supplied her with a dressmaker from Paris. Her gown of a warm brown velvet was the perfect match for her complexion but it seemed almost drab beside the many-coloured fabrics in the rich attire of both sexes. She wore no jewellery other than the collar with four strings of pearls to hide the unfortunate mole on her neck. Over her beautiful black hair she wore only her habitual half-moon head-dress which by its simplicity stood out among the extravagant plumes worn by most of the ladies. I had no explanation of this strange modesty till the next day when I told her my joy at having seen her thus, virtually proclaimed as queen.

"Don't excite yourself," she said with a drumming of her fingers. "It's far from settled. The king deceives himself if he thinks he can impose me quite so fast. Catherine is inflexible. Gardiner has walked out on me. Thomas More disapproves the divorce. Norfolk and Suffolk don't want to compromise themselves. I must efface myself and avoid all provocation, use great self-discipline and count on no-one but myself."

"And on the king," I corrected her. For Henry had just sent Thomas Boleyn, Earl of Wiltshire, on a mission to Bologna to plead the cause of the divorce. Not this time with the Pope but with the emperor, who was there; he had strong influence with the Holy Father now that the two were reconciled and since Charles's coronation at the Pope's hands. Wiltshire took with him some learned doctors of the Church and was to ask that his theologians be allowed to discuss the case with the Roman cardinals. Then if the cardinals rallied to the case put forward, ought not the emperor to abide by it as well and advise the Pope to do the same? Walking with Wiltshire in the gardens at Greenwich Henry had broken out angrily against the Pope: "If he wants to defy the King of England he will be ripe for a drubbing" and added that he, Henry, might well seize the Church's possessions and attach them to the Crown. The emperor would be wise, then, to restrain Clement's intransigence and allow the cardinals to hear the English doctors.

But Anne, with better foresight, regretted the embassy to Bologna: "As always, whatever he desires, Henry thinks is his already. My father is not more sensible. They would not listen to me and I much fear that the result will be a disaster."

So truly was her forecast borne out that Wiltshire returned

from Bologna more discomfited even than she had feared. Right at the start the emperor had interrupted him to ask, giving tit for tat: "And if you and your theologians fail to convince the cardinals, King Henry binds himself to abandon the divorce?" Caught unprepared, Thomas could only stammer out that this question went beyond his mandate. And that brought the venture to an end.

Then when Wiltshire, already much disheartened, was about to leave Bologna an usher from the tribunal of the *Rota* handed him a summons to the King of England to come to Rome to appear in court or else be represented. Wiltshire hurried to protest to Clement but the Pope had him received instead by his chief of staff and after an interminable discussion all that the unhappy earl could obtain was a suspension. So Wiltshire had to make known to the king not only the piteous failure of his mission to Charles, but also this insulting summons to justice.

In his wrath Henry threw the whole blame for the failure and the insult on the incapacity of the wretched Thomas Boleyn, and Anne's position was in consequence shaken. He blamed her now, almost, for the disgrace of Wolsey, of whose cleverness and know-how they had had so many proofs. Capricious as ever, Henry experienced a revival of affection for the man he had banished; and when Dr Butts, the king's doctor, reported that the cardinal, old and sick at heart, was dying of his exile Henry melted so far as to give him money, presents, "get-well" wishes and the promise of pardon for the prelate. He even made Anne do the same. She consented so as not to make things worse; but this threat of a return to favour of Wolsey made her painfully conscious of a decline in her own influence.

The pardon was signed in February. In March the cardinal was given back the revenues of his diocese of York; his vermilion crockery; his silverware; his furniture and tapestries. Generous as this might seem in Henry, there was a motive for it. Wolsey, in the hope of softening the rancour of his most powerful enemies, had distributed a part of his fortune among them, and had given up to the king personally his most important source of income – the pension paid him by the French Treasury. Like all treasuries it found itself constantly short of ready money: so that the payments were generally in arrears. Henry for his part was always in need of money. But he had no desire to compromise his royal dignity by having to harass the French ambassador, as Wolsey had had to do at every payment date. So he relied on his ex-chancellor to continue doing this as though he were still the beneficiary. When Wolsey was informed of this intention he saw in it a real chance to win back the king's friendship.

But he grasped at this idea too soon. Despite having recovered a part of his riches he was still strictly confined to the diocese of York. But this did not stop him from living once more in great style. In his episcopal palace he was already discussing ambitious plans with his architects for beautifying his country residence. When the king came to hear of this his vindictive sentiments returned. Was the incorrigible cardinal once again by his splendour going to make the king feel small? Wolsey took fright when he heard of this recrudescence of Henry's hostility towards him. He dared not ask for an interview. The opportunity could have come all the same when the king was staying not far from Richmond Lodge, the prelate's summer residence. But Norfolk and Suffolk were on the lookout for trouble. Henry was quite capable of letting himself be hoodwinked again, so they sent word to the cardinal to go back at once to his distant diocese of York. For want of any support Wolsey had no choice but to obey.

This was the moment too when he saw his last hopes melt away. Having nothing further to lose from the King of England, he resolved to take his chance with the King of France. To win his favour he proposed through one of his agents to remit his pension to Francis including all sums already due and those payable in the future. This amounted to taking back with one hand all that he had given to Henry with the other and of course it irritated the king more than ever. Henry, as it happened, had just sent the Earl of Wiltshire to France in hopes of winning the king's support at the Vatican, with propositions so advantageous that Francis did not even give Wolsey's proposal an acknowledgement. Now frantic, the old prelate turned to the Emperor Charles and told him that he was prepared to ask the Pope to excommunicate Henry if he did not submit. He received no reply from Charles either. Like an animal caught in a trap that looks for an escape on all sides at once he sent a messenger to London at once to warn the king that Norfolk was taking part in some intrigue and that he, Wolsey, was confident that he could foil the plot. Whereupon the messenger, afraid the king might hand him over to the duke, made haste to betray his master by going to warn Norfolk of the whole business.

It was time to make an end and the duke decided to apply the death-blow. He had Dr Agostino, Wolsey's doctor and confidant, arrested. Under interrogation the unfortunate man could not long withstand the torture and made a complete confession of the overtures made by the cardinal to Francis, the emperor and the Pope. In the face of so much treachery Henry blew up. He issued a warrant for Wolsey's arrest and to crown the cardinal's humiliation gave the charge of it to Percy, Earl of Northumberland, whose happiness with Anne Wolsey had long ago destroyed. Percy of course acquitted himself of this mission with especial rigour and satisfaction. He had the cardinal mounted on a mule and was intending to bring him to London to be judged but the old man gave him the slip in a way that there could be no disputing this time. The arrest had frozen him with fright, old age had laid its hand upon him and the interminable journey in the worst of weathers had worn out his nerves and broken his spirit. He fell ill on the road and had to be put to bed in the nearest abbey, that of Leicester. His sickness would not mend; on the contrary, it grew worse from week to week, and the fallen chancellor, without the strength or perhaps even the desire to climb the slope again, allowed himself to sink gently into unconsciousness. He remained in that condition for several days; then, without further resistance, he gave his soul back to God.

\*

At the news of his death Anne's friends and relations gave free rein to their joy – sometimes in a fashion so unseemly as to shock the French diplomats on duty in London. Wiltshire wrote a satire which he put on stage, showing the dead prelate on his way to hell. Norfolk, who had never ceased to tremble for his offices as long as the cardinal was alive, was so enthusiastic over this farce as to have it printed. But to my surprise Anne herself was the first to react against this exhibition of bad taste.

"I had to fight Wolsey," she told me, "to the point of driving him from office; but despite his failings I felt respect for him and almost friendship. I do not forget that during the Sweat he had the courage to come and see me when I was ill, while the king was running away as fast as he could. Besides, his death does not solve my problems as much as you might think. For you will see. They will all walk out on me: Gardiner, Fitzwilliam and a dozen others, with Uncle Norfolk at their head. While Wolsey was alive he frightened them and they supported me against him. But now it is I who will alarm them and they will support Catherine against me."

This was well conceived for in fact Catherine, sensing now that she had support behind her, took advantage of the king's being with her over Christmas to tackle him vigorously with the demand that he should separate from his favourite. It was usual in these quarrels, the queen having much the stronger character of the two, for Henry to lower his flag. Fortunately for Anne, this time Catherine let herself be carried away by the violence of her feelings and her arrow overshot the mark. In her exasperation she unwisely accused her husband of adultery and Henry could reply triumphantly that his intimacy with the Lady Anne was purely intellectual; it had always been chaste and so it would remain. He had not touched his favourite and never would until he had married her. For he wanted a son and cried out in a fury that "this marriage must and will take place". Not the Pope, not Catherine nor her nephew would make him go back on that. Then letting the quarrel drop, he withdrew, still nursing his anger.

Since among her other amiabilities the queen had defied him to impose a girl of so low an extraction on the court he immediately set his heraldic experts to work out a genealogical tree, authenticated and official, tracing the nobility of the Boleyns back to the celebrated Norman knight whom William the Conqueror had brought over with his baggage. It was too much; the court laughed it to scorn and Anne had to put up with some gibes from her aunt Norfolk. In a defiant answer the king had a motto, one that he had heard spoken of in France, sewn on the livery of Anne's servants: *Groigne qui groigne* ("Thus it shall be, mutter who may".) A new gaffe; for when he learnt that this was the motto of the House of Burgundy he had to have it removed in a hurry. Anne chided him for all these blunders which made the situation worse. When the king declined to give Norfolk some new prerogative the old man blamed it on his niece and loaded her with crude abuse. Suffolk, Henry's brother-in-law, gave out that the little goose who had now taken precedence over Mary his wife, the king's sister, had been the mistress of the Earl of Northumberland before having the same relationship with Thomas Wyatt. Anne had always expected these accusations and she had long since forestalled them by telling Henry that she had loved Percy, and Wyatt had loved her, but that neither the one nor the other had ever touched her. She urged Henry to call them both in; whereupon Percy swore on the Bible that Anne had granted him no favours. Wyatt did not even have to do that, for the king, who loved him well (they enjoyed their games together at tennis and bowls), was only too happy to believe it. Suffolk was made to leave the court, followed by Anne's aunt Norfolk who was too fond of making mock of her. Thus for the moment the *beau monde* found itself checkmated.

But it was no longer only the court who made difficulties. It had come to the knowledge of the English bishops that the Faculty of Theology in Paris (duly tutored by Francis) had declared Henry's marriage with Catherine null and they had vigorously denied the competence of these Frenchmen to pronounce on an English case. Invited in their turn to declare in favour of the divorce, they had shown themselves resolutely opposed. In Rome the emperor's agents at the Vatican – as Henry was soon to learn – were asking the Holy Father to threaten the king with excommunication if Anne were not immediately banned from the court. This so scared Henry that he thought of complying before the notice had even reached him.

Under this avalanche Anne had withdrawn to Hever where she kept quiet in hopes of better days. There she received, smuggled (no-one knew how) on to her dressing-table, crowns made out of gilded cardboard accompanied by verses tartly critical of her behaviour. I would have liked to inquire among her housemaids so as to discover who had made an accomplice of one or other of them. But Anne took less seriously than I did these displays of hatred touched with irony and advised me to have patience. I obeyed but I could not refrain from keeping a sharp eye on all the servants in the castle.


After the death of Wolsey Anne had been approached by one of the prelate's secretaries who had shown himself very able in his service. He was called Thomas Cromwell. A man in his forties, son of a carder of wool at Putney, he had taken up a course of studies which he had rounded off in France, Holland and Italy. After being employed for a time by a Venetian money-lender he had enrolled in a body of *condottieri*. Thus he had sown his wild oats and returned to England apparently more settled. He put himself under the protection of Wolsey who taking note of his energy and his intelligence had retained him in his own service. After his master's disgrace it was Cromwell who, being in a good position to exploit his talent for diplomacy, had won the king's pardon for Wolsey. Again it was Cromwell who after the death of the fallen chancellor had distributed to good purpose the dead man's fortune among clergy and nobility. Norfolk, one of those whom he enriched, had him elected to the House of Commons. Soon after he became a secretary to the king and it was then that he put himself at the service of the favourite.

That a man so evidently shrewd should elect to support her at a moment when all might seem to have been lost was the first encouraging sign that had come Anne's way for a long time. "This wily man," she thought, "would not have bet on my future if that future had not had a great chance of being royal." So it was with full trust that she saw him propose to Henry a new plan of action for the divorce.

Cardinal Wolsey, by appealing to the emperor and the Pope against the king, had incurred a charge of high treason. Cromwell proposed to institute legal proceedings against any ecclesiastic who had received any delegation of power from the traitor, no matter of what kind. As it turned out, they all had. They were all therefore guilty of the crime of *praemunire* against the king. It was a little far-fetched; but coming from a vindictive king with docile magistrates around him it was menacing enough to worry all the clergy. Besides, the lords hated the bishops, who competed in their dioceses with the lords. Cromwell's project, then, by curtailing the power of the episcopal body, was sure to win the lords' support. Even those who in the king's Council were far from favouring Anne Boleyn could be guaranteed to approve this measure, while taking care not to see into its real purpose.

The bishops were convened and thought at first that this was a new device for getting money out of them. They expected to get off by offering the king a sum of £100,000 sterling to be paid in five annual instalments. To their extreme surprise and causing them at first a surge of panic, their offer was refused. But on reflection they came to understand what the king was getting at. They revealed this to the lords who thereupon became less zealous for the king's plan. Covered on that side, the bishops were now in a position to bargain over their act of supreme submission to the Crown. Cromwell could obtain it only by agreeing to add to the text this saving clause: *Within the limits of what God's laws allow.* This obviously robbed the act of its intended purpose, since divorce is contrary to those laws.

Strong in this initial success, the bishops went on to obtain signatures from a majority of priests to a declaration objecting to any attempt by the Crown to free itself from the authority of the Holy See. This semi-reverse for Cromwell was a complete one for the king. It aggravated his subjection to the Church. It was the clinching reminder that over all sovereign monarchs there reigned one supreme sovereign and he was in Rome.

Anne was concerned at this, naturally; but its effect was rather to deepen her reflections.

"You are aware," she told me, "of the absolute power of the Church of Rome and you can measure how widely it extends. It is truly a spiritual continent which governs the whole of secular Europe. If England does not yet sense herself as an island, it is because she still feels included in this vast incorporation. Whether the Pope's authority exerts itself in favour of Spain, of the Empire, of France or even of England, it is still a hindrance to the destiny of this kingdom. To become herself, queen of the four seas, Albion must break out from this vassaldom and the king become her sole master under God. And to that end, he must not implore the Pope, as he is doing, to sanctify his royal will; no, that will needs to be in itself the single decider when the good of the kingdom is at stake. Right up to a break with Rome, if that must follow. But Henry is too frightened. The thought of being excommunicated appals him. So it is I and only I who can and who must drive things on to that point. It will take a long, a very long time; but the day will come when Henry and England too will thank me for it."

I was like the king. The idea of excommunication appalled me. When that happens to you, anyone in the street – no matter who – has the right to kill you. Besides, at the Last Judgement your chances will be pretty thin. So I urged Anne to reflect on her salvation.

"Done," she said; "all the reflecting has been done already. My salvation depends on no mortal in the world, were he the Pope. It does not depend on Signor Giulio dei Medici, called Clement VII. I am a Christian and my faith is sincere. It is God who will judge me and my salvation depends on him alone."

*

127

Cromwell's failed attempt had of course aroused Clement's anger. He went back on the reprieve granted to Henry by his chief of staff and instructed his nuncio in England, Baron Del Borgho, to inform Henry that the procedure of the *Rota* had been set in motion against him.

There was a fine explosion. Foaming in anger, the king swore that he would not give way and that if he went to Rome it would be at the head of an army. Del Borgho of course did not believe it, nor did Henry himself. But for once Anne did not rebuke him for this blustering; she even gave him her congratulations. For she could see in this reaction the first beginnings of a movement towards independence from the Holy Father and the Roman Curia.

Nursing his wrath and swept along by his enthusiasm, Henry convoked the members of his royal council that same day and ordered them to visit the queen and charge her in the name of the whole government to submit and to abdicate her rights. The delegation consisted of a dozen lords including the Dukes of Norfolk and Suffolk, accompanied by the Bishops of London, Lincoln and Winchester (this last was Stephen Gardiner) and various doctors of theology. All led by Cromwell himself, thickset and harsh under his square skull-cap, wrapped in his ample black coat, and tightening that powerful jaw which so impressed me. He had not been able to choose the members of the delegation, all of whom were there as of right. Moreover, they were of very different persuasions, so that as soon as she saw them Catherine was little disturbed. Confident and in a good humour, she had little difficulty in convincing one lot by argument and the other by her charm. At the end one of them, Guildford, proposed agreeably that Cromwell and his doctors should be sent to Rome with the mission either to make the Pope change his mind or submit to his censure. The only one who did not laugh at this was Cromwell.

In fact the queen's position remained strong. She reigned still, if not over Henry's heart, over his cowardice, and she continued to supervise the running of the household and many small matters; she would often mend with her own hand the

128

king's linen or the lining of his garments. Anne had fought for a long time to wrest Henry from the influence of these old habits. She remained Catherine's principal maid of honour and was often called on to be her partner in some game of faro. Each time it was a double trial for Anne who could not help feeling a kind of filial attachment for this ageing woman while she was impressed at the same time by her tough Spanish character. It was becoming urgent, if she and the king were to escape this spell, that the queen should be exiled not only from Whitehall but from all the other royal residences; from Hampton Court where Henry loved to stay; from Greenwich where Catherine lived; from Windsor where they passed the summer together.

Once she had made up her mind, Anne persevered till she had won her point. Now was the right moment to act. The king was leaving for a long round of visits through the kingdom and for a whole month Anne would be alone with him. I did not go with her so I was not there to witness how she set about making up the king's wavering mind for him. Did she grant him some new intimacy? I do not know, but however it was, before they returned to Windsor the queen was informed it was the king's wish she should reside there no longer. And that she must withdraw with her suite to The Moor, the residence of the Abbot of St Albans, where Henry never went.

# Secret Marriage

Sending the queen away was an important stage on the road to the divorce. Catherine's friends, not having her presence to support them, very soon lost their posts and were replaced by men loyal to the king. But in the five years of her struggle Anne had taken the measure of a courtier's soul; she was under no illusions about such people.

"Stupid Henry again!" she said to me with a flash of anger. "When he thinks he is being clever he refuses to listen to me. What he should have done was the exact opposite and so I told him: instead of dismissing Catherine's friends he should have promoted them to higher posts and thus secured their devotion. As it is, he has made mortal enemies of them without obtaining any balancing extra support from those others, who spoke up against Catherine only in the hope of supplanting her friends in their jobs. You will see; now that they have got what they wanted, they will be much less enthusiastic over the divorce."

Anne's perceptions had been correct; the conduct of the newly promoted went even beyond what she had anticipated. Several wrote to the emperor assuring him of their loyalty to the queen his aunt; one of Henry's agents at the Vatican, a Dr Bennett, while pretending openly to urge the divorce upon the cardinals, was at the same time whispering to the Holy Father that he ought resolutely to hunt the king down and force him to give way and come to Rome to plead his case. Thomas Elyot, Henry's recent appointment as ambassador in Vienna, published a lampoon against the divorce and had it sent to Charles in Spain. These defections scarcely surprised Anne; and besides she had more immediate causes for anxiety. One of her agents

130

with the emperor assured her that Charles was waiting only for his aunt to be formally repudiated before going to war against Henry. A fleet to carry soldiers was already in a state of alert in the Dutch ports and was waiting only for the word of command before getting under way. If the emperor's troops landed, that would be the end both of Anne and of her hopes for the future of the kingdom. The English forces, being too few in number, would have no means of resisting. Henry would be deposed, the Crown would revert to his daughter Mary, aged fourteen, Catherine would govern in her name, and Albion be turned into a province of the Empire.

There was only one chance of avoiding this catastrophe: the alliance with France. Anne therefore urged Henry to strengthen the bonds of this alliance as soon as possible. She thought – with good reason – that Francis would be well disposed to it for he had a strong interest in not seeing England, across the Channel, fall into the orbit of his dangerous rival. In fact the demands he made were not exorbitant and a treaty was swiftly concluded.

Now that the emperor's forces were pretty well held in check it was deemed possible to risk decisive action and to have the English bishops pronounce the divorce. Anne was approaching her thirtieth year. Her experience and her political acumen were blossoming into a calculating subtlety that still evokes my admiration. For a long time as I watched her pile up, one after another, intended slights directed at both Pope and clergy I had to ask myself what goal she was pursuing. This goal was precisely that Henry should so thoroughly provoke the Pope and push him to extremes that he would finally have no alternative but excommunication. Thus the rupture with Rome which she judged indispensable to England's sovereignty would be accomplished.

But Henry, one suspects, was the last to have wished for so radical an outcome. He therefore had to be led up towards it, as it were, unawares. Besides, the moment was well chosen and the king's mood matched it. Had not Henry quite recently proclaimed that he, King of England by the grace of God, was in line with all the kings of England who in the past had had none but God over them? So he would not be averse to calling Parliament together in order to give the force of law to a declaration so suited to his pride. A vote would still be needed to achieve this result. But it was the right moment. Anne sensed among the public a growing irritation at seeing foreign priests meddling overmuch in English concerns. One might well find fault with Henry for his plans for divorce but this did not make it any the more acceptable that an Italian bishop, Campeggio, whose vast revenues came from English dioceses where he never set foot, should presume further to dictate orders to the King of England. Henry's friends among the peers had in fact little difficulty in convincing the Commons of the Lower House and a decree was soon issued, forbidding members of the clergy to obey any edict without first having obtained the king's assent.

This was a flat defiance of the Pope's authority. The Bishop of Winchester – our friend Gardiner – made an effort to raise a hue and cry among the bishops against the decree but he was called to order and did not persist. There was more trouble with old Warham, Archbishop of Canterbury and Primate of England who, up till then, curiously, had shown himself among the most accommodating to the Crown. But he had fallen gravely ill and since with death in front of him he had no more to lose he dictated a solemn protest from his bed claiming for the Church of Rome an inalienable primacy in diocesan administration. It was the old man's swan-song; he died soon after.

Without the power to call into question the decree that Parliament had voted, the Primate had nonetheless made its application more difficult. Henry and Cromwell were therefore agreed that the successor to this post should be one more willing to oblige. They found such a man in the person of a bishop named Cranmer, who had always shown himself in favour of the divorce. Intelligent, clever, hardworking, with a noble visage, assuredly this man would turn out to be the best of all archbishops of Canterbury. At first glance, with his deep blue eyes in a perpetual state of astonishment, you would have thought him candid, but his twitching lips that drooped at the corners and smiled only rarely belied the impression. And what belied it altogether was the eventful existence he had led hitherto, no more austere than it had been candid and open. After studies at Oxford and a Chair of Theology at Cambridge he had become chaplain to Rochford. Later, when Rochford had been made Earl of Wiltshire, the young prelate, happening to be in the king's company at a hunting-lodge, was presented to His Majesty by some ministers who had known him before. He knew how to catch the ball on the bounce. Bringing the conversation round to the divorce, he suggested that it might be possible to obtain the agreement of the Universities of Oxford and Cambridge.

Henry did not take up this idea immediately but he was sufficiently struck by it to attach Cranmer to his person. He began by sending him, more than a year before the time we are talking about, with Wiltshire to Bologna. Then when the latter had gone back to London the young bishop found himself dispatched to Germany with the emperor's suite. His mission was to try to rally as many as possible of the German doctors to the cause of the divorce. For this purpose he made numerous contacts but by the end of the year he had not had time fully to exploit them, for the emperor had taken him with him to Vienna and then to Italy. It was at Mantua that the news finally reached him of his recall to London.

Now Cromwell knew through his spies that during his stay in Germany Cranmer had fallen in love with a beautiful girl – no shrinking violet – and had married her secretly. This grave contravention of the celibacy of priests would become graver still and a criminal offence in an Archbishop of Canterbury and Primate of England. So when the mitre was offered him – an offer too good to be refused – Cranmer was careful not to tell the king about this secret marriage. On their side Henry and Cromwell pretended not to know. In this way they made sure of having a zealous and obedient Primate; for if, like his predecessor, the idea occurred to him of supporting the primary of the Church over the king he would be offered his choice: either comply or be dismissed from his post, and sent to the Tower of London, brought before the judges and condemned for felony.

But after nomination and before he could be enthroned in his diocese of Canterbury, he had still to obtain from the Holy See the bulls of investiture. Now Clement was wary and if he were to suspect the true motive behind this promotion he would make inquiries about Cranmer and, on discovering his past history, would assuredly refuse the bulls. The affair, then, must be handled in such a way as to avoid arousing his suspicion; or rather, and more difficult still, since the suspicion was bound to occur, they had to drive it right out of his mind. Here it was that Anne's cleverness, her extraordinary inventiveness and her experience of men worked marvels. She got the king to assign her a marquisate which would carry with it lands and the title "Marquis of Pembroke". She was known as the Lady Marquis.

To all those people who had for so long thought Anne was the king's mistress, this would be proof that Henry, grown weary, was shaking himself free of her with a shower of gifts. So sudden an elevation, accompanied by an annuity of £1,000 sterling and presents in gold and jewels, could hardly be explained in any other way. It is in fact what was believed. The Pope was informed and he believed it too: at last this affair was sorting itself out for the best! With Anne put at a distance there would be neither divorce nor re-marriage to fear. When, a little later, an English deputation solicited the bulls of investiture for Thomas Cranmer the Pope neither suspected a trick nor made any closer investigation. He would not of course be ignorant of Cranmer's efforts in Germany on behalf of the divorce but he would also know that at the emperor's court he had declared himself its resolute opponent. This sort of double game or turnabout did not surprise the crafty tenant of the Vatican. Had not Thomas Elyot and Dr Bennett, seemingly so devoted to Henry, behaved in just the same way?

With the bulls obtained in this manner, Anne could pass on to the next chapter. It was then that she prepared to set out on a course from which there would be no returning. To wait any longer would have been difficult for her in any case. For something that befell her on French soil where she had gone with King Henry to meet Francis had been too unpleasant for Anne to remain any longer in the situation in which she was.

For the reason we have noticed – the emperor's warlike preparations – Henry had wanted a radical strengthening of the French alliance and in the autumn the ambassadors of the two countries had met to prepare the ground. But this time Francis had declined any ceremonial such as that at the Field of the Cloth of Gold. So as not to upset the emperor overmuch he wanted the meeting to look as if it had happened by chance. The teams accompanying the two monarchs would accordingly be on a very modest scale. Anne and Henry agreed that her retinue should be on a scale equivalent with his and she would wear the royal jewels that he had recovered from Catherine. Thus the French would have to treat her as the queen's equal; by implication the divorce would have been approved in advance.

It followed that the "Marquis" of Pembroke should be welcomed at Boulogne, in default of the queen who obviously could not do it yet, by some French lady of the highest rank. The negotiations were difficult. Margaret of Navarre, the king's sister, had great need, if she were to win back her territories beyond the Alps, to keep the emperor's goodwill and so she must decline. She was in any case opposed to the divorce. At an equivalent rank the only one who would have been acceptable was the Duchess of Vendôme. She would undoubtedly have asked nothing better but her scandalous life, prolonged into middle age, was notorious. Anne Boleyn's fortunes would thereby have been compromised rather than furthered. The discussions were still going on when Henry, his "Marquis" and their suites set off to embark at Dover.

The crossing was good and they arrived at Calais sooner than expected, so that Francis came late. This gave the favourite time to realise that no princess, however insignificant, was waiting for her at Boulogne. This could have wounded Anne three times over: as a Frenchwoman at heart, as a friend of

Francis and as pretender to the crown. But she concealed her feelings and even seemed to take the misadventure with a smile. She decided all the same that in the circumstances she would not leave Calais.

The meeting of the sovereigns had been set to take place at a boundary point between their two territories. Henry and his suite proceeded there without Anne, and the two kings made their way together to Boulogne. Henry wanted to ride on the left of his host; Francis insisted it should be on his right. But the English king would not be persuaded and there ensued an excellent climate of mutual respect and allegiance which the monarchs did their best to maintain. Three days of conference followed and the results appeared to be happily balanced. A treaty of alliance – not too precise – was to be signed by Henry against the Turks. In return Francis would send two French cardinals to Italy where the Pope was to have another meeting with Charles; their mission would be first to cool the sovereign pontiff's ardour for satisfying the emperor, then to bring him round to a meeting with the King of France. To put Clement in the mood for this, they would dangle before him the old project of a marriage between his niece, Catherine de Medici, and one of Francis's sons.

Henry therefore returned to Calais well satisfied. Before leaving, he showered liberal presents upon the French courtiers, pensions, jewels or gold objects. Francis on his side tried to make the "Marquis" forget her disappointment by sending her a girandole bedecked in pearls and diamonds at the hands of the Provost of Paris. He was profuse in the kindnesses he showed Anne, promising her in particular that once she was married to the king he would use his prestige at Rome to offset the emperor's influence and persuade the Pope to accept what had become a fact. Henry himself, assured henceforward of total support from the King of France, brimmed over with self-confidence. Normally so vacillating, for once he felt ready to take the boldest decisions. Anne for her part, seeing her lover at last ripe for action, was resolved to learn a lesson from what had happened at Boulogne. Once back in England, she went and shut herself up in Hever Castle, declaring that henceforward she would quit it only to be led to the altar.

It was a rash decision, one for make or break. But the king had the same impatience to be wed and the outcome showed that her bid had been well calculated. If on his return from Calais Henry still hesitated a little, he could not long endure this retreat to Hever: an absence which, knowing how strong-minded Anne was, he might well fear could go on for ever. A new and ardent correspondence confirmed him in this fear and a few weeks later – it was the end of January and the roads were under snow – he sent discreetly to summon his beauty from her retreat. Anne was very cold on the journey but her heart was warmed by the thought of what was so soon to follow. And sure enough, next day, under the roofs of one of the towers of Whitehall and in the presence of several tried friends – I was one of them – a friar of the Order of St Augustine celebrated the secret marriage; to persuade the priest to do it the king had promised to appoint him General of the Order of Friars Mendicant.

I must admit that during the whole ceremony up to the "I will" of the king, pronounced in a vibrant voice, I had been much more affected than the bride appeared to be. So Anne, my friend Anne, had well and truly married the King of England. I had witnessed this spectacle myself; there could be no doubt that it had taken place, and yet I could still hardly persuade myself that it was true. Was it not a dream?

That same night and for the first time Anne shared the sovereign's bed. That, had it been needed, would have been enough to wake me to the truth; but in the morning when I was helping her to dress it was she who seemed to me deep in thought. I was alarmed; had the night gone well?

"Yes, yes," she said; "it's not that, even if I had to make believe that I enjoyed that kind of thing. But don't run away with the idea that just because here I am, married, all my troubles are over. Far from being a *dénouement*, this impromptu marriage is at best only a beginning. The king has married me, yes; but that hasn't made me queen. Catherine still holds the title; and to take the crown from her and wield power I shall need more than ever to fight, without respite or weakness. I shall still have against me, as well as the Pope and the cardinals, most of the ministers, not to speak of a large part of public opinion. And as support I will have only the most opportunist, all ready to betray me if the wind turns. So I don't need to tell you to keep your lips sealed. This marriage must stay secret for a long time yet."

At first nothing essential appeared to have altered in the relations between the king, Catherine, Anne and the court as a whole. What I had not realised was the extent to which the new bride was going to find herself in a delicate situation. For she was still Catherine's maid of honour and when Catherine, breaking the ban for a few days, was present at Greenwich or Hampton Court, Anne had still to be at the queen's disposal. And she who still bore the title took a malicious pleasure, though she had not yet divined the whole truth, in choosing Anne to play with her all kinds of games – *primero*, Pope Julius or chess. One day when Anne had just taken, one after the other, her castle and her bishop Catherine suavely remarked to her: "You are in a position now to lay your hand upon my king; but for you, unlike the others, it's a matter of all or nothing". That evening I saw Anne come back shaken to her depths.

"If this goes on much longer, it will tax me beyond my strength. I thought I was battle-hardened; but I had not calculated the extent to which I must dissemble and be cruel if I am one day to impose my policy." Yet it was no more than she had told me earlier, when she had seen me shocked by the way she was behaving: that in the struggle for power one must acquire a heart of steel.

Though she had not been able to go quite so far as that, she still laid her plans with Cromwell. The marriage was to be kept secret so long as the Pope's bulls for the enthronement of Cranmer had not come to hand. To keep the Pope in ignorance and allay any fears that he might entertain, Anne had the nuncio invited to the opening of Parliament with a seat on the king's right. This was to give the Holy Father's representative precedence over the French ambassador, seated on the king's left. After thus providing for Del Borgho and the Pope this reassurance which could last only for a time, Anne prepared the next episode. The plan was little by little to accustom the court to the idea of the marriage, so that it should not one day burst on them as a scandal. A few weeks later, in the presence of all the courtiers, she told one of her favourites, laughing, that the day before she had been seized with an irresistible craving to eat apples:

"The king told me it was a sign of pregnancy; but I replied to him, No, no!" She meant it to be understood that she might perhaps have the joy of bringing into the world a son, when Catherine could no longer do it and had given the king only one solitary daughter. What would the sovereign, desperately anxious as he was for a male heir, not do to keep the crown in the Tudor line? The remark, when reported to the nuncio, plunged Del Borgho into confusion. Realising that he had let himself be duped, he hesitated over whether he ought to confess to the Pope; then after thinking about it he chose to keep the news to himself.

Meantime the two French cardinals had succeeded in persuading Clement to meet the King of France. This would be such good news for Henry that Francis straightaway sent off a delegation to England. Whereupon Henry with his customary exuberance was so delighted that he promised the messengers forthwith that he would sent Norfolk and Wiltshire to assent to any wishes of Francis in the matter of Scotland, and on some minor issues. He begged his dear brother above all to instruct his cardinals to impress upon the Holy Father to take no action until these talks had been held. Francis agreed, with the rider that Henry should take none on his side either.

When all this was already in hand and halfway to being accomplished Henry suddenly became very embarrassed. His first instinct was to conceal everything – marriage, pregnancy and the rest. But Anne made violent protest against this childish back-sliding, the cowardice of which would be exposed by the first indiscretion. Francis would certainly be informed of Anne's pregnancy; he would deduce from this that there had been a secret marriage and would never forgive them for having fooled him. Instead they must take the initiative and send him an emissary who would reveal the truth to him. It was George Boleyn, become Viscount Rochford since his father's elevation, who was charged with this delicate mission.

Perhaps Francis might have felt a certain pleasure at this news. He feared Catherine as the emperor's aunt whereas he would be glad to see Anne Boleyn, whom he liked, on the throne of England. But he could not help pondering on the unforeseeable consequences which an excommunication of his ally Henry must import for France. Then when George went on to ask for a promise of help in case of need, Francis was put off by the conceit of this young and inexperienced diplomatist. This did not stop him from appearing to consent but George was shrewd enough to read between the lines. On his return to London he asked that his sister should first give him audience alone. Before she had even seen him, Anne gathered from this that the news was bad; that it was accordingly becoming urgent to put an end to a situation which was no longer tenable; and that she and Henry must prepare the court for news of their union.


She impressed this on the king; and as an initial step, the lords were invited to a sumptuous banquet at Whitehall. There, while the servants passed round a dish consisting of hundreds of larks and buntings, the king called out to the Dowager Duchess of Norfolk – the same who not long before had made a mock of Anne when the Boleyns were ennobled – and invited her to admire all these silver dishes, these golden goblets, the rich gold plate, not to mention the treasures shut up in the cupboard: the whole belonging to the mistress of the house:

140

"So well endowed," he exclaimed, "is not the Marquis of Pembroke the best of all matches?" After a disconcerted silence the courtiers stood up and applauded. Anne lowered her eyes, affecting the false modesty of one who knows well that homage will be coming to her, which made the company still further convinced that Henry was in fact announcing a royal engagement. A little later, in church, in the presence of Anne and the king these same courtiers heard the minister in his sermon implore the king to separate from Catherine for his own salvation and so put a term to twenty years of mortal sin; then for the salvation of England offer to his subjects a worthy and virtuous queen. Whereupon the congregation assumed that not only the engagement but the marriage had already taken place.

When finally in mid-March Anne and Henry were assured that the bulls signed by the Pope were on their way to England Parliament was asked to pass a package of laws restricting Rome's authority over matrimonial causes and assigning these to the supreme jurisdiction of the Primate of England, the Archbishop of Canterbury.

The Commons of the Lower Chamber were already convinced, being only too happy to withdraw from foreign priests a right of scrutiny which they judged excessive. It was not the same with the Lords of the Upper Chamber. Hand-picked though they had been, it took a good three weeks to bring them round to pass the new laws. But passed they were.

The consent of the ecclesiastics had still to be obtained. Cranmer had drawn up two proposals: one on the full judiciary powers of the Primate, to which the lower clergy, like the majority of the Commons, would willingly consent; the other on the illegitimacy of the union with Catherine, which the bishops would be as little disposed to endorse as a majority of the Lords. The bishops must therefore be chosen with care. When this had been done one hundred and twenty churchmen, vested moreover in the powers of two hundred others not present, were convened under the presidency of the Bishop of London. To make things still more certain, the presiding

141

bishop produced a brief published three years earlier by the Pope, authorising certain ecclesiastics to make their own decisions now; he omitted however to add that since then the Holy See had annulled the brief. After some debates put through for form's sake the two proposals were adopted, the first almost unanimously, the second with a number of abstentions.

A royal commission was appointed by Cranmer, with Norfolk for president. This set off to find Queen Catherine and inform her that, deposed by the bishops as well as by Parliament, she was no longer King Henry's wife and must retire into the county of her choice. In the face of her resistance she was promised the greatest favours if she gave way; the threat, if she persisted, that she would find herself deprived of all her revenues. To which Catherine replied that if her worldly goods were taken from her she would beg her bread from door to door.

But nothing came of it; everything went through as it had been decided, and on a Saturday in April Anne appeared in the royal apartments robed in all the insignia of sovereignty. Her train was held by the Duchess of Richmond, Norfolk's daughter and wife of the king's bastard; she was followed by eighty maids of honour. Thereupon, though Anne had not yet been crowned, the courtiers were invited to come and pay homage to her as loyal subjects.

But next day, Easter Sunday, it was otherwise in church where the majority of the congregation were not of the court. There, when the Prior of Cheapside had prayed for divine protection for the Marquis of Pembroke, King Henry's wife, the majority of the faithful bustled out noisily, not even waiting for the elevation of the Host. It was proof of the general aversion, as much against Anne herself as against the repudiation of Catherine. The king had commanded that henceforward prayers should be said in the churches of all parishes for the safety of the Marquis of Pembroke, and the same scene of rejection was repeated everywhere. Nonetheless it had to be recognised that the repudiation and marriage were accomplished facts. Yet although there was neither hope nor means of going back on them nor of preventing an early coronation, this popular resistance continued. Anne certainly felt it painfully. But she had foreseen it and it seemed that nothing could now dispute the power she had won against such grave odds.

# VIII

## (1533)

# The Coronation

But Anne still had a long way to go before she could exert in reality the power she craved. The months that followed were fertile in setbacks of one kind or another.

In the first place there was the question of the coronation. It was not a matter only of giving it glamour but also and above all of imposing it on a public opinion that was fundamentally hostile. To achieve this Anne and Henry judged it essential that the divorce as well as the marriage should be sanctioned in advance by the official findings of an ecclesiastical court. But the setting-up of such a court ought to be the subject of a request from the highest religious authority in the land. This would mean that the Primate, the Archbishop of Canterbury, should address a petition to the king requesting that he be made judge in the case. But to achieve its object the petition must be made public, and this would expose Cranmer personally to the censure of the Pope. Therefore to persuade – or rather to oblige – Cranmer to agree to do it regardless, he must no doubt be given a gentle reminder of his clandestine marriage. Even so he could not be sure, if he obeyed the king, that no-one else would discover the secret and put himself in a still worse predicament by revealing it to the Pope.

Hence the efforts he made to persuade Anne and Henry to allow the business to lie over until after this interview since Clement was due to meet Francis and might let himself be convinced. I myself was much of this opinion; why rush things along when they could come all right by themselves? When I discussed it with Anne:

"No, no," she told me. "We can't wait any longer. I could

have a son in the meantime, and his legitimacy would be contested and he would be yet another bastard. More than that, don't you see, from now on Henry can come to my bed when he likes; the familiarity will cool his passion for me and then how much longer will I be able to hold him? Suppose that, weary of struggle, he is tempted once more to make submission to the Pope and comes round to repudiating me? All my projects would be ruined. No, no," she repeated. "I absolutely *must* be crowned; and for that, the divorce and the marriage must be ratified – and the sooner the better."

Having failed to dissuade either Anne or Henry, Cranmer was in no position to hold things up any longer. Either he must submit or lose all. So he set the procedure in motion. And since the first thing to be done was to draw up the petition to the king this was duly written, sent and made public; whereupon Henry with equal publicity made a show of protesting that he recognised no other supreme judge on the validity of his first marriage than God; but that nonetheless he was authorising the Archbishop of Canterbury, in his capacity as Primate and representative of the divine will, to hear the case and to pronounce.

The deposed queen was then cited to appear before the Primate at Dunstable, not far from where she was residing. But Catherine had found a highly valued and influential friend in the person of Eustace Chapuis, the emperor's new ambassador to London. After taking counsel with him she refused to comply and signed two protestations challenging the Primate and his right to sit in judgement: first as traitor to the authority of the Holy See; secondly as judge and party to the case in his capacity as former chaplain to Anne Boleyn's father. After which she declared that she was not concerning herself in the matter any further.

Chapuis for his part had gone to find the nuncio and get him to alert the archbishop to the papal brief forbidding any cleric, of no matter what rank, to judge in this case. If the nuncio had done it the unhappy Cranmer, caught between two perils, would still have had great difficulty in guarding himself from the more immediate one. But once more the timid Del Borgho, fearing what would happen to him in London if he took so bold a step, sent word to Anne's chaplain that he would not be providing the brief in question. Given this assurance, Cranmer declared Catherine in contempt of court.

It took a few months after that to bring the various stages of the legal process into line with all the requirements of Catholic law. Finally, at the beginning of spring Cranmer could pronounce his judgement, annulling Henry's incestuous marriage.

After a decent interval the second action could be opened, this time concerning the legitimacy of the marriage with Anne. It followed from the previous annulment that the reasons requiring to be adduced in court were now fewer and so the judgement authenticating this legitimacy could be given within a few weeks, in the early days of May.

There was now nothing to stop the coronation from going ahead.


Nothing, except the continuing apathy of public opinion. And that is why the new queen, with the king's agreement, wished the ceremony to take on a splendour that would go down in history. For if her coronation did not outmatch Catherine's in pomp and solemnity Anne might be written off as a "discount queen". Whereas a superior exhibition of splendour would stamp her in the eyes of all as the undoubted queen of the kingdom of England.

But, as Anne realised, this luxury would itself be provocative. So she prepared herself for some painful incidents.

Tradition had it that the actual crowning should be preceded by a preparatory halt at the Tower of London where the queen would be understood to have gone on retreat to pass a night and a day in prayer. Anne therefore left Greenwich before the king, to join him two days later at Westminster. Preceded by a gunboat decked out joyously with flags, she embarked on a vessel which resembled the gondolas of Venice, though it was larger and less tapered in appearance. Its canopy was adorned on the left with armorial bearings hastily put together for the Marquis of Pembroke – a hooded falcon holding a sceptre and issuing from a crown turned upside down and sprinkled with oak-leaves; on the right, with royal armorial bearings – a crowned shield held on the right by a griffin, on the left by a leopard and quartered into twelve sections with lions rampant and fleurs-de-lis. A cloud of small craft with ladies and gentlemen on board followed the royal vessel in convoy on its way to the Tower.

With other maids of honour I had embarked in attendance on the queen who, under her canopy and half stretched out on enormous cushions of white and gold satin, smiled at me from time to time. Her smile was a little tense, owing perhaps to the discomfort of a pregnancy rather far advanced, perhaps to disappointment or maybe to both together; for, apart from a sky which seemed to have become a cloudless blue for the occasion and the Thames which by reflection intensified the blue, the countless boats of the flotilla around her from which one would have expected songs and acclamations to ring out, glided on in a profound silence which struck me as most strange. For a funeral it could not have been more profound. So the journey to the Tower, several miles upstream, seemed to me interminable. Our vessel reached its destination in full view of the river bank where a crowd of the common people, drawn by curiosity, stood squeezed together, and the silence of this crowd appeared to be deliberately echoing the silence of the courtiers. No waving of handkerchiefs, no cheers. It was lugubrious indeed. Setting foot on the steps of the Tower, the queen was received by a deafening fanfare of trumpets, drums and salvoes fired from ten blunderbusses, not to mention a couple of dragons vomiting flames – a cacophony which, bursting out suddenly upon the silence, had the effect on me of a cannon-shot in church.

I do not know just how far Anne was affected by this icy welcome. All that she said to me about it in the luxuriously appointed room where we found ourselves alone, she and I and a half dozen other young girls, was (with yet a touch of bitterness in her voice) "To think what one has to go through before being able to seize the reins of government! And to-morrow will be worse". Then with a snap of her fingers she proposed, "Let's have a song!" From then on she was the jolliest of us all and the rest of the day passed in amusements of one kind or another.

She withdrew early and spent the evening genuinely in prayer, then slept (she told me next day) "like a log". In the morning – it was the last day of May – a chamberlain came to conduct her to Westminster. The sky seemed resigned to the mood of the day; it had gone grey. On a litter with a canopy and drawn by two mules the queen, still wrapped in satin of white and gold, began her journey through the town. The king had had the streets decked out with banners and standards, the windows with flags, the house-fronts with garlands of roses. Through this festive setting the litter proceeded while along the walls a crowd of spectators was lined up, with members of the corporations in the front row.

All silent, these too. Not a smile. Not a cap doffed, prompting the queen's jester to call out to them: "Are all your heads eaten up with scurvy, that you're afraid to let us see them?"

The procession was headed by the guild of French merchants in London; they were robed in velvet of violet colour with the crowned falcon embroidered on their breasts. Anne had wished that these Frenchmen should be gentlemen, but all had declined. Behind them rode the Lord Chancellor Cromwell, the ambassadors of Venice and of France, the Primate Thomas Cranmer, Archbishop Stokeley and – who would have thought it? – Bishop Gardiner. There followed by itself the royal litter, flanked on either side by the Duke of Suffolk as Earl Marshal on a bay horse and the Grand Seneschal William Howard on a piebald horse. Lady Wiltshire, the queen's mother, and the Dowager Duchess of Norfolk (she no longer gibing) followed the litter in a carriage – themselves followed by the ladies of the court on their mares decked out in brocade studded with gold.

Approaching Fleet Street the procession halted to allow the

queen to admire the monument put up and paid for at large expense by institutions both English and foreign. There on the top of Parnassus, above grottoes and springs whence spouted the golden streams of a wine of the Rhine country, Apollo played on his lyre, surrounded by the nine Muses singing verses in honour of Anne. But at the very top, what was that? The imperial eagle with wings spread out over the escutcheon of Aragon and Castile – the escutcheon of Catherine! That of King Henry came lower, that of Pembroke lower still. The insult was deliberate: the work of German merchants annoyed at having been made to pay heavily while no-one had ventured to tax the Spaniards, devoted as they were to the deposed queen.

But any protest would have been out of place, since the emperor in fact had the highest rank. All the same, Henry was for punishing the insolent foreigners. Anne opposed this, since the English had been no better. Halfway along the route St Anne and the Holy Virgin sat enthroned on an altar surrounded by little girls in the colours of Mary. One of them had come forward and recited a complimentary speech comparing Anne to her patron saint and wishing her a no less glorious progeny: a mischievous forecast that her child would be a girl, when the king was so eagerly wanting a boy.

The queen no doubt was sensitive to these slights but she had expected them too much to attach the least importance to them. If the coronation ceremony and still more the feasts and entertainments that came after had a slightly bitter taste in consequence, it was rather Anne's relatives and friends who felt it. One thing alone counted for her: she was crowned. Even if the displays of spite went on for more than a week – and in fact a dozen German and Spanish merchant vessels with Eustace Chapuis on board dropped anchor at Greenwich under the palace windows and a hullabaloo of shouts, songs, big drums, rifles, trumpets and cannon to salute the imperial eagle continued without stopping day and night – even if, after dissuading Henry from giving orders to put in the fleet, Anne had to take refuge with him at Windsor, far from the hubbub, she laughed at it all, rather than wept. She was crowned, she was crowned; she was going to be able to carry things forward briskly at last: the rest was merely stupid pranks.

And as if the coronation had been a signal given to destiny, events followed fast. At all this news the Pope had exploded in anger and again set in motion against Henry the process of the *Rota*. Our ambassador at Rome was summoned to appear immediately as a stand-in for his king, now judged to be in contempt of court. When Henry heard of it, he was struck with fright – not simply at the idea of being excommunicated but above all at having to face the flare-up that he thought would follow all over England.

When she saw that I too was frightened, Anne cheered me up:

"On the contrary, it's fine. The king is too proud to give way and go to Rome as a penitent. As for what scares you both, I can reassure you. The kingdom is quiet. The agitation among the people has died down. And Cromwell's spies are positive – no plot is being hatched at court." She added, a little darkly: "The climax is near at hand, after which I can disappear; the rest will follow by itself."

"*You* disappear! What an idea!"

"Once more, be comforted; I'm in no hurry. But for too long now I have been for the king as much his mistress as his wife. His desire for me has lost its edge. And without violent desire this fire-eater is not up to much. He always needs something new. Do you know that he almost strangled Eustace Chapuis?"

She told me how it happened. Charles's ambassador had sought an audience with the king and under cover of his diplomatic immunity had tackled him with a certain insolence. Telling him that in his treatment of Catherine he had violated the sacred character of marriage, he went on to say that even if he could trample down every human consideration his conscience could not forget what it owed to God. Keeping calm, Henry had replied that his conscience and God were on good terms. Chapuis insisted that at the least the Princess Mary, now sixteen, be married as early as possible so as to ensure a male heir to the crown. Still master of himself, Henry told him that he needed no-one's help to give him an heir. Whereupon Chapuis had the impertinence to ask him if he was sure that he had the power to beget. At that, Henry had sprung up: "Am I not a man like any other?" Chapuis made no answer. "Not a man like any other?" Lips still sealed. "Not a man like any other?" Henry had bellowed and he was about to take this obstinate mute by the throat when he guessed what it was that Chapuis was hoping to hear. Calming down, he said: "You won't drag my secrets out of me". These words were enough and Chapuis could assure Charles that "the usurper" was pregnant.

"I *am* pregnant," said Anne as she ended her story with a laugh, "and for the time being it's my safeguard. All the same, I must move fast. For the king makes having to do without me a pretext for seeking out something new, of which there is no lack among the maids of honour. I do not blame him. But it could well be that one of them might turn out one day to be as much a danger to me as I was to Catherine. And that's why I have to hurry."

Therefore in retort to the insult implied in the Pope's convening of the *Rota* she persuaded the king to call together a General Council of the upper clergy of England. Without loss of time Henry charged Cranmer to put this in hand. When the council had met, the king, in the presence of the Primate, appealed to it against the Pope in the matter of the legal action of which he was the victim. But when he came away after making this appeal Henry was trembling so much at the defiance he had launched against the Pope's authority that Anne took pity on him. And she made no objection to this decisive step towards the rupture between England and the Church of Rome being kept a secret – at least for as long as that was possible.

It could not be possible for long. For the Pope to be informed little more time would be required than it would take the courier to reach him. At the news Clement felt as if he had come down to earth with a bump. He must crush this king who flouted him! All his agents in France and in the Empire were urged to denounce the sacrilege. He made every possible promise to Francis if he would ally himself with the emperor to put in force the decrees the Pope had issued against Henry. He even thought of betrothing Mary Tudor, Catherine of Aragon's daughter, to the Earl of Surrey, son to the Duke of Norfolk, with the aim of rounding up enough supporters to enable the princess to overthrow her father. On being informed that Surrey was already married, Clement felt sure that he could easily annul a marriage. But it was pointed out to him that this would create a precedent to stop him from upholding thereafter the marriage of Catherine of Aragon. As for Francis, he turned a deaf ear. Nor was the emperor much inclined to intervene in his support. Anne had known all these things beforehand, having learnt from her spies how each of these individuals was thinking.

The secular arm having failed him, Clement had to forgo his illusions and be content with the means at his disposal. He assembled consistories and congregations with the purpose of denouncing the illegal council convened by Cranmer and declaring it invalid. Anne was delighted when she heard this. The Pope then announced that if within six weeks, Henry, the Primate and Anne Boleyn did not repeal judgement, divorce, marriage and coronation they should all three be excommunicated. This delighted Anne still more.

For now there could be no possibility of going back. She had brought him up against the wall, and now there was no way out but to take the offensive. Henry besides had become so exasperated with the Pope that he needed little spurring on. An initial setback, far from damping his ardour, only heated it further. Having appealed to Francis for support, like Clement he received no answer. This defection outraged him and he feared some action on the emperor's part; he therefore dispatched two friends of Cromwell, one English and one German, to half a dozen Lutheran princes to negotiate with them treaties of mutual assistance against Charles. At the same time he recalled his two ambassadors from Rome, after they had first formally notified Clement of the appeal that Henry had launched against him. At one stroke this put out of question any reconciliation or even compromise. Thanks to Anne's will-power and tenacity the thread was cut for good and all.

## IX

## (1533–1534)

# *The Schism*

If the rupture was now assured, it was not yet an accomplished fact. To make it so beyond a doubt the King of England had to be proclaimed sole spiritual head of the kingdom by an Act of Parliament and with the agreement of a council.

Apart of course from Anne, no-one was yet ready for this. Not the lords, or the bishops, or Cromwell, or above all Henry himself. Particularly as the king's appeal against the Pope, aggravated by the understanding he had reached with the Lutheran princes, had had the effect all over Europe of a boot thrust into an ant-heap. Francis, Charles, Clement, not to mention Henry, no longer knew where they stood. There ensued between them a constant permutation of figures, as in those surprise-dances where there is endless changing of partners.

First, a new character had appeared upon the stage – John du Bellay, the bishop ambassador of France. This man had acquired a special partiality for England, and for Anne in particular – perhaps because their names, Bellay, Boleyn, both derive from the *bouleau* (birch) – and he tried throughout, and with more or less success, to make the different figures of the diplomatic dance evolve in favour of the English sovereigns.

The first figure in the dance had been the appeal that Henry had launched against the Pope.

"It was time," Anne said to me, "for my confinement will be coming soon. If it's a boy, all will go well. If it's a girl, I shall be out of favour. Luckily, I have now got the schism so thoroughly under way that the king cannot go back on it. That's what matters."

"What name will Your Majesty give to it?"

154

"To the schism?"

"To your child."

"If it's a boy, either Edward or Henry; the king hasn't yet decided. If it's a girl, which he refuses to contemplate, I will give her the name of his mother: Elizabeth."

It was a girl. The king felt deeply humiliated. In the face of the world he had gloried in the birth of a Prince of Wales, and now he found himself exposed to every kind of raillery. People were quick to seize the opportunity. Knowing how disappointed he was, they exaggerated their demonstrations of rejoicing; there were flags all over the streets with the name of Elizabeth; congratulations flowed in from every side.

It was I who had to announce the bad news to Henry. When I saw him, his eyes flashing like lightning, his enormous fists raised high, he frightened me and I ran to escape. The queen was asleep, the baby at her breast. Doctors and midwives had fled too, just as scared as I at having to face the king in the first blaze of his disappointment.

"Ah, you are there," Anne said, opening her eyes. "No luck; but we don't need to dramatise. Given time, Henry will come round to it. Only, the war to the knife between Catherine and me will now extend to Princess Mary and my little Elizabeth. Which will be the legitimate heir? I shall still have to fight on that front unless meantime I have a boy." Silence, then a pout of disappointment: "And I shan't have Cromwell to support me any longer. He's betting either way. He pretends to approve the divorce from Catherine but in order to win the emperor's goodwill he's already confessing his preference for a princess of royal blood on both sides. I cannot count on him any more."

She knew from her agents that in the previous summer Cromwell had had discreet interviews with Charles's ambassador, from which it was clear that Chapuis had been hinting at what the emperor's gratitude would be worth to him if he went over to Catherine's cause. Had not the powerful Wolsey fallen for the want of just such a support? The respect that Cromwell was displaying towards Mary was a sure sign that the minister was letting himself be tempted. His influence with

155

the king, now that after two years in his post Thomas More had resigned to return to theology, made this temptation highly dangerous. The day that Henry began to tire of Anne, Cromwell might well be able to persuade him that in marrying and crowning his concubine he had given proof enough to the world of his manifest independence; so that he could now without loss of face, or sacrifice whether of dignity or prestige, take back Catherine of Aragon and be reconciled with the Pope and Charles. With a character as volatile as Henry's, the danger was far from being a remote one.

Then Anne had many other perils to think of. Fisher, Bishop of Rochester, the great theologian, had brought together the opponents of the divorce to join him in urging the Emperor Charles to intervene by force. The king's rebellion, they maintained, was as much a danger to the Catholic faith as the Ottoman invasions. If Charles would not be persuaded, Fisher had in mind a marriage between Mary, the Princess Royal, and Lord Reginald Pole whose descent gave him the right to lay claim to the throne of England. Happily, the threat to his crown that these manoeuvres imported obliged Henry to leave no-one in any doubt either of his authority or of his tenacity. And that – for the moment – tied him effectively to Anne and to Elizabeth.

Moreover, Anne could see that the birth of a child – even though a girl – was after all a help to her with the king. Once the disappointment was over, Henry had realised that in bringing this sturdy infant into the world Anne had given proof of her fertility and so could be capable of giving him further offspring – one day, perhaps, a boy. The little Elizabeth, baptised in September, had continued ever since to grow and prosper. She derived vigour, so Henry believed, from her father and he was increasingly surprised to find himself loving his daughter with his whole heart: "You could well one day", he would tell her while he caressed her laughing cheeks with his beard, "reign over some prince with a grip as masculine as mine!" So saying, he would picture her already marrying the Dauphin and becoming Queen of France or else the Infanta and becoming Queen of Spain. He was so proud of the "baby" that when some trouble-makers put it about that Anne Boleyn had had given birth to a monster, he even called up a group of diplomats and let them see the child quite naked: "Ha! What a strapping wench!" he said to them. "Now go and tell those rascals to shut up." All this led Henry to feel some revival of tenderness towards the mother, and Anne took advantage of it to renew her influence over him – an influence which increased in proportion as the relationships between Henry, Francis and the Holy Father became more and more embroiled.

First of all, to satisfy Henry, Francis had made use of Clement's presence at Marseilles to try to persuade him to revoke the brief that condemned Cranmer and his judgements against Catherine and in favour of Anne Boleyn. Expecting a blunt refusal, he had been careful not to press his request, which Henry in his irritation reckoned a betrayal.

Meantime Clement wanted to have Anne cited to appear before the tribunal of the *Rota*. But Gardiner warned him that Cranmer had enough juridical devices at his disposal for her defence to draw out the process almost indefinitely. Clement had to give this up and Francis, at Gardiner's insistence, persuaded him to make an effort to renew the dialogue. At Francis's dictation the Pope composed a brief allowing Henry to have his case heard at Avignon. Two legates would go there for that purpose. But when the Holy Father wanted to make it a condition that the king would bind himself to submit to any decision the legates might reach, Gardiner (like Wiltshire before him) had to confess that he was not empowered to give this guarantee.

Francis felt that he had been duped and warned the ambassador that he would give Henry no further support against the Pope. This made Clement think the moment had come for him to seek military aid from Francis against this shifty and ever-restless King of England. And to decide him he promised to make Henry give up Calais. But it was an empty promise, for the emperor, on being consulted, sent word that he was less afraid of the harmless little English fleet in the Pas-de-Calais than of the powerful French warships.

At the same moment John du Bellay, informed by Anne, told his king about the secret interviews between Cromwell and Chapuis. Francis feared that if he and the Pope pushed Henry up against the wall he might reconcile himself with the emperor by taking Catherine again as his wife – while keeping Anne as concubine – and seal with Charles an alliance against France. Therefore despite his irritation he decided he would be ill-advised to drive Henry to that extremity and that in consequence his best course was to renew his old ties with England if it were not too late.

He accordingly instructed du Bellay to plead his cause in London, to encourage the queen to trust him (du Bellay) – she already did – and to vindicate Francis in the eyes of Henry. Perhaps he could also persuade the two of them not to be in a hurry to burn their boats by breaking with Rome. Du Bellay achieved this on condition that before Easter – we were now in December – the Pope should issue a brief revoking the one that annulled the judgements of Cranmer; if by that time no brief had arrived, the schism would be proclaimed. Du Bellay was satisfied with this reprieve, confident that he could extend it from month to month. The main thing, he told himself, was to keep Francis happy and to gain time.

However, if Henry had been able to pluck up spirit to force the Pope, within so short an interval, either to give in or to break with him, this was because meantime in the autumn events had occurred which seemed to open up golden opportunities.


For almost two centuries the Hanseatic towns had been waging war after war against the Scandinavian nations. Lübeck, whose fleet had once been the strongest in the Baltic, had for a long time been going through a period of ups and downs. She had seen her port decay and her commerce reach a state of collapse. The goodwill of Gustavus of Sweden and Frederick of Denmark helped to set her on her feet and she had just armed a fleet which in the course of cruising along the coasts of Holland was causing havoc among the population. At the very hour when Queen Anne was being crowned in London a squadron sailed up the Thames and captured three vessels of the Empire. It then departed to anchor at Rye on the Channel with a view to trapping a dozen Dutch merchant ships known to be on their way back from Spain.

The commander of this more or less pirate fleet was a buccaneer called Marcus Meyer. When Chapuis complained to Henry that Rye was giving its support to brigandage an order went out to arrest Marcus as soon as he set foot on land. Deprived of its commander, the squadron went off to seek shelter in Denmark, and Meyer was taken to London. He was already resigned to a death at the gallows when some remarks of his were reported to the king, who was intrigued and had Meyer brought to him.

Meyer seemed to be well versed in the rivalries between the various powers of northern and central Europe. Were the pretensions of Pope and emperor, not to speak of France, a source of anxiety to England? No less were they to Lübeck and Denmark. Frederick had just died in Copenhagen and it should be possible to impose a prince friendly to Henry as his successor. A solid alliance between Albion, Lübeck and Denmark would be a match for any coalition you could think of.

These fabulous projects, which Meyer felt sure of realising, set Henry's ambitions afire. Confident from now on of being strong enough to act as he pleased, he waited neither for the term he had granted the Pope until Easter nor for conclusion of the alliance with Lübeck. With Anne he set to work to provoke the schism as early as January and had the two Houses summoned in order to pass the bills that would trigger it: the first acknowledging the king as sole spiritual head of the kingdom; the second validating the marriage with Anne; the third proclaiming Elizabeth (in default of a boy) as heir to the throne.

Before being submitted to the Houses, the document had been presented to the lords and the bishops without sparing either threats or promises. And despite an anathema from the Bishop of London (who nevertheless came round shortly after) signatures were assembled in sufficient number to allow the matter to be referred to Parliament.

In order to disarm the opposition Mary, Catherine's daughter, was invited to renounce of her own free will, if she did not want to be forced to it, her title of Princess Royal. She protested in writing but was nevertheless banished from the palace and installed at Hatfield where the little Elizabeth was already residing. But she declined absolutely to go and see "the nice princess". Stamping her foot she declared that she knew no other princess of England than herself. To bring her to heel Henry gave her a governess (a Lady Shelton: we shall come back to her later) who was told to stand her in the corner every time she called herself Princess of Wales and to stop her from corresponding with her cousins, Charles or the Plantagenets. The king had not resigned himself to this treatment without his fatherly heart bleeding a little. Despite the adolescent's surly character and its disagreeable consequences to herself Anne felt some pity for this innocent victim of political necessity. She intervened therefore with Lady Shelton to have the orders less strictly enforced (to which the governess lent herself so well that she got on famously with her pupil – so much so that Henry had to remind her of her duties). Still, Anne understood quite well that Mary's banishment was unavoidable. Cromwell and the court as a whole remained too partial to the princess of the blood whose obstinate resistance showed how confidently she relied on the emperor's support against her father and Anne. This led Henry to intensify the watch he kept. He stationed agents around his daughter with instructions to allow neither person nor letter to come in or go out of the castle.

A demonstration by peasants arriving en masse to acclaim the prisoner at her window drove the king to adopt more rigorous measures. In particular, when it appeared that a sort of plot was hatching round a nun of St Paul's Cross, Elizabeth Barton, who claimed to have had visions signifying the early death of the royal couple, Henry was pitiless. He had the visionary arrested. Under questioning she revealed the names of a number of nuns and gentlemen. Under the same treatment

these revealed many others. In this way a widespread conspiracy was brought to light around the visionary. And what
names! John Fisher, Thomas More, the Marchioness of Exeter,
the countesses of Derby and of Salisbury with a legion of other
lords and ladies of lesser rank. While the visionary was formally
charged, all the others were arrested. But they were all released
(except of course the madwoman who was condemned to the
stake). Anne had persuaded the king that once discovered they
ceased to be dangerous, and their gratitude would be more
rewarding than the curses of their friends. No name was made
public and this discretion had the result expected; everyone
was afraid of becoming involved and the entire opposition
kept quiet.

Anne, as we saw, had secured du Bellay both for herself and for
her cause. In point of fact the ambassador's original instructions
had been to sound out Henry's feelings in regard to Madame
Renée, sister-in-law to the King of France. But at a grand ball
given in his honour at Greenwich – in the course of which a
surprising *masque* had been enacted: the Pope a prisoner and
St Peter come in chains to kneel at the feet of Cromwell – he had
seen Anne Boleyn, superbly got up in ermine and cloth of gold,
directing the dance. From this he easily deduced that Henry's
approaches on the subject of marrying Madame Renée were not
genuine. On his return to France he had made haste to advise
the king accordingly and to submit to him a plan of his own
devising.

Clement would be won over for a start by the proposition of
a marriage between his nephew Alexander de Medici and
Princess Mary of England. In exchange for a substantial dowry
the princess would abdicate her rights to the throne. If the
Pope were then to show himself amenable, Henry on his side
would be more amenable still. One could again moot the
idea of a tribunal at Cambrai where two French cardinals
would discreetly give judgement in Henry's favour before
Catherine and her supporters had time to hear of it.

This would be a way for Francis to recover Henry's confidence, at the same time making impossible any future understanding between Henry and Charles; Alexander, indebted to Francis, would (together with Florence and Tuscany) come under the French king's influence. Du Bellay made no reference to his personal assurance of being well rewarded by all the parties concerned; from Francis he counted on some new promotion; from Henry a comfortable pension; from the Holy Father a cardinal's hat.

Both the ambassador in putting forward these suggestions and Francis in lending an ear to them were ignorant that in London Parliament was already on the point of reassembling. Without waiting for Henry's agreement which he took as a matter of course, and although he was rather unwell, du Bellay travelled post haste to Rome. He was not able to see the Pope immediately on his arrival but he represented to the chief of staff and the cardinals the danger that a schism provoked by King Henry must pose for the whole Church of Rome. Would there not follow a federation of Protestant churches which one day might even infect the Vatican?

Those around the Pope were not much impressed. Perceiving this scepticism, du Bellay pressed his point a little too far. Was it not known, he said, that already the Flemings were tearing down papal briefs that had been posted on the doors of their churches? And that quite soon it would be the same with churches in England? Continuing to support Catherine against the king and Queen Anne would produce this result all the sooner; a support the more futile because Catherine, so he claimed, was very ill.

But the harder he pressed, the less he was heeded. Bishop though he might be, he came to realise that he had misunderstood the nature of Vatican man; then when he was finally admitted into the holy of holies the character of Clement so astounded him that the man he had described to his friends six weeks earlier as "the old fellow" he could now only describe as "the old fox". Indeed the Pope dealt with him as he had with Dr Knight; while making a show of toning down his requirements, he fooled du Bellay too with honeyed words. Silently he went ahead with his action against Henry and did all that lay in his power to bring it to as speedy a conclusion as possible.

Meanwhile du Bellay, having let himself be taken in by the apparently friendly dispositions of the Pope, had already invited Francis to make discreet preparation for the proceedings at Cambrai; he had even urged him to send selected cardinals there in advance while informing Queen Anne of the good turn the discussions were taking. But in all this he had failed to perceive the hidden purposes of Clement, the hesitations of Francis, the will-power of Henry and above all the strong resolve of Anne herself.

For, as we have seen, she by no means wanted du Bellay to succeed in his efforts. By no means did she want Henry to escape being excommunicated. No doubt she could not, without alienating Francis, have said this to his ambassador. But she threw herself vigorously into supporting Henry in his intransigence, knowing full well that the Pope would never slacken in his own. Poor du Bellay was thus, without suspecting it, misled on the one side as on the other.

Meanwhile Parliament, having met in London at the end of January, was dragging its feet. Although care had been taken not to summon to it any of Catherine's friends, the complaint that had been lodged against the visionary's accomplices had aroused among the lords such a passion of resentment that it was sure to encounter opposition. The lords indeed showed scarcely less repugnance at promulgating the bill which, by reducing the title of the deposed queen to Dowager Princess of Wales and granting her a dower as such, implied the annulment of her marriage with the king. As for the dower, it could not be paid without putting in pawn with the banks possessions on the Continent which the emperor would then have the right to seize. This would compromise trade with Spain and the Netherlands, vitally affecting English interests. Here the lords were at one with the merchants.

Anne had the genius to draw some advantage from every

difficulty. She made the king understand how everything, even his divorce from Catherine, was being held up by the want of a fleet strong enough to make itself respected. Certainly this fleet, virtually non-existent thirty years earlier, had been developed a little by the two Henrys, father and son. But in vessels only moderately armed, intended less for artillery warfare than for boarding, and in numbers far too few.

"Your Majesty," Anne kept telling him, "lays out on pageantry and entertaining enough to multiply your fleet ten times over and fit it out with cannon rather than with swords and axes." But this irritated Henry, who had never any concern more pressing than to surpass his rivals in luxury and pomp. Moreover, all these complications tended to sap his vital energy. He fulminated and scolded Anne for having plunged him into this imbroglio.

"Did I not tell you so?" she confided to me. "I am queen but I have no authority. I have even rather less now than before. For a long time Henry has put himself under my influence, which has saved him the trouble of thinking. But now he is dying to shake it off. He is dying to extend beyond Easter the term he granted to the Pope, to send some apologist to Rome to plead his cause and so escape being excommunicated. My excellent du Bellay thinks he is serving me when, in letter after letter, he assures the king of the Pope's friendly disposition towards him. He writes that the Pope even complains of the untold menaces from the imperialists which this goodwill is costing him. Francis backs all this up of course, for there is nothing he wants so much as a compromise. I am going to have my work cut out to put all that right."

Anne knew only too well all the twists and turns of the king's character. Equally she understood the tortuosities of the Pope. She would gain nothing by tackling them head on. On the contrary, she must play the tortuosities of the one against the equivocations of the other. The queen accordingly pretended to support the efforts du Bellay was making towards a conciliation. Because all this was causing him so much irritation, the king, on his side, promised Francis to extend the session of the Houses and to put off *sine die* the proclamation of the schism. He would propose to Clement that he send an apologist to Cambrai to plead before the two legates – *for* the king, however, not in the king's *name* since this would impinge on the crown's sovereignty: a reservation which, as Anne saw it, would have the double advantage of flattering Henry's pride and of further compounding the Pope's exasperation.

It remained to persuade the Houses to vote the bills without attracting the attention of Henry who would rather have deferred them. The king had a high regard for Thomas More and no great animosity against a number of the others, so it was not too difficult to persuade him to leave out their names in the plea of treason being brought against the visionary. Thankful to see their friends come cheaply out of that affair, the lords were more amenable to Cranmer's negotiations over the Act demoting Catherine to Princess Dowager. It was the lords themselves who, with the same idea of wiping the slate clean, then brought pressure on the Lower House to pass the Act. When Anne reported this success to the capricious king he was stirred to be daring again: resolute once more to yield nothing to the pressures of either Francis or Clement. The Pope in any case was encountering the greatest difficulties in proceeding with the business of the *Rota*. The legal formalities were full of many minor irregularities and the documents were in grievous disorder. Du Bellay, still confident, was nevertheless rather shaken when he heard, towards the end of February, that a consistory had been summoned with the task of resolving these points of law so as to get the proceedings moving again. The Pope, to reassure the ambassador, told him that in allowing a month for the cardinals to think it over – which would take them forward to Easter – he was on the contrary giving proof of his goodwill to Henry. Du Bellay was only too happy to believe it; moreover, he was confident that a month would not be long enough for the prelates to unravel the web. He felt sure that by the time they had delivered their verdict Henry would have sent him such an answer as would bring the proceedings to a halt.

The good du Bellay passed all this on to Anne, who was

careful in her replies not to pour cold water on his illusions – which therefore remained intact at the time when the consistory met for its March session. Still positive that nothing would come out of it, the bishop-ambassador was expecting their deliberations to be prorogued for a month. When their meeting had dragged on for seven hours he was all the more confident in his belief. It struck him therefore like a thunderbolt when at the end of the day the cardinals pronounced their sentence: Henry was condemned!

In an instant the wretched du Bellay saw his card-house in ruins. He had become too intimately involved in the case and saw himself condemned with the king and his reputation wrecked. To try to salvage it he went around Rome, telling everyone he met that he had not come to the Vatican to plead in favour of the concubine, still less against the legitimate queen. No-one had charged him with a task so disagreeable, one that he would never have agreed to undertake. All that he had wanted was to warn the Pope and the Roman curia of the danger that King Henry might secede from the Catholic Church if he were condemned for his divorce and his remarriage. In so saying he flattered himself still with the faint hope that Henry would be so scared by the sentence that he would empower du Bellay to patch up a compromise.

But he was at Rome a week too late. Anne had not waited for the consistory of March and three days before the verdict the game had already been played out. The two Houses had met and had voted the bills. Catherine was deposed along with Mary; Anne was acknowledged Queen of England, Elizabeth the legitimate heir; and Henry proclaimed sole possessor of spiritual authority in the kingdom.

The schism had been achieved.


But once more – it had become almost the rule – Anne surprised me by her way of greeting this success. She did tell me that evening: "It is done; we have crossed the line. Whatever may happen, England is going to understand at last that she is an

166

island. Henceforth the rest will follow, for better or for worse. In short, my task is finished."

But when I asked her why, in that case, she had shown no joy when the result of the voting was announced her answer was at first only a long and sceptical sigh. Then she said, as much to herself as to me; "Because the immediate outlook is worse, rather than better. England remains stripped of everything and her fleet is pitiable. To become a formidable power she must labour long and hard."

She looked at me with a smile at once sad and mocking that moved me deeply, yet disturbed me. Then she added *sotto voce*: "And I shall no longer be there to keep watch".

# PART II ⬟ HENRY

## X
## (1534)

# *Francis I and Charles V*

What had Queen Anne meant with her "I shall no longer be there"? Had she a foreboding that her destiny would be tragic? Was it only that she dreaded the reactions at home and in Europe that must inevitably follow the proclamation of the schism; the effects upon Henry of these reactions; and the consequences of these effects for her? She knew the king too well not to fear them. Rarely had he taken a bold decision, under pressure from Anne, for which he did not afterwards reproach her angrily as soon as the first difficulties arising out of that decision had to be faced.

Announcement of the schism had quickly produced those confrontations so easy to foresee. Catholic Ireland came to the boil, Scotland looked fierce and even in England riots broke out among the people here and there. Only the lords, strangely enough, seemed to keep cool; but even this calm could be a source of uneasiness – was it not a cover for something being plotted secretly among themselves?

As a counter to this, how much support could Anne and the king be sure of? That of the Protestant princes of Germany was not yet forthcoming. Nor was the alliance with Lübeck. If Francis were now to abandon Henry the situation would become alarming.

Rochford and Fitzwilliam were sent as ambassadors to France. Francis and his sister Margaret gave them the warmest of welcomes, laying on innumerable feasts and all manner of delights, but so overwhelming them that the two envoys could not find a single moment for serious discussions. They were asked to put in writing the particular requests with which the king had charged them, the implication being that the answers would be given in the same style, leaving no room for talks.

And so, to Henry's request that his good brother Francis should break his alliance with the Pope the answer was returned that there was nothing to break because there was no alliance.

To the request that Francis should refuse subsidies from the Pope for invading the duchy of Milan the reply was that the moment for such an enterprise had not arrived.

To the request that Francis should adopt for his own kingdom the new reforms and laws passed in England the King of France said that these were not necessary in France.

This was a good number of rebuffs; but on other issues the replies testified to more goodwill.

A meeting with the King of England would be considered favourably.

If it would reassure his good brother Henry, Francis would give up his project of marrying his daughter Madeleine to the King of Scotland.

If Henry should wish to raise his own contribution to the pensions the two kings were paying jointly to the German princes, the gestures would be duly appreciated.

With acquiescences and rejections thus nicely balanced, Francis in his turn posed a question of good faith: if the Pope were to ask Charles to carry out the sentence against Henry and if (because he, the king of the French, was supporting his excommunicated brother) the emperor were then to ask the Holy Father to excommunicate Francis as well and were to use that as a pretext for invading France, what help would the King of England bind himself to furnish to Francis in that case?

This put Henry in the most acute embarrassment. He was by no means anxious – for the sake of flying to the aid of his good brother – to weaken his own forces against a possible attack by the emperor. This led to a brisk quarrel with Anne. The queen wanted a positive answer to be given; for if Francis could not count on England, how could England expect to count on France? But this sort of binding engagement was something that the fickle Henry had avoided all his life. Despite Anne's insistence, he would go no further than what is called in France a "Norman answer", promising all without in fact promising anything. And following his natural bent he so handled matters as to make friends with Francis against Charles but at the same time with Charles against Francis.

By way of protection when he went over for their next meeting he asked the French king for a naval squadron to convoy him by sea and, on land, for troops to be stationed around Calais so as to deter the emperor from any attempt at making him a prisoner.

At the same time he sent word to Charles that he had given orders to restore to Catherine of Aragon, besides the full use of her royal apartments, the service of all her attendants and also her diamonds, jewellery and silver.

"It would be obvious to anybody," Anne said to me in dismay, "that both Charles and Francis are fully apprised of these approaches Henry has made to each of them. But the king has a wonderful gift for turning a deaf ear to what he doesn't want to hear. Besides, this way of behaving and the indulgence shown to Catherine are signs there can be no mistaking. Henry is gradually escaping from me and from my influence over him."

So at the first symptoms of a second pregnancy she lost no time in letting the king know. It was to give him hope of a son and thereby bring him back to her and allow her to recover something of her old ascendancy over him. Henry in fact could not contain his joy. Everything seemed to brighten up.

"I gain time," Anne said to me, "but it's a matter of luck; a miscarriage or a girl, and the king will make me pay a hundred times for the pleasure he now feels. At the worst I shall have had nine months in which to forward my policies. And one lucky chance gives me a bit of room for manoeuvre. He has promised to entrust the regency of the kingdom to me while he is away."

"But won't his time away be very short?"

"Long enough for me to lay down the foundations for a solid independence. How? By opening ten yards for shipbuilding, setting experts to work, architects, carpenters; by extracting from the Treasury the sums at present wasted on ceremonial and by borrowing the rest from peers and banks so that, involved up to the neck, they will be bound to give my policy their support. On his return the king will have no option but to carry on along the path I've laid out for him."

But there was no return, for there was no departure. Therefore no absence, no regency; no shipyards, no fleet. At the very moment of leaving, Henry changed his mind. By way of excuse to Francis – an excuse very readily accepted, since a conference with this unpredictable Henry no longer held any pleasure for him – he used the pretext of Anne's pregnancy. But the real causes were very different. First, the fear – not unreasonable – that Anne might take advantage of the regency to pack Catherine and Mary off to Spain, so as once and for all to render them harmless; then the feeling that since the schism the royal authority had been shaken and put under threat, so that it would be unwise for him to go abroad at this moment. In fact, a revealing incident had just occurred which went some way to justify this vigilance.

A certain Lord Dacre of Greystock was known as one who spoke openly and vigorously against the divorce; he was suspected also of being secretly the head and brain of a seditious clique. A list of complaints against him, weighty enough to involve him in a charge of treason, had been built up over the course of months. He was accordingly arrested and the Duke of Norfolk, as Grand Seneschal, constituted a jury made up of twenty-one lords among those most loyal to the Crown. The king's prosecutor called for a capital verdict. As Wolsey had said when they came to arrest him: "If the Crown is accuser, you may be sure the jury will find Abel guilty of killing Cain". The accused, therefore, persuaded that his fate was sealed, did not take the trouble to plead. It was without illusions that he resigned himself to the judgement of his peers. When these withdrew to deliberate they were away a long time but neither the accused, nor the king, nor Anne nor anyone had any doubt what the verdict would be. The more astonishing was it, then, when in answer to the formal question of the Seneschal on their return the jury replied unanimously, the Duke of Norfolk only excepted, "Not Guilty". And Lord Dacre was acquitted.

When this incredible verdict was announced Henry felt as though he had been struck by lightning. He saw his absolute power called into question and the wound to his feelings came at a bad moment. For some time he had been feeling the effects of advancing years. He had headaches and above all a painful abscess on his leg which would not heal. This caused him mental suffering even more than physical, as he foresaw in the near future an end to his hunting, his tournaments, his tennis and his fencing; balls and masquerades would lose the charm they had had when he was young. Any voyage, especially by sea, although it did not alarm him, had lost its attraction; and to go abroad just when the acquittal of a traitor seemed to shake his throne appeared a suicidal idea. There could no longer be any question of running such a risk.

In this disturbing affair Anne saw a danger rather to herself than to the king. Confronted with this defection of his most faithful friends, Henry would take the warning as a sign of an unyielding resistance to the divorce and a decisive condemnation of his second marriage. Would he have enough character to stand up to it? Anne could no longer be sure. And this acquittal of a notorious dissident under the king's very nose appeared to the queen as the prelude to her own fall.

We looked anxiously for the first signs of it. The weeks seemed long, to me as much as to her; but when nothing happened, I slowly regained confidence. Would the hope of Anne giving him an heir offer him a foothold on the slippery slope down which events were pushing him? At last my fears were genuinely set at rest when I saw him carry the queen off to spend the summer in the Midlands and make a progress together through those rich provinces.

During this happy time of her absence and right up to September I had no further news of her. I had spent those weeks saying to myself "No news is good news", when she appeared suddenly at Hever alone and in a state of great agitation. "Catastrophe," she announced as she threw herself into an armchair. "My sister Mary is pregnant and expecting a baby any day."

"But she has been seven years a widow!"

"Just so; and that's what makes it a scandal. She has got herself with child by a good-looking trooper. She has been dismissed from court. I could do nothing to help her; all I obtained from the chancellor, and with great difficulty, was a niggardly pension for her and her trooper. Barely enough to die of hunger on."

"What does your father say?"

"He rolls at the sovereign's feet, swearing that he has given her a taste of his tongue and will never see her again."

"Still so fond a father. And the king?"

"He hunts from morning to night, till his horses drop, and does not speak to me any more." Then, with a grimace in which I could detect a sob repressed, the irony of disillusion and a black and bitter mood: "And to make all sweet, if my sister is pregnant, I no longer am." As I remained dumb, my mouth wide open: "Perhaps I never was," she murmured; "I must have wanted to believe it, or else it was a false alarm."

I was of course utterly dismayed. Everything was turning against her. I could picture the king's anger when on top of the scandalous news of Mary he had to be told that Anne was not pregnant after all. What would he do? The man was brutal and in his wild anger was capable of strangling her. As if she had read my thoughts she nodded in agreement: "Ah yes . . ." she sighed sadly, "the royal fleet will not be built."

Thus when calamity menaced her person, when her crown and her life were compromised, it was of England that she was thinking first! I was amazed. Never perhaps, so much as on that day and at that instant, had I perceived how noble was her soul, how lofty her cast of mind.

Anne went on thinking aloud: "And Francis too is going to desert me. He likes me well enough but I have little credit with those around him: without the hope of a male heir I will have still less. Once again we shall have only pleas in defence of Catherine and attacks on me and Henry, and he will be made to listen to them."

"Aren't you looking at everything in the worst light? The peers on either side of the Channel feel a certain solidarity and the French ones owe you gratitude for having saved from the scaffold the lords and bishops who were implicated in the plot."

"They will forget it very soon. All they will remember is that I was not able to stop the execution of the Observantin Friars, whose Order is already raging loudly about it all over Europe. And Francis will not want to risk losing the advantages he has gained in Germany at so high a cost."

"I thought Luther had got the upper hand there?"

"Over Münzer, yes, and over the peasants. But the whole region is still in a state of upheaval. In the south, Zwingli has stood aside from the rising and made links with Luther, but the north has not yet thrown in its lot with the Reformation save with many reservations. Francis has made use of these uncertainties to obtain strong contingents of Swiss from Zwingli, from Luther his support and from the reformed princes alliance against the emperor. He has plenty of more important things on hand without bothering about a Boleyn lady in distress. But for last year's sudden incursion of the Turks, against whom Charles has united all Germany behind him, on seeing his rival so threatened internally Francis would already have clamped a war on him by now. Victory over the Turks has done no more than put it back. And how much do you think my poor person would weigh in such a situation?"

In fact, though Anne did not yet know it, the war was already ablaze. The stake was the Wurtemberg. Three years earlier, Ferdinand, King of Bohemia and Hungary (brother of the Emperor Charles), had unexpectedly been elected King of the Romans. His first care had been to have the Duke of Wurtemberg banished and his son Christopher captured. But Christopher had managed to escape and, knowing that he had supporters in the King of France, the Duke of Bavaria and other

174

German princes, demanded that the duchy be returned to him. In another quarter, the Landgrave of Hesse, from whom Francis had just bought back, at a price in gold, the county of Mont-béliard, had lost no time in using this money to raise an army. And at the hour when Anne was relating her story the forces recruited by this means were already on the march to the Württemberg.

A little earlier, the secretary whom Henry had sent to Lübeck had come back with good news. Meyer had been making no idle boast when he had claimed that Lübeck was well disposed to form an alliance. The king had set himself at once to elaborate some grandiose plans with him. The idea would be to take advantage of the troubles in the south and start in the north by deposing Christian of Denmark. There one would levy troops who could be maintained easily on the resources of the country. Meanwhile the Hanseatic fleet would cross to England to pick up contingents of mercenaries. Then with one contingent starting from the coast of England, the other from the coast of Jutland, the combined force would have no difficulty in making a landing in Norway. Thus a vast league of Protestant powers of the north could be created under the aegis of the King of England.

Agents were exchanged between London and Lübeck. Others then set out to visit the Baltic ports; to meet the Voïvode, King Sigismund, in Poland; and the princes of Prussia, Brandenburg and Pomerania, so as to enlarge the league in every possible direction and dimension.

Meyer himself, meantime created Knight of the Rose and supplied with a comfortable sum of money, embarked for Lübeck to persuade the burgomaster Wullenwever to reach an early understanding with Henry and thus enable the campaign to be started without delay. Wullenwever at once sent a secretary to London to make sure of Henry's intentions and ask him for subsidies.

Given an audience immediately on arrival, this man explained to the king the conditions for a loan. As soon as Denmark was occupied the loan would be repaid twice over. And if Henry did not want to appear formally as leader of the expedition there was a good fighting man, a neighbour of Lübeck, Count Christopher of Oldenburg, who would be happy to conduct it in his name.

From the start Anne had not concealed her opposition to this campaign. But it was useless her warning Henry of the setbacks to which he must expose himself without the cover of a powerful fleet, and how deceitful as well as rash a part he played in urging the burgomaster on to war while keeping open the option of leaving him in the lurch if things looked dangerous. Henceforward Henry would act only as he pleased. Without heeding Anne, he had already secretly dispatched his agent Dr Lee to press Wullenwever to act. On his side Marcus Meyer, fearing that the burgomaster might either hesitate or back out, had swiftly recruited a band of freebooters like himself, left the town by stealth, marched upon Denmark and made a night attack on a border fortress in the duchy of Holstein. This forced Wullenwever's hand. He now had no choice but to declare war on the duke, having first made sure of the support of his neighbour Christopher. Thereafter, without further delay, the conjoined troops of Lübeck and Oldenburg invaded the duchy.

So as not to risk running out of money the burgomaster and Christopher sent their ambassadors to Henry. But, as always, when the news was brought to him that hostilities had begun, the king took fright at having become too far involved. Finding himself being hustled sooner than he had expected, he evaded their demands by confronting the two envoys with unacceptable conditions.

The envoys were furious and on the point of re-embarking when word arrived that Christopher of Oldenburg had entered Copenhagen! Leaving half his troops on the battle-front he had taken to sea with the remainder and landed close to Elsinore.

Henry saw himself about to miss the boat. He recalled the ambassadors in haste but he could not now with any credit go back on the conditions he had stipulated. He got out of it as best he could by standing fast on points of lesser importance while giving way on the principal point. So he allowed Lübeck the loan she had asked and loaded the two envoys with presents.

What Anne feared in all this was the likely reaction of the German princes of the north. Exposed as they already were to uprisings in their towns and to peasant revolts in their countrysides, a defeat of Denmark and the setting-up of a vast democratic confederation at their doors was certain to alarm them. She feared also that Francis, irritated by these unaccountable pranks of Henry, might think of coming to terms with the emperor, as Pope Clement was vigorously urging him to do. And Charles, afraid of being caught in a pincer movement between the Turks (whose incursions were on the increase) and the French with England to back them, might well be inclined to an understanding with the King of France.

So accurate was her judgement that soon afterwards she heard from du Bellay that the German princes had sent troops with Philip of Hesse in support of the Duke of Holstein while others were on their way by forced marches to Lübeck and Oldenburg; and that meanwhile Charles had sent the Count of Nassau to urge upon Francis a marriage between the royal Duke of Angoulême and Princess Mary of England. It was a means of dangling before Francis the throne of the Tudors and since Henry would of course oppose this union the emperor in suggesting it had hopes of setting the two at odds.

Certainly du Bellay had assured Anne that Francis had behaved loyally, declaring that he was bound in honour to Henry. But Anne knew only too well how much an engagement of honour was worth in politics. Therefore by the same channel she let Francis know that the emperor was counting his chickens too soon: Mary was not free either to decide for herself or to go where she pleased; the proposal could even cost her her life if her father felt his throne to be under threat. If Francis had ever thought of listening to Charles he must have understood the warning, for matters rested where they were.

This was no doubt a success up to a point, but all danger was far from averted. At home the news that Anne was not expecting a child had removed the one obstacle holding back her enemies. They must surely think the moment favourable for an armed intervention by the emperor. Some twenty or thirty earls and barons of the north sent their wives to Chapuis – to foil the spies of Cromwell – to invite him to make discreet inquiry of Princess Mary's former chamberlain, Lord Hussey. This man, with Lord Darcy to back him, did actually tell the ambassador that (apart from the Earl of Northumberland, who could easily be got around) he knew no-one who was against the plot in the whole of the north. Further, that he undertook on his own personal account to raise a force of eight thousand men; that assuredly the King of Scotland, having certain views on Mary and the throne, would not withhold his help; and that if the emperor were to send contingents with arms and ammunition to land on the coast of England from the Thames in the south to the Tyne in the north a majority of the lords would rise up and join the emperor's troops.

Henry, warned of this by his spies, became greatly agitated and wanted to raise an army without delay. While the queen might have profited from this disposition in the king's mind to bring home to him yet again how badly he was missing a strong fleet she nonetheless did her best to damp down this costly warlike ardour. Though she was quite as aware as he was of these intrigues and goings-on, they made no great impression on her. She knew just as well as the emperor how involved the situation was. Certainly Charles might at first glance see in a landing the opportunity to realise his dream of bringing all Europe under his sceptre. Once master of England he would soon be master of France too. The Roman eagle would spread its wings over the entire west.

Only it was too good to be true. To attack England would be to risk letting loose a general conflict in which the Turks on one side and the French on the other would attack Germany. A war against Henry was only possible on the day when the emperor could be confident of an alliance with France: something that must be out of the question for a long time.

So it was no surprise to Anne to learn that Chapuis had been taken to task by his master and ordered to put a check on the conspirators' ardour, while not discouraging them altogether.

178

But if it followed that on that side of things the queen had nothing to worry about, nearer home she had become aware of a more immediate cause for fear: the king had a mistress.

In truth this was by no means the first since he had married Anne and he took small pains to conceal from her the successes he had had with one woman or another. Anne was not troubled by them. But now there was a new fact: one that made her feel, if not already certain of disaster, at least profoundly apprehensive. It was the dawn of a presentiment. For Henry was hiding this new mistress not only from Anne but also from the whole court.

# XI
## (1535)

# *Margaret Shelton*

The new favourite was so well hidden away in some castle of Sussex that we could never discover her name. Nor the true reasons for a discretion so foreign to King Henry's practice in these matters. The court naturally spent a great deal of time conjecturing; the queen and I likewise. People even asked if it might not be an incest: had Henry fallen for some bastard daughter of his father's who had come to light? All that Anne was able to deduce from the king's altered behaviour to her was that the hidden influence of the lady was being exerted at her expense and in favour of Catherine and Mary.

The king's new manner towards Anne was rude in the extreme. So far from conducting himself in the presence of third parties, if not with dignity, at least with a certain courtesy towards the queen, he overwhelmed her with proofs that he was not only tired of her but positively hostile. To the point sometimes of reminding her of the low origins out of which he had rescued her and into which he could plunge her again if he chose. What helped the queen to while away her time was the little court she had built up for herself: a youthful group, full of gaiety and talent, a court, moreover, which attracted the king more than did his own. It was a last bond subsisting between Anne and Henry, of whom the poet Thomas Wyatt, a friend of Henry in their younger days, would say "that he was every inch a king but would never be a gentleman".

All the same there was no reason yet to fear that Henry would be as good as his word and genuinely seek a divorce. First because his marriage to Anne was, for foreign powers, the proof of his independence of the Holy See, secondly because it was evidence of his authority over the clique of those who affected to despise him; further, because in repudiating her he would find himself married again to Catherine; finally, because he had not lost hope that Anne would give him a son. And so he made a point from time to time of still sharing the marriage bed with her.

The one genuine satisfaction Anne could still feel was that she had caused the king to involve himself so completely that he must now, whether he would or not, continue acting with the same goal in mind as hers. When Clement died in the autumn and Paul III who succeeded him let it be known that he was inclined towards a reconciliation, it certainly crossed Henry's mind to make his peace with Rome, thereby, he hoped, disarming his enemies within the kingdom. But the rumours reported by Cromwell's spies pointed quite otherwise. A return of the Prodigal Son would be interpreted not as a settled act of allegiance to the Church of Rome but rather as a weakness which the lords would exploit by making fresh demands. And this first retreat would bring others after it. Acts of Parliament would become a dead letter for a start; then with Anne repudiated, Catherine would be taken back: proof, in short, of an authority so tottering that it could cost Henry his crown. This agitation made it imperative for Henry to let himself be seen not as an appeaser but as a strong man.

Thomas More and the theologian John Fisher, Chancellor of the University of Cambridge, Bishop of Rochester and friend of Erasmus, had protested openly against the bills the king had in mind. Henry had both arrested and shut up in the Tower of London. The purpose was to discourage anyone who should dare to follow their example. Anne was dismayed but when she tried to intervene Henry rebuffed her harshly. She had to give way all the more because the sovereign's spiritual authority in England was still a pure formality; it required corroboration by a law both binding and repressive, proclaiming the King of England supreme head of the Church in the kingdom and subjecting offenders to punishment. It would come to be known as the Act of Supremacy.

To forestall any rebellion by the lords and the bishops, Parliament was recalled at short notice, hand-picked as before, and was induced to pass, as a matter of urgency and without debate, the statute putting King Henry rather than the Pope at the head of the Church of England.

By this enactment, Henry had well and truly burnt his boats; there could be no question in future of going back. The royal chariot was committed to a track which henceforward it must follow to the end. "But this end," Anne said to me, "is a little like a game of pitch-and-toss. All now turns on Henry's determination to make the kingdom of the Four Seas an impregnable fortress. Otherwise he, and England with him, is going to be floundering in the mire. But steady determination, alas, is what he lacks above all. He is at once weathercock and turncoat. The last thing we can expect from him is perseverance."

"And so?"

"And so I look beyond him. What he will have failed to do, another will do."

"Another?"

"Elizabeth."

"But she's still only a babe-in-arms!"

"She will grow; and you have often told me yourself that you saw in her tenacious little character a reflection of my own. If God gives me life and I have no son I shall know well enough how to bring her up to see things the way I do. Or else it will be you if I am not there any more."

"Why should Your Majesty not be there any more?"

"For a thousand possible reasons. Now listen to me carefully. Because we still have to ensure that Elizabeth is heir to the throne. It looks impossible that Henry should come back to Catherine, to Mary; but the man is unpredictable. Elizabeth must cling on, she must impose herself and once in power secure for the kingdom what perhaps I never can: command of the seas. That is what my last will and testament will tell her. That is what you, dear, will go on repeating to her in season and out of season."

I felt, as you can imagine, immensely honoured by this

expression of trust; but even more was I anxious and troubled for the future, which seemed to me to have about it the smell of death.


The first priority now was to make of the Act of Supremacy a law of binding force by depriving its opponents of any means of challenging it. A supplementary bill was therefore put to the Houses, whereby anyone who, in contempt of the Act, refrained from paying due honour to the royal family, Henry, Anne and Elizabeth, or, again, dared in private to call the king a heretic, a schismatic or an infidel, would be charged with high treason and hanged.

But the bill's wording had been too brutal, so that before voting on it the Houses sought and were allowed two amendments: first, that the Act of Supremacy should not come into force for a full three months so that everyone should have time to hear of it and not be at risk of transgressing it through ignorance; and second, that any breach of this law should count as a crime only if "committed with a guilty purpose". This obviously had the effect of watering it down a great deal and would save the skins of many now compromised – among them Thomas More and John Fisher in the Tower of London.

Despite this provision Anne feared that a tightening up of the law, unavoidable as she knew it to be, might aggravate the fate of the two captives. In fact, by reason of events abroad their lot was, on the contrary, improved.

For Henry was receiving no reply to his proposals from the King of France; moreover, his agents at the Spanish court were sending him alarming news. A large number of ships was being constructed in Portugal and fitted out for the transport of troops. Was it Charles's intention to make a landing on the English coast? Worse still, such an invasion could be supported by a local rising. This twin peril had some fortunate consequences for Anne. First, to appease his enemies at home Henry was prepared to give them a proof of his clemency. Despite the obstinacy of More and Fisher in refusing to acknowledge any supremacy other than that of Rome, the king, far from having them sentenced and put to death, saw to it that the rigours of their prison life were somewhat alleviated. They were allowed to read and write, to correspond with their friends and receive visits. Secondly, and most importantly, in view of the manifest inadequacy of his navy to intercept that of Charles, Henry took fright and consented to cut down on his luxury expenses, devoting the money to the fleet instead, and to set about the building of new warships. It was at last the beginning of that powerful Royal Navy for which Anne had battled so hard.

An ill wind can produce some good, but while Anne could rejoice in this awakening of the king she had plenty of other reasons for sharing his anxieties. She knew for certain from du Bellay that though Francis had rejected the emperor's idea of marrying off his cousin Mary to Francis's youngest son, the Duke of Angoulême, he had proposed a worse one in its place: to unite her to the Dauphin.

"If this marriage takes place," Anne said to me, "it will be all over with England. On the death of the two kings there will be nothing to stop England and France coming under the same sceptre. Admittedly these kingdoms, joined together and masters of the Channel on both shores, would isolate Spain and to that extent reduce the power of the emperor. But I know what would happen then. Since France is still her superior in all domains England would become, like Brittany or Aquitaine, one of her provinces. And the funny thing is that to avoid such a merger there is almost no-one I can count on except the emperor, since he would be bound to fear it. So here he is, obliged to act to the detriment of his cousin whom he wants to put on the throne of England and by the same token in favour of my daughter whose right to the crown he denies. You often find such paradoxes in politics."

While Anne was speaking, there was a question I was burning to ask and finally I came out with it: "Am I wrong, or was this engagement between Mary and the Dauphin not the subject of a treaty more than fifteen years ago?"

"Yes, and it is precisely that treaty that Francis would like to revive. Henry denounces it with good reason but in so doing he creates another difficulty for himself; for it means pushing the Dauphin into the arms of the Infanta, thus fortifying France with the whole power of Spain at our expense and bringing Francis and the emperor together."

"Then what ought he to do?"

"That's what Henry is asking himself. And alas, I know only too well what he will do: nothing. As usual, he will allow things to drift with the stream; he will submit to them instead of directing them."

But for once Anne was wrong about her husband. For if the king lacked singleness of purpose in his ideas he was not wanting in either subtlety or industry – now he let us see it.

What he did was to summon Chabot, Admiral of France and one of Francis's agents, and remind him that Mary was illegitimate; that the Dauphin would gain little from marrying her – something that in any case he, Henry, would never permit; equally that talks about betrothing the Dauphin to the Infanta would meet with no less opposition from him and would oblige him to marry Mary at the earliest to Philip, son of Charles, thus bringing about a union between England and the Empire. Whereas if the Duke of Angoulême were to marry the Princess Elizabeth, heiress to the throne and furnished with a handsome dowry, that would be for the best for France as well as for England.

I thought Anne would be pleased with this unexpected proposal, since it legitimated Elizabeth at Mary's expense. However, I found her scarcely less hostile to it than to the other. The duke might be the youngest of the French king's sons, but the possibility remained that one day, if his brothers died, the throne of France could revert to him. Elizabeth would then be Queen of France as well as of England and the risk of Albion turning into a French province would be greater than with Mary.

Queen of France, so I told myself, was not such a bad position to be in! But Anne put the destiny of England above that of her child and I admired the resolute spirit in which she pursued her aim: to build up an *English* England, powerful, independent of any connection with the other nations of the Continent and protected from the shocks to which that connection at present exposed her.

"Were it only the language," she said to me. "Think it out. Charles V speaks French and hardly knows either German or Spanish; you and I talk French between ourselves; I talk French most often with the king and he writes to me just as often in that tongue; and the whole court follows its sovereign's example. Married to Angoulême, and supposing even she becomes only Queen of England, Elizabeth will speak French and her children also. That is not what I want. I want a court where what is spoken is the language of the English people."

"Your Majesty is worrying unnecessarily. You are by no means being the only one to think like that. Why, one day when du Bellay expressed astonishment that Lord Shrewsbury spoke no French, the other replied: 'Let this son of a bitch take note that if there were in my frame a single word of French I would have it out with my sword!'"

"Amusing, yes. But from the very fact that that has struck you, you must see it's an exception. A touch of the provincial about it too. At court all the rest prefer French and so naturally they see themselves as strangers to their own people more than to the French nobility or even to Charles who speaks as they do."

And in fact, as though the king had heard her, he was redoubling his efforts to reach an accommodation with the said Charles. Anne was aware of the advances Henry had already made, some months earlier, to the Viscount Hanart, ambassador for the Empire to the court of France, informing him that Catherine would see her property, her rank and privileges restored to her. From one concession to another would Henry not go on finally to making a deal over the body of Anne Boleyn? Love was no longer there to hold him back and a compromise of that sort could well have its attractions for the emperor who was just then in serious negotiation with the King of France.

Francis was accusing him of having spread word in Germany that he, Francis, was abandoning the Lutheran princes, whose friendship he clearly needed to retain in order to recruit in their territories the mercenaries that were indispensable to him. He had therefore demanded from the emperor that he refute the claim, but Charles continued to prevaricate. For the need to draw these princes into his camp was even more urgent for him than for Francis. But he could have reason to fear that if he delayed too long over the refutation Paris might forestall him by an accommodation with London. And in fact, a few days before Epiphany, Francis had already sent his treasurer Palamède Gautier on embassy to Henry.

For her part Anne felt herself to be in some degree the stake, if not already the victim, in these triangular intrigues. At the ball given in honour of Gautier she had a brief talk with him, but under the mistrustful eye of the king and the malevolent scrutiny of the courtiers she could neither prolong nor find an opportunity later to resume it. She had barely time to explain to him the more than precarious situation in which she stood, to complain that Francis was abandoning her and to ask him for some prompt help. She could say no more, nor could Palamède reply, for at that moment the king came up with three of his counsellors to take Gautier off to the library.

What came to the queen's ears of their discussion did not threaten her directly; rather, it went to confirm the legitimacy of Elizabeth. Palamède had told Henry that Francis was not rejecting out of hand the project of a marriage between that princess and his youngest son; nevertheless the little girl's titles had still to be clarified from all points of view. Whereupon Henry had retorted with some violence that she was well and truly heir to the throne. Moreover, if Francis wished to be sure of it, all he need do was to persuade Pope Paul to revoke Clement's sentence and declare null the marriage with Catherine. And that, for Anne, savoured rather of good news.

The sequel moreover did not contradict this impression, making as it did the threat of an understanding between Francis and the emperor even more remote. But the negotiations took a rather sour turn from then on. If the marriage were to be concluded Francis laid down two severe conditions. The first, in the queen's eyes at least, was by no means impossible of acceptance: the King of England must renounce his title to be also King of France, a claim never abandoned since the time of William the Conqueror. Anne considered that this outworn title, merely symbolic though it was, kept a last link alive with France and the Continent which she wished to break. But the second condition had a sting to it; for it trenched on the money-bags: it would require abandonment of all the claims which, under earlier treaties, Henry held over France in the form of a permanent pension and annuities for life, all in sizeable amounts. Henry came near to choking. Then, realising that demands of this kind must be the subject of bargaining, he took heart and said he must be given time to reflect – without specifying how long a time. By not being in a hurry to say either Yes or No, he had good hopes of inducing Francis to meet him halfway.

Left thus in uncertainty, Gautier proceeded to every quarter of the kingdom to influence the powerful in favour of Francis's point of view. He was received by Cromwell at Austin Friars, by Norfolk and Suffolk at Westminster. All pensioners of Francis, they assured Palamède of their friendly dispositions. Finally at Candlemas Henry had him sent for and without reverting to the main question reminded him in the most amiable manner of the project for a meeting with the French king in France. Palamède, no less amiable, said that, to receive Henry, Francis would have his daughters and his sister Margaret of Navarre with him. Henry's vanity was flattered and the same evening he called the council together to work out with them the counter-proposals to be made to Francis. To show himself accommodating, he said he was ready to drop the illusory title of King of France and there were few objections to this. But when Henry suggested restricting the money claims to life-annuities only, there was resolute opposition. The council would admit no reduction of any kind. The king did not press the point but decided at once in his own mind that when he met Francis he would ignore this restriction. It was agreed with Gautier that at Pentecost representatives of the parties should meet at Calais to prepare for the talks between the two kings including advance arrangements for the union of Elizabeth and Angoulême.

Anne followed these marriage preparations in a way that struck me as strangely passive and I told her so. "When one can do no more," she sighed, "one has to watch from the window what is going on in the street."

"Without a struggle and without a fight, then, Your Majesty is going to let the little Princess Elizabeth be married contrary to your own wish?"

"And what would you have me do?" she replied in some irritation. "Don't you see that my position now is much worse than at the worst moments before the marriage? Then Henry desired me and I could play on his desire. I have grown older, I have wrinkles, he has had his fill of me. Would you wish me, by trying to thwart him, to get myself repudiated? That is all the king thinks of."

"But he can't do that any longer. He would find himself married to Catherine again and would have to recognise Mary as his heir; it would look like giving in to his enemies, to the Pope, to the emperor and this apparent weakness would fuel a rising!"

"You're coming on, my dear. But what he can't do today he will do tomorrow, if Catherine dies."

"Why, is she ill?"

"That's what they say."

The king might have had his fill of Anne; certainly he was rebuffing her more and more, but this did not stop him of course from knowing that so long as Catherine lived he could not repudiate Anne. But to be obliged for this reason to show her some courtesy in public only stoked up the fires of his irritation. The king's attitude naturally served as a model for the whole court, whose bearing towards Anne was attentive or cold in line with what they could observe of the sovereign's temper. One day when Princess Elizabeth and her half-sister had been brought to Richmond, Anne went up to kiss her child and was followed by Norfolk, Suffolk and a crowd of ladies and gentlemen. But when the king pointedly refrained from joining them they all went at once to present to Mary the tokens of their allegiance, before bowing to her sister. Anne said not a word but she could not conceal a twitching of her face which gave me a cold shiver. George, Anne's brother, stood apart with his wife Lady Rochford for the good reason that no-one would speak to them. Worse still, when a little later Lady Rochford had begun to chatter about the king's invisible mistress she found herself at once banned from court. The next thing was that when some lord brought an action against Rochford which formerly Rochford would have won by royal favour, this time by disfavour he lost it. With the whole Boleyn family thus fallen into disgrace, the isolation of the queen was plain to see.

Nevertheless, Cromwell still appeared to remain loyal to her, if not out of constancy, then at least from motives of self-preservation; he had indeed everything to fear from a return of Catherine. Norfolk, who had caught the prevailing wind and was reproaching Cromwell for the encouragement he had given to the schism, was now lining up against him the powerful and dangerous party of the nobles. With the conspiracy every day growing in numbers, the chancellor attached himself increasingly to the Boleyn clan.

"Even including my dearest friend," sighed Anne, "Percy of Northumberland, who has just joined the plot. He's the one peer of the north who had stayed loyal; they must only be admitting him under suspicion. But I cannot count on him any longer, and on Cromwell still less."

From day to day there were more and more disquieting signs. If the chamberlain of the royal household – I forget his name – fell ill and left the court it was so that he could send his doctor to Chapuis and have word passed to the emperor that the kingdom was in so weak a state militarily that its conquest would be easy. And he added the promise that the Marquess of Exeter, the chamberlain himself and a number of other lords, disposing between them of several thousand men, would fight alongside the imperial troops. There was no-one, even Dr Butts, the king's own doctor, who did not assure Catherine's doctor of his loyal sentiments "for the real queen".

All this, Cromwell learnt from his spies. He knew that a plan for Mary to fly to the Netherlands had been put off only because of a sudden indisposition of the princess. Chapuis had supported this out of fear that Henry in case of an insurrection or invasion might forthwith send Catherine and her daughter to the Tower of London where their lives would be a guarantee for his. When a new opportunity came up – Mary was to be taken to Eltham – the ambassador flattered himself that he could effect her escape from there by night and have her taken to the Thames. With the princess on board ship he was sure that any attempts to recapture her would be dropped.

Chapuis founded this assurance on a recent illness of Cromwell and the want of vigilance which ensued. In fact the chancellor – taken with a shivering fit on Ash Wednesday, in bed until after Lent and then catching a still worse fever after Palm Sunday – was in no condition to keep a close eye on things. But the transfer of Mary to Eltham was not due before Low Sunday and the sick man had by then had time to leave his bed. His first care was to have the princess's dwelling guarded by a squad of loyal servants under the command of Sir John Shelton. This made any escape impossible.

All these alarms, fugitive attempts and shrewd devices had, curiously, the effect of leaving the queen a breathing space. For it was not by chance that Cromwell had chosen Shelton for this last assignment. And if he had felt he could count with absolute confidence on Shelton's loyalty he had a strong reason for it: the man had Margaret Shelton for his daughter.


Now that I come to speak of Maggie I am the prey of scruples. I have known her very intimately and if I say too much good of her I risk flattering my model; but if I cannot bring myself to speak the truth of her I risk what would be worse – doing her an injustice.

I am embarrassed too in giving you her portrait. Regarding herself in the mirror, Maggie would have seen a girl neither tall nor short, neither beautiful nor ugly, with quite a good figure and a very gentle expression. I can say, because it is true, that a peach-like skin, but of peach exposed to the weather, made the charm of her face – with the nose just a tiny bit short – "very Parisian", so they said. Her mind, I suspect, was not of a very wide range but she had been creditably instructed and above all, above all she was devoted to Queen Anne. Younger than Anne by a few years, it was through Anne's eyes only that she saw and this absolute fidelity is the mainspring of the friendship that I feel for her.

Now everyone, Anne and I among the first, had been aware for some time that Henry had his eye on Maggie. At a ball he would choose her more and more often for his partner. Whereupon Cromwell, the queen and all the Boleyns saw a chance for them to return to favour. For the king's favourite of six months' standing, however well concealed she might be, was exerting an increasing influence in favour of Catherine. To have her replaced by a new mistress devoted this time to Queen Anne could do nothing but good. Margaret understood this without needing to be told; and when George and Cromwell encouraged her to make a conquest of this attentive sovereign I joined my voice to theirs. Realising that by this means she could help her royal friend to recover her lost influence – could save her perhaps from a disaster, if not from worse – she thought it would be treachery to Anne if she lingered too long about it. She did not. Bringing into play all the coquettish arts common in this class of enterprise and with the mysterious favourite losing something of her interest to so changeable a lover, Margaret had no great difficulty in taking her place.

If this required little effort of mind certainly it cost her still less of feeling. For to put it mildly, she had no taste at all for the king. In fact, out of love for Anne she had to overcome a degree of repugnance. But although these games of gallantry were – and still are – current coin at the court of England (more even than at the court of France) still Maggie's conduct has been condemned by some as frivolous if not mercenary. It was a risk she had to take: and she took it. Thenceforward her one thought was to devote herself while in the sovereign's arms to telling and re-telling to him faithfully, as I would have done it myself, all the good things that came to her mind about his royal consort. This certainly was something of a surprise to Henry but he was not displeased that his new mistress should approve his good taste in the choice of a wife.

But every coin has its reverse side. To keep the king in good humour with them for a full half year, the courtiers had been depending on the influence of his clandestine mistress. They sensed that with Margaret the wind was veering completely round and that Henry's new feelings for the queen were going to leave them badly exposed. To counteract this they tightened their ranks; any who had hesitated to join the conspiracy now resolved to do so as quickly as they could.

Having foreseen this development which he set his spies to watch, Cromwell proposed some rigorous measures to the king calculated to intimidate the ring-leaders. An edict announced that any person suspected of fidelity to the Pope or who pronounced his name or his title in church should stand trial for high treason.

The lower clergy accepted the edict as it stood but the priors of several Carthusiasn monasteries made a joint protest. They were called before Cromwell and because they maintained their protest they were – to set an example – thrown into the Tower of London, accused, tried and condemned to death. Their long agony – disembowelling and breaking on the wheel – then their execution by hanging took place in the presence of an imposing number of bishops and peers of the realm. But the queen, despite Henry's vigorous insistence, refused to attend.

For some weeks Anne and I had been seeing one another less frequently and in a more or less furtive fashion. Still, she had found occasion to express to me her horror at these barbarous procedures.

"No sentiment in politics," I ventured gently.

"But politics doesn't come into it," she protested with vehemence. "It's a question of abominable manners, manners which have lived with us from the Dark Ages. Besides, if it were politics, it is a monumental error. The Carthusians, whose priors have been assaulted in this way, are not exclusive to England. Their Order covers the whole Continent. And the atrocious death of these monks is going to have an appalling effect in France. No doubt human life is treated with not much greater consideration there; but at least the thing is managed with more attention to form, if not to elegance. It is perhaps because I was brought up to finer manners that I find these of England so odious."

The torture and execution of the priors did indeed arouse the greatest resentment in France. Rochford, sent by Cromwell to Calais to meet Chabot and three other emissaries of high rank, found them implacable. Far from reducing the rigour of his conditions, Francis made them sharper still. The annuities and pensions owing to Henry were now to stand as security for the marriage: these debts would lapse if the King of England should fail to keep his word.

When Anne had the news from George she rejoiced to think that the high line taken by Francis must now kill off beyond any doubt this project which she dreaded. To make yet more sure she suggested to the king, who was already in high dudgeon about it, that he should pay him back in kind. Let him stipulate that the young duke of Angoulême be sent immediately to London as a pledge of his father's good faith; further that if one day Elizabeth came to the throne the duchy of Angoulême with its possessions be annexed to the kingdom of England.

Clearly this put a stop to the negotiations but Henry's one thought was still to pay Francis back in his own coin. He considered he had been made a fool of and ill-treated, and now more than ever he feared an alliance between France and the empire. Upon whom, then, to vent his anger? He had victims within his reach: the prisoners in the Tower of London; Thomas More and John Fisher, Bishop of Rochester; Catherine of Aragon's former chaplain; the former tutor to Princess Mary. All were

194

brought before the royal council and called upon to make their submission within two months. When that interval had expired they would be handed over to the judges, with the fatal consequences that anyone could foresee.

"They won't give way," Anne said to me in great agitation. "The king will not give way either. And to cap it all, Pope Paul has just accorded Fisher a cardinal's hat. Henry takes that as a provocation; he won't cool down. As for me, I can do nothing any longer, for them, for anyone, to any purpose whatsoever."

To mitigate the offence the Pope promptly conferred the cardinal's purple on two friends of Henry and of England, the Italian ambassador Ghinucci and John du Bellay, the ambassador of France. But it was too late; the harm had been done. Paul made one more effort to obtain Francis's intercession but without success, for Francis had no desire to appear as having suggested to the Pope the gaffe over Fisher. All that he consented to do on Paul's entreaties was to set John du Bellay to work on the new cardinal. He was to urge him to submit to the royal edict, for which the Holy Father would there and then absolve him. But John Fisher was not the man to buy himself out by a pretended oath, even if the Pope should give it his blessing. Proudly he held to his refusal.

Henry, moreover, was furious with du Bellay, reproaching him for accepting a cardinal's hat for himself too at the Pope's hands and thereby implying that the honour paid to Fisher was no more than his due. And he held Francis responsible if, as he suspected, the Archbishop of Paris had advised the nominations. In brief, in his wrath against the Pope, against the archbishop, against Francis, against du Bellay, against the friends, relatives and gaolers of Fisher whom he accused at large of having tried to save him, Henry vented his fury on those who were close at hand. He could do nothing against the Pope, or Francis or du Bellay; but relatives, friends and gaolers were arrested, charged and put to torture. The cardinal was called upon one last time to make submission. He refused and in the face of his resistance was sent before the judges at Westminster.

A jury, carefully chosen, and stuffed with promises and with threats, returned a capital sentence. Everyone, Fisher the first, expected that he would be made to suffer on Tower Hill the terrible tortures of men condemned for treason. But a good number of the bishops gave Henry to understand that if the cardinal were tortured they would all take care to qualify for the same treatment. Even those peers friendly to Henry began to grow restless. Anne wept and implored. At last Henry agreed to be merciful and commute the penalty: the cardinal should simply be beheaded. For the last time, Fisher, already on the scaffold, heard his life offered him in exchange for his submission. He declined again, spoke a few words to the assembled crowd, knelt down, laid his head on the block and was beheaded.

A fortnight later Thomas More appeared before the judges. Throughout the proceedings he never weakened for an instant, losing neither his good humour nor the fine edge of his irony. Even before the executioner he kept it up, joking with him on the trouble he was putting the man to; and the smile was still on his lips as his head rolled upon the dais.

Anne had always had an implacable opponent in Thomas More. But his execution caused her sorrow nonetheless. In him she mourned the choicest flowing of the English spirit. All her entreaties for him to be delivered from the royal anger had not been able to save his life.

And yet from the time that her dear friend Margaret Shelton had become the favourite Anne had recaptured just a little of the king's ear: something even of his heart. Henry was charmed by this triangular set-up; he found something spicy in passing from one woman to the other with the goodwill of both. Anne, however, had no illusions; this would last only so long as Henry did not tire of it. Whereas she needed time: to consolidate the Church of England, to get the Treasury afloat again and to watch over the building of a fleet. Then the execution of More and Fisher that had brought tears to her eyes would surely awake in Europe as in England a storm to counter which she would need a free hand. So with Maggie's help she laid on a flow of balls, festivities and masquerades of which the king with his taste for luxury was still so fond. The queen took all the advantage she could of this precarious interval to forward her policies and smooth their path.

Henry for his part cared little about storms ahead; he preferred not to think about them. All that mattered to him was the present. He was vastly intrigued by a piece that a troupe of travelling comedians were playing. It was called *The Apocalypse* and in one of its scenes the king was shown cutting off the heads of the clergy. Henry had come barely disguised. At this scene he roared with laughter, applauding vigorously, and the audience laughed with him. It is true they had been incensed by the injustice done to More and Fisher, but executions in themselves were of daily occurrence and excited little feeling. The parody struck those who saw it as funny and at the end they cheered the king. On his return to the palace he said to the queen: "You would have found it very amusing." To his surprise and annoyance she had no inclination to think it funny.

When the storm came to a head and erupted, it was suppressed quickly enough in England, but in France men's minds were disturbed by it for a long time. Francis, his ministers and even the loyal du Bellay let Henry understand the vehemence of their indignation. Cromwell learnt from his agents in Rome that the French cardinals who up to then had been on Henry's side were now at one with their Italian colleagues in approving his condemnation by the *Rota*. Joined in consistory with the congregations, they prepared a bull which, on top of his excommunication for the crime of heresy, called for the king's deposition and condemnation for the crime of lèse-majesté.

For Rome always reckoned the kingdom of England as a fief of the Vatican. Thus Henry's deposition would mean that the vacant throne would revert to Pope Paul. Neither the king nor the queen troubled much about this, since a deposition could not be made effective without help from the emperor Charles, and if the throne of England were transferred to the Holy See the first effect would be to deprive the emperor's cousin Mary

197

of her right to the crown. It was therefore very unlikely that he would intervene.

When the cardinals urged Charles to act this was indeed the answer that he gave them. They pressed him then to depose Henry in favour of Mary. But since the princess was in her father's hands the king could move first and safeguard his throne by putting her to death. Then if Henry were deposed and no successor named? That could result in the Crown not falling to neither Paul nor Mary. The result was that at the end of the day, as Henry and Anne had expected, the impracticable bull remained in the drawer.

XII
(1535)

# *Lübeck*

What all Europe was calling the "assassination of More and Fisher" had caused a stir even among the Protestants of Germany whom the two theologians had consistently opposed. But many Lutherans, despite their differences on theology, had continued to hold the two in admiring, often even friendly, regard. They perceived in the author of "Utopia" a rare elevation of thought, which they found again more especially in his correspondence with Erasmus. Fisher had been open to no compromise on the sacred character of marriage and thus on the validity of the union with Catherine, and accordingly the Lutherans had no fault to find in him: nothing in either Testament authorised the use of the term "incestuous" as applying to the marriage of a widow with her brother-in-law. Quite the contrary: the Bible had much to say on the duty of such a union. This pretext that Henry had put forward for the divorce, and then for his marriage with Anne, appeared to them (as well as to Catholics) a pretence impossible to condone. In fact they were drawn by the Gospels far closer to these two Christians loyal to the Catholic Church than to this usurper of a spiritual supremacy – which, if they did not acknowledge it in the Pope, far less would they admit it in a layman, though he were the King of England.

"What they fear above all," Anne said to me as she thought aloud, "is that if no bar is raised against a supremacy of that kind we shall see springing up all over the place eighteen popes instead of one. Every new sect will be for having its own." Such a consequence had not occurred to me. And I must admit that I still have no very clear idea how I would begin to get round it.

199

"After all," I said, "on a matter of this kind we need concern ourselves only with what happens in England."

"You are right, but not entirely. If one day Henry is only one pope out of eighteen you will see springing up even here some dozens of sects with a dozen other popes. The king will lose his authority. And in this area of religion England will no longer stay sharply distinguished from the Continent. It will be all to play for once more. What is wanted – and the sooner the better – is the birth of a Reformed Church clear-cut and English, growing ever more strong with the king as its sole head."

If Henry recked little of this kind of danger it was because it had not even crossed his mind. He meant all the same to win back the goodwill of the Lutheran princes of Germany. And he set about it in his own manner.

The princes were at grips with the determined opposition of a dissident sect calling for the baptism of adults only. Members of this sect were hunted down, arrested and banished. To escape these persecutions a number of the Anabaptists had taken to the sea from Dutch coasts and sought refuge in England where they had found a welcome. Henry remembered their presence and thinking to please the Lutherans he had a couple of dozen of them arrested, judged by an ecclesiastical tribunal and then burnt on Tower Hill as heretics. And despite the warnings the queen had given him, it came to him as a huge surprise when he was made to understand that so far from winning back the favour of the German reformers this fresh act of cruelty had only set them against him still further.

Driven to become aware of the hostility he was incurring all over Europe, Henry had recourse to other methods no less shrewd. He had two documents drawn up, published and widely circulated, the first in praise of himself, the second in denigration of his victims, particularly More and Fisher.

In the first the king was presented as the most pious, the most just and the most clement of monarchs. It recalled his kindness to the young James of Scotland in not having exacted retribution for the crimes committed by his father. It recalled his generosity to the King of France, towards the cost of whose ransom after Pavia he had contributed on a royal scale. It made the point that at Florence or Venice such as More and Fisher would have been removed by poisoning without further ceremony; that after judgement and condemnation according to the rule it would have been quite in order to have had them boiled alive in molten lead or else flayed alive, disembowelled, quartered or at the least burnt at the stake; whereas King Henry in his goodness and mercy had had them gently put to death on the block. In short, all that was lacking in this portrait of Henry was the halo.

The second pamphlet claimed to remind the German Lutherans that John Fisher and Thomas More had never ceased to be their cruellest enemies; how they had called heretics any who had impugned the doctrine of the Church of Rome on even a single point; how they had had these people searched out everywhere in the kingdom, giving rewards to informers; how finally More had thought up, for use against those who refused to admit their errors or having admitted them, then retracted, the most horrific tortures such as burning the soles of their feet with red-hot irons. In short, as compared with the remarkable leniency of the king, his two victims were made to appear under the cruellest colours.

In one of the two pamphlets – I forget which – the writer reproached the Pope for a shameless lie: namely, the assertion that Henry, the Most Noble King of England, had rejected with mockery an urgent petition in favour of Fisher from His Most Christian Majesty the King of France; whereas no such request had been made. He appealed, on this point, to the conscience of the said Most Christian Majesty.

So challenged, Francis was exposed to grave embarrassment with the Holy Father. For it was true, he had not intervened. But to acknowledge this would be to confess to the Pope the little trouble he had taken to save Fisher; on the other hand to claim that he had made a request which had not been granted would be to acknowledge his total want of credit with the King of England. Either way he would look small in the Pope's eyes. He was therefore extremely resentful of his good brother for having landed him in this embarrassment.

With the German Lutherans the pamphlets had had no better success than Henry's treatment of the Anabaptists; less still with the people of England: the response on all sides was of utter disbelief. The noble character of Thomas More, his sense of honour, his generosity had been admired by all; no less abominated were those bloodthirsty prosecutions brought by King Henry — for which the queen was naturally held responsible.

"Could Your Majesty," I asked Anne in some surprise, "not have stopped the king from publishing these two lunatic pamphlets?"

"Henry does not listen to me any longer," she said with that pained smile which was becoming customary with her. Then the smile turned to sarcasm: "Except however in theology." When I looked surprised she said: "The king remembers my existence when he is discussing some obscure point in the Pentateuch with the Bishop of London. He then makes me read through a quantity of works which he is too lazy to consult himself. And woe betide me if I do not find the argument which proves him right. But for the rest," she went on, "the little that thanks to you, I may have regained from him in goodwill, I have not regained in influence. He has discovered a taste for independence and follows only the promptings of his own head: one full of extravagances which are going to cost him and all of us very dear."

While she spoke those words the price was already beginning to be paid. The political set-backs were mounting up. Henry had made himself so unpopular with the Lutherans that he could not hope for their support; and the alliance with Lübeck, far from bringing in what he was expecting of it, was turning to catastrophe. Marcus Meyer had been defeated under the ramparts of that Hanseatic town by the united forces of Christian of Denmark and the Landgrave of Hesse, thus reducing to extremities the burgomaster Wullenwever.

Finding all the grist he could for his mill, the burgomaster, while sending word to Henry that he was eager for his alliance, at the same time treated secretly with Christian. For nothing succeeds like success and the victor prince found himself approached by numerous new allies from Sweden, from Prussia and many a German principality. If it was a league he wanted, he now had it, ready made.

However, Christian's victory had to be balanced against serious difficulties nearer home. In Jutland insurgent peasants had got the better of his legions in a sanguinary battle. This sapped his confidence, and so, while still making his approach to England, he was careful to keep on good terms with the Hanse. He despatched his counsellor Schwaben to propose to Henry an alliance much more advantageous than that of Lübeck.

But deaf as always to news that he did not want to hear, Henry was still dazzled by that mirage of a League of Northern Europe with which Marcus had deluded him. So he gave Schwaben no cordial welcome. He had every possible motive, he told him, to occupy the throne of Denmark himself and would keep faith with his good friends in Lübeck. Christian, he added, would do far better to lay down his arms at once.

Schwaben had let him talk. When finally Henry stopped he took a courteous leave, but not before calmly letting the king know that Marcus had been routed and killed on the battlefield.

Still in his dreams, Henry simply refused to believe it (on one point only he was right: Marcus was only a prisoner). He had yet to learn that Christian, having pacified Jutland shortly after Schwaben's visit, had taken control of the region; moreover, that Wullenwever had gone over – lock, stock and barrel – into Christian's camp. Henry in his rage had now to contemplate how blind he had been to fence himself in with so many delusions.

Accordingly, when Marcus Meyer – freed by a peasants' assault of the castle of Warberg where he had been imprisoned and of which he was now the master – offered the castle to Henry in exchange for immediate support in taking up the struggle again, the king this time resolutely turned a deaf ear.

He was glad he had done so on hearing that Marcus was now besieged in Warberg. Dismissing this dream for another, he pictured himself as mediating between the different factions of the Reformation and bringing together under his wing all the Protestants of Europe. A series of ambassadors had already been charged with the mission of winning over all this gentry to his views and preparing a general reconciliation when report came to him of the Hanseatic fleet's disaster in the Skagerrak. This virtually put an end to the fighting (only Copenhagen still held out) and rendered obsolete these grand plans for mediation.

"And now," Anne said to me dolefully, "what new dream is Henry going to come up with? How lucky for us in all this business that Francis does just as many stupid things and has had his own fill of embarrassments!"

"Serve him right," I said. "He had only to remain faithful to Your Majesties after having encouraged the schism; faithful also to the Lutheran princes after ranging them against the emperor."

"It was to please the Landgrave of Hesse and the Dukes of Bavaria; to make a counter against Austria and the King of the Romans. But he has been beaten at his own game. Ferdinand has stolen a march on him; the new Elector of Saxony has just been to see him in Vienna."

"With a view to an alliance?"

"To propose to him a marriage between a son of the Landgrave and one of the emperor's daughters. If this marriage takes place, Francis will have lost his most faithful allies."

"What a carry-on!" I said in joyless mirth. "Like schoolboys stealing each other's marbles."

"Yes, but so far as I am concerned there's not much fun in it. For I know very well what Francis will do. It's an idea that he's been toying with for a long time. He is going to take all these fine folks by surprise and try to bring the Pope and the Lutherans together. This, if he can manage it, will win back the Protestants to his side and turn them against the emperor. But to persuade the Holy Father to listen to him he will have begun by giving something away – by saying no to the schism and throwing us, Henry and me, to the dogs."

This sombre prediction was by no means unfounded. It was based on what Anne had just learnt from John du Bellay whose brother William and another bishop – I forget his name – had begun, under Francis's direction, a correspondence with Luther and the great theologian, Melanchthon. The aim had been to establish the points in common, far more numerous than those of difference, between the Church of Rome and the Reformed Church. One of these differences, and the most serious, had of course been the primacy of the sovereign Pontiff. Now Melanchthon was confident of bringing the Lutherans to admit it *de facto*, since obviously they could not admit the Pope's authority *de jure*. This gave Francis an opening to try to interest Pope Paul, less opposed than Clement had been to any negotiation, in the project of an understanding between Luther and Rome and to nurse the hope of one day seeing it come about. But meantime he needed to contrive to deal a fatal blow to the schism and by consequence if not perhaps to Henry, at least to Queen Anne.

That is why Anne tried to put off for as long as possible the initial steps intended to prepare the way to this dangerous accord. Francis, so du Bellay informed her, had already sent to the German theologians, and in particular to Melanchthon, an invitation to come to his court. This must be prevented at all costs, at any rate as regards Melanchthon. A piece of luck, if one may venture so to call it, was that a number of his co-religionists had just been burnt in Paris as heretics. An emissary should therefore be sent to him in Saxony to tell him about this, dissuade him from the journey to France and persuade him to come instead to the court of England where the king, so the envoy should say, was desirous of discussing with him certain points arising from the Old Testament.

For this mission Anne chose a friend of du Bellay's, by name Robert Barnes. But when Barnes landed in Hamburg the plague was rife in Wittenberg. He therefore waited for several weeks where he was, making use of the time to confer with numerous theologians and overcome their prejudices. When at last he was about to go to Wittenberg he learnt that his mission was no longer needed, since Melanchthon would be going neither to France nor to England. John-Frederick, the Elector of Saxony, probably for fear of offending Charles and Ferdinand, had just forbidden him to quit the territory.

That, for the moment, was the essential – at least, as the queen saw it. For meantime the king had mounted another hobby-horse. Marcus Meyer's brother, Gerard, had come from Denmark with a captain named Mores and tried in vain to secure for Marcus a military and financial contribution. Henry was about to give a vigorous refusal when another captain arrived with a message from Marcus. The buccaneer now offered to hand over to Henry besides Warberg four large towns with their fortresses, Copenhagen with Elsinore among them.

And there was Henry once again totally bedazzled by the heady prospect of imposing himself militarily on all the northern powers and uniting them under his rule. He was already having two ships fitted out for transport of troops, with supply of cannon, powder and ball, arquebuses and ammunition of all kinds when news came that four English ships had been seized by the Swedes at the exit from Copenhagen; twelve others boarded and captured in the Sound; all carried into Swedish ports, the vessels disarmed, the crews held prisoner and the goods on board confiscated. To send two new ships in these conditions would expose them and their cargo to the same fate, if not to be sunk with all on board. Henry had to give it up. He discharged his wrath on the two captains, ordering them to sail back up the Thames and dismiss the mercenaries.

Anne's mere presence was enough to fuel his anger, for she seemed to be telling him: "See, that's what happens when instead of pressing on with your naval construction you divert the money voted for that purpose to useless pomp and ceremony." The queen did not breathe a word but her silence spoke for itself and exasperated the king who on the slightest pretext abused her coarsely. He could never admit that he was wrong without getting angry.

And the news that was coming in to him was not of a kind to make him forget his misjudgements. He found himself more isolated than ever. At Hamburg, at Brunswick, finally at Wittenberg, Robert Barnes had had little success with theologians still under the shock of More and Fisher's execution. At Lübeck Wullenwever and his party had just been put in a minority. He kept his seat on the council but none of the rest of his party did. Soon afterwards anyway the burgomaster, after struggling as best he could, had had to resign his office which was taken over at once by his rival, Broemse, a man hostile to England.

As if that were not enough Wullenwever, left with only the small rural districts attached to Lübeck to administer, had not put up for long with this humiliation. He made his way secretly to Hamburg where he got in touch with the English ambassadors. He told them that on the outskirts of the town there were eight or ten roving companies of mercenaries commanded by a rough-neck soldier of the name of Uvelacker. He was confident that with ten thousand florins he could enrol them in his service, return in strength to Lübeck, drive out the unfriendly burgomaster and re-establish King Henry's influence there. Thereafter with these five thousand men he would raise the siege of Copenhagen and regain control of the area.

This plan enchanted the English diplomats, who paid the ex-burgomaster a substantial advance. He left Hamburg by night, intending to meet Uvelacker next day. Alas! Putting up at an inn to sleep, he was recognised, informed on by the innkeeper and arrested at dawn. That was the end of the hopes both of Wullenwever and of Henry's ambassadors, who had to confess to the king how their scheme had gone wretchedly wrong and the money been lost.

Shorn of his best allies and encountering setback after setback, Henry was afraid that the isolation in which he found himself might tempt the emperor to make a landing, depose Henry and have the emperor's cousin crowned. Anne feared likewise, for herself of course, but chiefly for England. In the hands of Mary, so of Catherine, so of Charles, Albion would be reduced to no more than a jewel of the Empire.

Assuredly that is how it would have been if by good luck Charles had not been at this moment too taken up with his expedition against the Turks in Saracen country. Wholly bent on achieving the fall of Tunis he entrusted the task of deposing Henry with the help of the rebel English lords to his sister, Mary of Hungary, regent of the Netherlands and a strong and determined woman. When Henry heard this he assumed that he was lost; she would surely make no more than a mouthful of the little English army. Anne on the other hand felt reassured. She knew that the regent was having to cope with Anabaptist unrest in Holland itself; in these conditions to denude the country of troops would be to risk an uprising: then how could she be certain that the rebel lords were as many as they claimed to be? Finally, what would Francis say of it? Would he not come to the help of his ally Henry? The regent, unlike her brother, would not have the rest of the Empire to support her. And if Charles marked time too long in Tunis would not the kings of France and of England jointly take advantage of his absence to attack her in return? In brief, neither the queen nor Cromwell felt unduly anxious, at least for as long as the Turks held good in Tunis.

In fact, from that point of view the news seemed good. Even the siege of La Goletta, the port protecting Tunis, was not over; the garrison under the direction of Khaireddin never ceased their murderous sallies. The imperial troops were suffering besides from fever and seemed near to breaking. The emperor had to put himself in person at their head. He worked marvels at first by his drive and energy and courage, until a general assault won him the port with all it contained in cannon, ammunition, food and galleys on the quay. Had he stopped there Charles would have deprived Tunis of its exit by sea and with patience he would no doubt have reduced it to his mercy. But he was pressed for time. He wanted to return to Europe as early as possible, but not without first having set free the twenty thousand or so Christian slaves of the Turks. He also had to fear a counter-attack that might perhaps win the day if Khaireddin were given time to regroup his forces. For all these reasons he took the initiative and launched his columns on Tunis.

But between the port and the town there was a vast and arid area to be crossed under the African sun. The air was suffocating. Soon the soldiers were tortured by thirst. They became breathless, slackened their pace and were too exhausted to continue marching. During the night putrid fumes from stagnant water and the stings of insects left them with a burning fever. When the dawn came they were shivering all over as they had to set out again. Cathing sight of a little greenery in the distance they tried to reach it. Whereupon they saw instead of water the dazzle of helmets and coats of mail of a large force of cavalry bursting out from among the trees and charging them from all sides. Headlong flight ensued.

These comforting reports reached the king, the queen and the chancellor only after a long interval. They had little time to rejoice, for the next report was disillusioning. Charles had kept fresh troops in reserve within whose cover he was able to regroup the fugitives. Given time to recruit a little strength, the imperialists resumed their march, but now by night. Surprised at daybreak, the Turks rushed out of doors in disorder and at the sound of fighting the Christian slaves, imprisoned in the citadel, threw themselves upon their warders. They overwhelmed them, bound them hand and foot and closed the gates of the ramparts. This meant that Khaireddin was not able to fall back into the town and there entrench his troops; compelled instead to make his escape in the direction of Algiers, he left some thousands of Turks on the field. And Charles entered Tunis in triumph.

He put his Moorish ally, Moulay Hassan, back on the throne while leaving a garrison to occupy La Goletta. Then, crossing the sea, he returned to Spain, covered in glory and bringing with him twenty thousand Christian slaves. From there he went on to be acclaimed all over Germany.

If this unexpected victory dismayed Anne and Henry, it dismayed Francis no less. When he was certain of the success of the Turks and of Charles's failure before Tunis he promised himself that with Henry's help by sea and land he would secure the Pas-de-Calais, attack the Netherlands, drive out Mary of Hungary and occupy Saxony and Thuringia. The emperor's triumph put all such projects out of the question. To go to war against him in present conditions would be to court disaster. There was nothing for it but to change course, reach an understanding with Charles at Henry's expense and think again about a marriage of the Dauphin with Princess Mary. Which would in the long run bring England and France together under the same sceptre.

If Francis could thus change his policy as a man might change his shirt it was that the situation was favourable. The emperor's victory had put life into the Holy Father. It came at a moment when, revolted by the executions of More and Fisher, the Pope was thinking of formally forbidding all Christian princes to keep up any relations with the apostate. But until now he had not dared. Charles's popularity throughout Europe gave him the opportunity and, rubbing his hands, Paul published and at once sent out the briefs signifying to all his interdiction of the English king. To Francis this came as a godsend, since it was the Holy See that constrained him and justified him in abandoning the schismatic and making up with the emperor. But full well every king worthy of the name knows that he has an obligation to the future. Rather than break openly, better to force his good brother Henry to become the author of the rupture.

With this purpose he sent to Henry the bailiff of Troyes, by name Dinteville, together with Villandry and Castelnau. Dinteville showed the king the brief that Francis had received. If Francis were to remain the ally of the excommunicated Henry, he must expect to be attacked by Charles and the Catholic princes. He was, he said, fully resolved to defend himself; but it would be necessary as well that the King of England should still be of a mind to take a share – one third, as had been agreed – in a campaign against the emperor. The costs, he made clear, would exceed a hundred thousand pounds sterling a month. Would Henry be willing to assume his share of this?

Now Francis was perfectly aware that the monthly revenues of the crown of England did not amount to twelve thousand pounds, namely one third of the third for which he put in a demand. Francis accordingly received the negative reply that he had angled for, and Dinteville and his companions quitted the soil of Albion forthwith.

But meanwhile in obedience to Francis's orders Dinteville had asked and obtained permission to go and present his homage to the two princesses, Mary and Elizabeth. The king saw nothing underhand in this, but the queen had her suspicions: would not the real instructions to the envoy be to sound out Mary's intentions as regards a marriage with the Dauphin? Now the princess made no secret of that being her dearest wish. Lady Shelton, the princess's chaperone (but also mother of Maggie, the favourite) had accordingly been warned to keep Mary in her room out of sight of the ambassadors. So she did, refusing leave to Dinteville to cross the threshold of Mary's apartments but inviting him instead to present his homage to Elizabeth in the other wing of the castle. In his fury Dinteville resolved at least to salute Mary on her balcony. But Lady Shelton, interpreting her instructions perhaps too literally, had had doors and shutters nailed down and Mary could not so much as show herself behind her window. All that Dinteville and his companions were able to overhear as they went by was a little French air which she played in their honour on her spinet.

On leaving Eltham, Dinteville hardly expected to find himself greeted all along his route by clusters of people cheering him as he passed and following his horse for some distance to ask him the date of Mary's marriage with the Dauphin. When they heard to their bitter disappointment that he had not seen her they cursed and swore against Queen Anne. The same scenes were repeated on arrival at the palace. Courtiers, domestic servants, even herdsmen and stableboys put the same question to Dinteville and were no less disappointed by his answer. Anne had not been mistaken in her apprehension about this visit to Mary, for on their return his envoys would be able to assure Francis that nobles and humble folk alike were strongly animated against the queen, to the point of saying a thousand nasty things about her.

I despaired for her but she said to me "What would you? I have told you already; one can achieve nothing truly great without being unpopular. People see the present; they have no eye for the future. They see the money that is taken from them to build a navy; they have no clear vision as yet of the purpose that navy is to serve. The poor see no connection between their poverty and what it is that is making England isolated and weak. They fail to realise that their very misery makes it incumbent on England to become both independent and strong. The rich are terrified that because of me Charles may make war on us and that their shops and warehouses all over the Empire will be seized. They shut their eyes to the fact that England is so enfeebled that even without a war their commercial interests in those countries are at risk. In Spain or in Holland the goods they deliver are often not paid for and if they bring a legal action they are non-suited on the spot. Increasingly our compatriots abroad are selling their businesses and coming home. This surge back into England in some ways suits me well enough. These are all men of boldness and experience and England needs them. She needs them to create business ventures here that will enrich our island, increasing its commercial power and thereby its power generally. But who do you suppose is going to understand these long-term consequences? And because they do not understand them, it is me whom they blame for all their woes."

# XIII
## (1535–1536)

# Catherine's Death

The last to be able to discern "these long-term consequences" was assuredly Henry himself. Wholly given up to his extravagant dreams, he could not see beyond the immediate present – any more, I should add, than the people of England, both rich and poor (and partly myself also, let me confess). And the present that he had to face was this accumulation of errors that had led to his being rebuffed on all sides.

Even apostates like himself and who earlier than himself had freed themselves from the papal authority, who should have been indifferent (to say the least) to what the Pope had ordered and should rather have opened every big port and trading facility to English vessels, even those seemed fully to have enforced Rome's ban on whatever carried the colours of the schismatic king. They went so far as to hinder his trade in fishing, especially in Newfoundland and off the island [Greenland] which belongs to Denmark. Henry thought that by way of reprisal it would be simple for him to seize the London warehouses of merchants of the Hanse; but these merchants exacted revenge at once by taking possession of any English vessels that happened to be in their ports. Worse still, when England that summer suffered so severe a drought that the plants died before they were ready to harvest, the countries that ordinarily supplied her with cereals refused to deliver their crops and sent them elsewhere. The Venetians did the same with wine and although they had always stocked up in London both with wool and tin, now turned instead to Madrid and Portugal. The ensuing shortage of foodstuffs and lack of income made England completely dependent on Holland and France, that is to say on Charles and Francis. This infuriated Henry but he could do nothing about it.

Anne made no comment. A word too much and he would have strangled her. But if she was distressed by the great difficulties that the succession of blunders had produced, what concerned her most for the kingdom's future was the projected marriage between Mary and the Dauphin. Mary thought of this union not as a project but as a fact. When Lady Shelton told her that there was an alternative plan to marry the Dauphin to a Spanish princess she had replied that her husband could not have two wives at the one time. This pretension, which did no more than annoy Anne, sent Henry into a rage. To bring his daughter to reason he told her that she was his worst enemy; that through her fault he was at loggerheads with the majority of Christian princes; and that if she persisted he would be obliged to use harsh measures. But this had no effect; Mary refused to listen.

For the vacillating Henry to issue a warning was one thing, quite another to carry it out. Irresolute as ever, he allowed mother and daughter to continue living in comfort and corresponding with whomever they wished, yet at the same time he summoned his council to consult on what he should do to bring the two women to terms.

When Chapuis heard of the danger, he at once informed the emperor. But Charles was not inclined to any precipitate action. He told his ambassador that his aunt and cousin were so far merely under threat but that if the danger took clear shape he would have to advise them to give in. He was no more disposed to pay heed to Pope Paul who – to please France from which he drew the major part of his revenues – was urging him to insist that the Dauphin be granted Mary's hand without further delay. Charles was keeping his options open. Anne knew all this but it did not ease her anxieties. For as soon as the emperor felt himself strong enough he would revert to this demand and perhaps make it a *casus belli*. Would Henry then, for love of the queen, take the risk of standing up to him? She had small hope of it and counted rather on his cowardly spirit: on his fear that if he gave way to the emperor his already tottering authority would weaken further to the point when a faction of the lords would have the power to deprive him of it altogether.

In either event, the king would hold the queen responsible. Did not all his difficulties spring from this ill-fated second marriage? Who gave rise to them in the first place and was now eternally multiplying them? The time was past when the queen could still rely on Cromwell. She saw that he too was gently distancing himself. Not that he had any greater wish than herself to see England pass under the tutelage of France by such a marriage. In dealing with Dinteville he had even shown himself one of the firmest; as soon as the Frenchman began discussing Mary and the Dauphin he had refused to listen further. When the other tried to insist, Cromwell had fulminated against France, declaring that England had no need of her; Henry's relations with the emperor, he said, were becoming rapidly more cordial.

In fact the king kept putting tempting offers before Chapuis; but they were so vague that the ambassador found them derisory and merely smiled at Cromwell's suggestion of marrying the emperor's son Philip to the Princess Elizabeth who was not yet two. Cromwell had not insisted, being aware that Eleanor of Habsburg* had met her sister Mary of Hungary at the northern frontier and that they had talked about the marriage of Catherine's daughter with the Dauphin. Proof that the emperor had not scrapped the project; and that his interest in it was still a danger.

Anne struggled helplessly amidst these complications without the power any longer to make either the king or Cromwell listen to her. She reproached Cromwell for not having confined himself, when he met Francis's emissary, to opposing the marriage but going on virtually to burn England's bridges with France. She sensed, moreover, that at Court the pro-French party was becoming weaker all the time; whereas in her

* After the death of Claude and the Treaty of Cambrai Eleanor had become Francis's wife and Queen of France.

view nothing but a cross-Channel alliance could keep the emperor quiet. On this subject she had a sharp quarrel with her uncle Norfolk whose support she was also losing and who now withdrew to his estates. But she could not hide from herself that even in his retreat the old man would now be numbered among her adversaries.

In these complicated relationships between Henry, Francis, Charles and Pope Paul one factor alone remained favourable: the bulls of excommunication and deposition had still not been published. The Holy Father hesitated. Neither in Francis nor in the emperor could he detect any eagerness to put them into force; and if the bulls were to remain dead letters, and the world knew it, he would lose face. Not that Francis had not promised, if Charles went ahead, to support him by sending auxiliary troops. But the emperor put small trust in this jerky and impulsive Francis. He demanded a written, irrevocable undertaking – which Francis was not disposed to give. And so Charles's forces remained at the ready.

If Anne, with her reliable sources of information, could breathe a little on the foreign front the unrest at home caused her deep disquiet. Such was the discontent that Cromwell hesitated to levy the taxes which he had with so much difficulty persuaded Parliament to pass. Other sources of income for the king's Treasury were likewise in default: the tenant farmers of the Crown, hit by the drought, were no longer able to pay their rents; the King of France, ill-disposed towards Henry, was holding up the payment of his monthly instalments. It followed that the tills were fast emptying. To fill them again rigorous measures would be needed.

For a long time – ever since the proclamation of the schism – the king had had his mind on confiscating the property of the Church. Several years earlier – but as always without the resolution to see it through – he had drawn up a petition demanding that the clergy should part with their wealth for the benefit of the kingdom; that priests should work like anybody else; and that they should be allowed to marry, and so leave the wives of other men in peace. All these measures would have been popular because of the general animosity towards high-ranking churchmen whose style of life was funded on the backs of the common people and whose opulence was considered out of keeping with Christian humility.

But when a number of monasteries were brutally dissolved this only aroused popular indignation, without bringing in much money. For Henry characteristically had not had the pluck to go beyond half measures. This kind of procedure, if resorted to, had to be carried through to the end so that at least there would be important advantages to set off against the violence used. (Henry was to reach this conclusion himself later; but it would take him – I anticipate – four years to come to that. Four years in the course of which the king would have dissolved close on six hundred ecclesiastical houses, freeing from their vows some thousands of monks and nuns. It was this, by the way, that was to set off a rebellion in the north called the Pilgrimage of Grace: one that would take a great deal of money to put down.)

The first wave of closures had brought in so little that it was not enough to pay the salaries of the officials, the costs of administration nor the debts incurred. The spoils from the second wave four years later far exceeded those of the first, but little even of this found its way into the kingdom's coffers. For the principal beneficiaries would be not so much the Treasury as the lords to whom the king owed money. It was among them that Henry was to parcel out the extensive properties taken from the monasteries; or else to sell the properties off cheaply to pay back with interest the sums he had borrowed.

Thus for four years and with almost no benefit to the kingdom, Henry was to bring that kingdom to a state of turmoil. The people may have had little love for the bishops, but they were nevertheless appalled by the way the convents were brutally and effectively pillaged; the monks and nuns dispersed; and all this in the end to enrich the lords, land owners and big merchants – a class for whom they had even less affection than for the bishops.

Furthermore, the "visitors" whom Cromwell sent to collect

(or rather, plunder) the property of the religious orders were heartily hated; first because they were brutal, cruel and corrupt; secondly because in carrying the relics away they would often destroy them. And it was Anne Boleyn, naturally, who was held responsible for all this.

Henry too was laying the blame on Anne for the many various and formidable difficulties with Francis, with the Pope, with the emperor, with the Lutherans, with Sweden, Denmark, Prussia, the Hanseatic towns, and finally with the people of England and the crown servants. Each new shock antagonised him against her the more. What had become of the renewal of affection he had felt for her under the influence of Margaret Shelton? It had disappeared along with the enthusiasm that that lady had once inspired in the king. For if Maggie were still the recognised mistress of the royal bed she had long ceased to reign over the sovereign's inconstant heart.

The court had for some time been noticing the rise of the Seymour family. Sir John Seymour was descended from a companion of William the Conqueror, of the name Saint-Maur. He himself came from Wiltshire. Like a fish in water, he felt at home in this court of intrigue and flattery, suspicion and ill-will, ostentation and petty meannesses. His cleverness had early won him the king's confidence. His son, Edward Seymour, was at Vienna in the service of Charles: a family link between Empire and kingdom that pleased Henry. Finally, Sir John's daughter, Jane Seymour, had become one of the maids of honour to Queen Anne.

We have seen how partial Henry was to these young girls now that he had reached middle age and grown finicky in his appetite. His desire for them reawakened those sexual urges without which he was no longer in a position to honour the marriage bed, nor the favourite's bed either. There might be many passing fancies of this kind, but a king so continuously spied upon and escorted found them difficult to fulfil. In all his movements from one place to another he had with him a retinue of lords and squires who left him very little time to himself. So, after being titillated by day with the young girls he would make up for it at night with the favourite or the queen. It was therefore in part owing to these young attendants of hers that Anne found herself pregnant once more – reviving in herself as in him the hope of a male heir. This state of affairs also brought back a renewal if not of affection for her, at least of a certain respect. This was no bar to many an amorous pastime: sometimes on the royal barge and even in the presence of Anne, who was not too much affected by these libertine games. But this queen who had been living on her nerves for seven years and always on the edge of an abyss now noticed with growing unease the manners that the young Jane Seymour had recently been adopting towards the king.

Anne recognised in this behaviour her own conduct of seven years earlier when Henry had singled her out from among Catherine's attendants; alone among all this squad of girls Jane was holding back, a shy violet. Same causes, same effects. Was not the king, as before, on the way to becoming impatient, then infatuated, then perhaps madly in love? What might follow could carry a threat. Anne had passed her thirtieth year, the other was in her twenties. She was not a beauty, but her youthful cheeks had so fresh a complexion that they seemed transparent. The slightest blush set them off, giving the impression of a delicate fragility that made you long to take them in your hands. What reassured Anne a little was that beneath these charms her rival was stupid. In the brilliant little court around the queen the young girl cut a pitiful figure. Discontented by the high-flown language, mostly French, that was used so as not to be understood by outsiders (for example, "I'm in the forest of Windsor", meaning that one has not understood) she scarcely opened her mouth. And the queen, remembering that she herself had kept a hold on the king, through the months and years before the marriage, only by her subtle and lively spirit developed at the French court, thought that Jane's doltishness would soon cause Henry to tire of her.

Anne then was not inclined to be too anxious when

Catherine's health, already rather shaky, began suddenly to collapse. The dropsy was spreading through her vital organs. I supposed that to the queen the ex-sovereign's demise would be welcome. But on the contrary I found her worried, even anguished.

"I never hated her," she told me; "and what's more, if she dies it could be the end of me and of my little Elizabeth."

"Come now!"

"Yes, yes. Two things still keep the king from divorcing me: my pregnancy and Catherine. If I don't have a boy and if Catherine goes (to whom he would still be married if he got rid of me) I shall not put a high price on my chances or my daughter's. With nothing to stop him any longer he will cast me off; and Mary will find herself once again the legitimate heir. In that case all that I have striven for will come to nothing. Let us pray, pray, dearest, and may God save Catherine."

This insight was more than borne out; events even went beyond it. A rumour circulated that Catherine's dropsy was simply the result of a slow poisoning perpetrated by Anne and the king.

These suspicions about Anne were absurd, considering what she had just told me. Less absurd certainly about Henry, who would in that way be ridding himself of the chief obstacle to his desires. So I would by no means stake my life on his innocence. That at any rate is how the insistent rumour ran.

Certain observations made a little earlier by Cromwell to the council were not calculated to dispel this suspicion. He let it be understood first that the disappearance of Catherine and of Mary would be a blessing both for the kingdom and for peace by removing at one stroke any *casus belli* with the emperor. Cromwell then pushed cynicism so far as to discuss with Chapuis this possibility, so beneficial to either party. The ambassador made haste, you may be sure, to report this conversation to the emperor whose hands were fortunately not free for immediate armed action because of the Turks. But for this he might have had recourse to it, so as to anticipate the tragedy envisaged.

Then when Mary in her turn fell ill the effect was to increase suspicion and rumour everywhere. Henry unwisely fuelled this by asking old Lady Shelton to threaten her pupil with severest punishment if she continued to resist. Chapuis, now more and more anxious, made contact with the governess, flattering her in every possible way, at the same time warning her that if the princess were to die while under her supervision the first person to be compromised would clearly be herself. Dr Butts, Mary's doctor, went further. He told her that she was suspected of preparing the poison; this so troubled the good woman that she could not sleep, becoming panic-stricken and seeing herself hanged if the princess had the slightest sneeze.

However, nothing came of it. Catherine did not get any worse, Mary got better, Chapuis was reassured, and the rumours died down; the emperor went off to fight the Turks. But the one who felt most relieved was assuredly Anne, since Catherine's life was warrant for her own.

For all that, she did not recover her peace of mind, for she had many other causes for anxiety. The one that was beginning to disturb her most was Jane Seymour. Day by day the queen had to watch the young girl's increasing influence over the king's heart. She seemed to be seeing herself again at the same age, and watched Jane playing on her virtue (as she had done herself) to bind the sovereign to her through his impatience and desire. In a bitter return to times past Anne was now experiencing what Catherine must have felt. From the moment that the king grew tired of her as he had tired of the deposed queen, everything about her annoyed and irritated him! Anne no longer doubted that she would suffer the same fate, with still fewer means of defending herself.

Although Catherine, far from growing feebler, seemed now rather to be mending, there were still rumours of poisoning. The Marchioness of Exeter wrote to Chapuis that she had heard the king make some frightening remarks about the sick woman, such as that he would not wait until the next session of Parliament to see to it that Catherine should no longer need either a companion or a household. The Countess of Derby recalled that the king had been in the habit of saying that "if his hat knew a quarter of his thoughts he would throw it in the fire". The ambassador spent his time either warning the emperor or reassuring him, as the state of the dowager princess either worsened or improved. Thus Christmas went by without any particular occasion for anxiety.

But on New Year's Day the sick woman relapsed with violent pains. She vomited all her food and drink and did not have an hour's sleep at night. At this news Chapuis asked permission to go to her bedside. Cromwell, while not refusing him this visit, replied that the king wished first to see him in private.

Responding to this invitation, the ambassador was a little surprised at the turn the interview took. In the course of an amicable stroll the king never ceased to hold Chapuis to his side, with an arm passed round the ambassador's shoulders. Saying no word about Catherine, Henry repeated what he had already told him twenty times. The French, he said, were offering him an alliance to which, unless the emperor had a change of outlook, he would feel bound to subscribe; he had loaded Chapuis' master with benefits, for which in return Charles had had him condemned by the Pope; he had proposed a union between his daughter Elizabeth and Charles's son, Philip of Spain, to which the only answer had been silence. Chapuis was wondering what this long and futile discourse might be driving at when he saw Suffolk hurrying up to announce that the queen was dying; accordingly it was too late for the ambassador to go and talk to her.

Chapuis pretended that he had noticed nothing; but realising that the king had wished to prevent a visit which he could not without offence have forbidden, he did not press his request. Next day, attended by his retinue, he rode up to the castle where Catherine was lying – and found her tired but still alive. Too weak, however, for any lengthy converse. Chapuis withdrew early but next morning he was recalled, and this time the sick woman kept him for two hours. She thanked him for his friendship which had meant, she said, that she was not going to "die in her corner like an animal".

222

Chapuis did his best to put her mind at ease both on the state of her health and on the zealous affection that her nephew felt for her. He departed but held himself ready to return at any moment.

Anne was kept informed about these visits by the friends she had made for herself among the ambassador's people. She knew that Chapuis and the Princess of Wales had met on four occasions. The comfort he had given Catherine had helped her to feel better; she was eating again and had passed some good nights. Since the doctor considered that she was out of immediate danger Chapuis packed his trunks again and prepared to return to London the next day. When he came to take his leave he found Catherine in a good humour, even laughing at her jester's jokes.

But before mounting his horse he made discreet inquiry of Dr de Lasco, Catherine's doctor, as to the suspicions of poisoning. De Lasco admitted that it was possible but that the symptoms were doubtful. In case of a relapse, he said, he would let Chapuis know at once.

But in the event he had no time to do it. On the second day after Epiphany, following two days when the patient had seemed much better, even sitting up on her bed to comb and plait her hair, the ex-queen called her servants during the night and said that she wished to receive the sacraments. The Bishop of Llandaff hurried in and wanted to say Mass straightaway. It was Catherine who reminded him that it was not the hour, but once the sun had risen the Mass was celebrated and while the bishop recited the service she made the responses herself. After communicating she fell to her prayers, calling on the priest to pray with her for the king: "I forgive him everything," she said. Then she sent for de Lasco and dictated two letters, one to Henry, the other to Charles. She then asked for extreme unction and prayed again until midday. It was while praying that she fell asleep and a little later she gave up her spirit.

Two knights rode at top speed to report the death to the palace. A young page gave the news to Anne while she was washing her fingers in a golden basin. She remained silent a long time, her hands held up and still wet, while she considered this news. Then with a sudden violent movement she emptied the water into the silver bucket and to the great astonishment of the boy threw the golden ewer and basin across the room, crying out: "Take them for yourself! I never want to see them again!" And throwing herself into an armchair she held her head in her hands.

The young page fled. He bumped into me in a gallery with his golden crockery, told me in a few words what had occurred and with a look of inquiry showed me his spoils. I signalled to him with a gesture to keep them and rushed into the room where Anne was now walking up and down. When she saw me come in: "Everyone will believe now," she said in an expressionless voice, "that Catherine died of poison." Then she said, but so low that I rather read it on her lips than heard it: "What's to do?"

Had anyone wished to promote the sinister rumour they would have conducted matters no differently. The body was stowed away so secretly as to strengthen my suspicions of Henry. Chapuis would have favoured a post mortem with particular examination of the intestines, whereas the body was hurriedly enclosed in a lead coffin. Neither the doctor nor the bishop had been granted permission to remain. Someone claimed to have come by chance on a minister who was saying to Cromwell: "It can't wait." Someone else had overheard the embalmer whisper to the bishop after cutting open the body and then sewing it up again that, surrounded by organs which themselves appeared normal, the heart was a horrible sight: all black and shrivelled, both inside and out. The bishop passed this on to the doctor who repeated it to his friends and Anne soon got to hear of it while I was with her. She had recovered her outer calm but not as yet her serenity. When I confessed to her my doubts about Henry, she answered: "Believe nothing of the sort; it would be most unlikely. Not that I think him incapable of such a crime, but he is far too much of a coward to have risked it. No, no; besides, what was he busy doing only yesterday? Planning to have Catherine thrown into the Tower of London, with a view to condemning her. She died just in time."

"Just in time?"

"To head off so crass a blunder. Catherine in the Tower of London; it would have been the signal for revolt. And the risk, for very many, of being massacred. *And the high-ranking state servants before any.*"

"Your Majesty accuses them?"

"I am not accusing anyone. The poisoning is still only a rumour. But if it really was so, who would have stood to gain?"

"A revolt could have been put down."

"Perhaps; but once the Tower had been taken by assault, with the complicity of a governor favouring Catherine, popular fury would have carried all before it. The next target would have been the palace; the garrison would have gone over to the insurgents: every one knows that except the king. Picture to yourself the carnage."

Anne went on to say that in that situation, with the king in flight leaving her behind, she would have been one of the first victims. Thus Catherine's death had saved her as well; and so she could not escape suspicion.

Then on another note she added that the principal beneficiary from Catherine's death was again the kingdom of England. For, once on the throne, Mary would have made herself even less popular than her father. Of a very poor intelligence and with little general culture, stuffed with prejudices and outworn ideas, unsure of her title, in her turn accused of having caused her father to fly or be put to death, Mary in the face of continuous and violent disorders would have had no option but to govern by terror.

At the palace not one person concealed his satisfaction. Henry himself went so far as to make display of a quite indecent joy. He publicly thanked Heaven for having removed with Catherine all differences with the emperor and so guaranteed peace. The courtiers naturally gave tongue to the same feelings. What especially alarmed the queen was to see all the Boleyns, with George and her father at their head, make a noisy exhibition of their delight, adding the hope that the dead woman would soon be joined by her daughter.

"But can they really be so blind?" said Anne in great agitation. "Do they not see that with Catherine gone we are left defenceless?"

For the moment, however, the king seemed to be in tune with this general satisfaction. After a single day of white mourning on the morrow he sported a brilliant doublet and adorned his head with feathers and ribbons; far from decreeing a season of penitence he piled on masquerades and banquets. While presiding at a ball, he had the little Elizabeth brought, took her on his arm and promenaded her through the hall, laughing happily. Then setting her on the ground he demonstrated that at the age of two she could walk like a child of four. Anne smiled, but it was a pinched smile. She made it plain that she found this gaiety out of place and disapproved it. It was only after Henry had been thrown from his horse in the course of a joust and remained for two hours unconscious that, bruised and hobbling on his game leg, he put a brake on these festivities.

Had he succumbed to his fall, who would have succeeded – Mary or Elizabeth? Anne had no illusions and during those harrowing two hours she was attacked by cramp and pains in the stomach. Then it became known that the bishop and the doctor who had seen Catherine die, Spaniards both of them, were preparing to go back to Spain, in dread of finding themselves mixed up in a case of poisoning. When the bishop was refused his passport he still hoped to reach the sea in disguise. But Cromwell's spies caught him, and both the doctor and he were thrown into the Tower of London. It was an open confession that they were being silenced because they knew too much. That evening I found Anne prostrate in her armchair; she said to me: "I'm lost".

# XIV
## (1536)

# *Mary Tudor*

That Anne should fancy she was lost seemed to me, for a long time, an exaggerated fear. For Henry's attitude to her unpredictable as always, changed from one day to another from hostility to its opposite and then back again. Each morning would find him in a different humour, so that the queen's nerves (and mine also) were put to a severe trial.

She was yet more certain of her downfall when, consequent on the fright that had struck her after the king's accident, she gave birth to a stillborn boy. With this ultimate misfortune she seemed to lose her one remaining trump. Henry's reaction was indeed just what could have been foreseen. Far from feeling sorry for her, he said it was clear to him that their marriage was accursed and that God was punishing them by refusing to give them a male child. Then, leaving the room in a fury, he added that he would have a few words to say to her when she was well enough to get up.

It was the only time that Anne lost her calm. She called him back, crying out that what had caused the miscarriage had been her fright at seeing him fall from his horse; that no-one had been so attached to him, not even Catherine, and that it broke her heart to see him take up with another woman. This clumsy outburst, so strangely unlike herself and induced certainly by the weakness following the shock of her still-birth, had of course no other effect than to fuel the king's irritation yet further. And to make his anger still more plain he left her alone at Greenwich and went back to London to have fun and games with Jane Seymour.

But a few days later when the queen was up this fit of rage had spent itself and Anne had the soothing surprise of finding herself once more the object of care and thoughtful attention. Nothing could account for this except the king's capricious humour.

Perhaps these changes of mood reflected outside events that were plunging Henry alternately into jubilation or gloom: events characterised as always by contrasts and sudden new developments.

A few months earlier Maximilian Sforza, the Duke of Milan, had died without leaving an heir. The King of France, taking the view that the duchy ought to revert to his second son, Henry Duke of Orleans, had notified the emperor of this claim and was awaiting his reply.

But the Dauphin's health was precarious and if the younger brother were one day to mount the throne, the duchy of Milan would become a French province. Further, the Duke of Orleans, by his marriage to Catherine de Medici, could advance a claim to Urbino and other neighbouring states. Should that occur the emperor would be confronted by a France dominant from the north to the centre of Italy, thus constituting a danger to the Empire: Charles could not accept this, since it would bring in its train new struggles, new wars. And so he disallowed this claim by Francis.

But he could not refuse him everything. The long siege of Tunis had weakened his finances without much affecting the position in the Mediterranean. He was in too great need of France's goodwill against the Turks to risk incurring her enmity. He therefore proposed to allocate Milan to Francis's *third* son, the Duke of Angoulême, not so close to the throne as his elder brother.

This offer of a compromise came up against the war party in France, led by Admiral Chabot. Now that Khaireddin had his fleet in good order again and was still holding Algiers Charles had a problem with the threatened coasts of Spain, Sicily and Campania. Chabot judged this to be the right moment to invade the duchy of Milan and annex it by force of arms.

Francis was tempted, but in two minds. He put a brake on this daring ambition and was satisfied to invade only Bresse and a good part of Savoy. Meantime the Swiss felt the urge to seize the canton of Vaud. This meant that the whole western side of the Alps was lost to the Duke of Savoy and so the road to Milan seemed open to all comers.

But the emperor was not slow to react. To protect Milan and Urbino he had set about organising a political and military power in the peninsula capable of coming to Savoy's rescue. He thought that a grouping of the small Italian states would meet this purpose and had arranged in Rome for Pier Luigi Farnese, the Pope's son, to be the co-ordinator. At the same time he had reinforced his army, now home from Tunis, with new troops levied in Germany and Austria.

With the threatened road to Milan no longer so easy to force, Henry saw a chance in this for himself. Francis would surely have need of his support and Charles of his neutrality. Charles therefore would take care not to give any active support to a revolt in England and this, so the king believed, would enable him to recover authority in the kingdom and influence on the continent.

But this was to miscalculate the balance of power and to forget that the emperor would long since have made haste to help Catherine and Mary if he had not feared that his doing so might bring about a break with Francis. Now that such a rupture had occurred there was no longer anything to stop him supporting the lords against the king. It was at this moment, it will be remembered, that Chapuis had made contact with the conspirators and tried, as a first move, to organise Mary's flight abroad. That plan, as we saw, came to nothing but Henry was perfectly aware that Charles's intentions had not altered and that the danger of an invasion accompanied by a rising was still very real.

He had also been forced to recognise that in France his good brother would not be seeking his aid any longer. Placed as he was in an embarrassing dilemma by the Pope's bull of excommunication, Francis's alternatives – according to whether he responded to the ban or rejected it – were either to break the English alliance or offend the Pope. He had not yet decided one way or the other and the Duke of Milan's death had not changed matters. On top of all this, Chabot had made a cruel mockery of the help that "England and her formidable fleet" could offer France. This jibe had made Henry explode in fury, especially against Anne.

Events taking place in the Baltic did nothing to put him in a sweeter temper. He had written a threatening letter to the Prince-Archbishop of Bremen calling on him to set free "his very dear friend" Wullenwever. This had been blithely ignored. In fact the officers who had arrested the former burgomaster had subjected him to a merciless interrogation and Wullenwever had had to own up to his dealings with England and the motives for his actions at Rottenburg. A second letter from Henry, still more violent, drew only the response that the archbishop was a prince of the empire and therefore anyone present on his territories came under his jurisdiction; if the writer should resort to reprisals on the citizens of Bremen in England, severe counter-measures would follow against the English in Bremen. If the king were dissatisfied he had only to complain to the emperor.

Henry might rage but he was finding at his cost that there is no worse mistake in politics than to utter threats which one has not the power to carry out. The first to pay for this mistake was the unhappy Wullenwever who, under torture, confessed to his dealings with the English ambassadors at Hamburg. Thereupon he was convicted of treason and – in his own words – even ten kings of England could not have saved him. He was thrown into a dungeon to rot.

Called together by the Archbishop of Bremen, the princes and delegates of Germany and Scandinavia met to decide on the attitude they should adopt towards Henry, for by his underhand conduct the king had extinguished the last flickers of friendship that the members of the Schmalkaldic League had retained for him. A majority of them now demanded that he be called on to give up all interference in the region and be made to pay a hundred thousand crowns to the Reformed States. Luckily for him, the opinions expressed were not unanimous and a more balanced decision was preferred by some: that Henry be asked to abstain in future from all opposition to the new King of Denmark but his face *be* saved by an offer of the title – once he had paid out the hundred thousand crowns – of Protector of the League.

The king, not knowing what line to take, came round again to confiding in Queen Anne whose intellectual superiority he was forced to recognise. She weighed up the situation at a glance; suspected that the League's counsels were divided; recommended the sacrifice of the hundred thousand crowns to make sure of having some supporters; and advised finally that the king not accept at any price the high-sounding but double-edged title of Protector of the League: not, that is to say, unless he could obtain an undertaking of reciprocal protection, so that England should be as much "protected" from invasion as she would in such a case "protect" the League. Henry should then be assured, if he found himself threatened, of military assistance financed as to half by the League: in effect, three thousand horse, five thousand mercenaries and ten ships of war. Finally, by way of mutual recognition, the League should proclaim and defend, in the world at large as in its own consistories, the validity of the divorce and of the king's remarriage.

Henry followed this advice, which was in any case acceptable to his pride. But when I wanted to read into this acquiescence the sign of a return of lasting favour Anne shook her head sceptically. "Certainly not," she sighed. "Lasting? Just so long as it will take to conclude the negotiations with the League. After which . . ." So expressive was her gesture that it made me shudder; then, knitting her brows, she said: "I must make good use of this interval of six months, or perhaps a year, to secure the crown for Elizabeth. And above all to take it from Mary; the daughter thinks like the mother, but without her highmindedness; and her first care, as I've told you, would be to bring England back into the bosom of the Church of Rome. Perhaps even to join it to the Empire. But will I have the time?"

This anxiety explains the precipitate, almost desperate attempts she made in the following weeks to have Mary renounce the crown of her own free will – attempts which may seem surprising in a woman so clear-sighted.

First she asked Chapuis himself to persuade the princess to listen to reason, to submit to the king her father, and so find herself treated with greater consideration and comfort in her retreat. Anne added that such a reconciliation would make significant contribution to good relations between Henry and the emperor. But as one would expect, the ambassador turned a deaf ear and took care not to intervene.

Unsuccessful in that direction, Anne decided to try a more direct approach. She told Lady Shelton to give her pupil, the princess, to understand that if she would drop her obstinacy and, like a respectful daughter, fall in with her father's wishes, she would find in the queen a second mother who would comply with all her desires and accord to her all possible honours; for example, on ceremonial occasions Mary would be placed not behind her but at the queen's side.

Mary's only answer was that no daughter in the world was more desirous of being obedient to the king her father – save in what would wound her conscience as a Catholic, her sentiments of honour or her fidelity to the memory of a beloved mother.

In a final attempt at conciliation Anne herself went to Hatfield to invite Mary to come to court where the queen, she said, would welcome her with affection. "I know no Queen of England," was Mary's answer, "save my late mother. But if you, Madam, as the king's concubine, were to intercede with him on my behalf you would earn my thanks." Anne kept her temper. She again made an offer of her friendship which Mary declined, and came away fully resolved to "humble this Spanish pride", as she expressed it to me on her return.

Now certain that she would get nothing out of the princess by gentle treatment, Anne had to decide to change her method. She wrote to Lady Shelton saying she must give up her charge of this recalcitrant girl since by her obstinacy Mary was ensuring an unhappy future for herself. If the king still had mercy on the princess it was solely for want of a male heir. But in nine months' time the queen would bring a son into the world and then nothing any longer would restrain the king's wrath.

It was a large commitment for Anne to make, for at the time she was not pregnant. But on her instructions Lady Shelton left the letter lying about where Mary could read it. This time she must have been frightened, for she sent a copy to her cousin Charles's ambassador. Chapuis reassured her that whatever happened the emperor would never cease to watch over her. And Mary did not give way.


Meanwhile Henry was no longer concealing his fondness for Jane Seymour. It was the gossip of the whole court; there was already talk of a new marriage and the common people made songs about it. They joked, telling one another that after these two matrimonial experiences and the extreme difficulty of a divorce the king would perhaps hesitate to tie himself down a third time, at least without the certainty of being able to go free again if he wished. Now Jane Seymour, naturally, like all the young girls of the court, must have reckoned it a sin to be still a virgin at twenty-five. So in order to marry Jane Henry need only require that her virginity be sworn on oath, and then, when the day came that he wanted to be rid of her, get together twenty young men to give evidence of perjury.

Jane meanwhile had the backing of practically the whole court in the expectation of a marriage. And I saw taking place before my eyes the very thing that Anne had feared from the start. Ministers and counsellors, following Cromwell, turned from the queen and gave their favour to Jane. They suggested to her how to conduct herself so as to achieve her ends, avoiding any blunders or awkwardness that could put Henry against her: behaviour modelled on that adopted in time past by Anne Boleyn. They pushed the young girl into the king's arms while encouraging her rigidly to hold fast to her virtue. Henry might have suspected that it was just an attitude, but this affectation of virtue seemed to please him. Or maybe in the increasing weariness induced by his ulcer he wanted to be spared from having to show what he could do . . . Whatever the reasons, Jane was rapidly securing her hold over the sovereign's heart.

One remark of the king's filled me with alarm. I overheard him telling one of the courtiers that his marriage with Anne Boleyn must have been the result of sorcery and that in consequence it could not be valid. Anne was a witch and the spell was proved by the fact that this wicked union had not been able to give them a male child.

When I repeated these menacing words to the queen she said nothing, as one resigned to her fate. Each day now brought her some additional poisoned chalice to drink. Among her new enemies she must now reckon the King of France. What! Her faithful friend? Du Bellay had had to confess to her in a tearful voice that his master was forbidding him to intervene on behalf of her and Henry.

So Francis had chosen, at least provisionally, to defer to the Holy Father's interdict. In fact when, at the beginning of winter, a consistory of the ambassadors of France and England had been held to judge the proposal to implement the sentence against Henry, du Bellay on Francis's instructions made a pretence of proposing extremely rigorous terms; this was to keep his options open, depending on how matters might turn out, between either applying the sentence or rejecting it as excessive. The cardinals deplored these uncompromising sanctions and wished Henry to be given at least the right of appeal. Many of them were apprehensive that at a time when a dangerous decline of the Church of Rome was becoming apparent all over the Continent this vindictive verdict would offend other princes in Europe and lead them to become heretics also. To the point perhaps of contaminating France, even Spain or Italy. But these prudential considerations had no effect whatever on the Pope's obstinacy. He did not want to alter a word of the sentence. When he was advised at least to consult Charles and Francis, who would have to apply the interdict, he gave a positive assurance that he had the agreement of both. Du Bellay knew well that his king had made no such commitment. And that is what he told Queen Anne, on his return, to soften the effect of so distressing a report.

The cardinals' entreaties moreover had made some impression on the Pope's irritated mind. After reflecting more sagely on the consequences that they feared he gave himself time and left the matter in suspense for several weeks. Most urgent in his view was that Anne should be repudiated and he pondered in his mind how this could be effected. Suppose, for example, Francis were to offer Henry the hand of his daughter Madeleine. He asked du Bellay to put this proposal forward. But Madeleine had just become engaged to James of Scotland.

Francis had nonetheless taken sides against Henry, and to draw closer to Charles he promised to sacrifice the alliance with England if in return Charles would sacrifice Milan. These by the way were the last confidences that Anne received from du Bellay; for the good cardinal was recalled to Paris as being too sympathetic to England.

Anne was aware that Cromwell too was secretly pursuing the hope of a warmer relationship with the Empire. Charles had made himself vastly stronger by his victory over the Turks in Transylvania. Moreover, an accommodation with him would benefit trade with Spain. Cromwell therefore asked Chapuis to let him know the emperor's terms for an agreement. Two were easy to accept: help against the Turks and for the rest a benevolent neutrality. A third condition – nomination of Mary as heir to the throne – did not seem to the chancellor totally inadmissible; for seeing Anne Boleyn on the way to being repudiated he had followed the wind and ceased to support Elizabeth. The last condition was harder to swallow: Henry was to recognise the authority of the Pope. Even so, for the reasons already mentioned, Cromwell took good care not to cause a rupture by a refusal. He asked only that discussion on the matter be postponed. And to show the ambassador how eager he was for an understanding he used the harshest expressions in speaking of Francis, the emperor's dreaded rival. He added that the cooling-off in England's attitude to France went beyond Norfolk and

Suffolk, who had always been against her; it extended now to former supporters such as the Boleyns and their friends.

All that I have just related (and much of what I have still to tell) I came to know only long after, when Anne was no longer alive. But we knew at once that the emperor was taking seriously the overtures that Cromwell had made. Catherine by her death had ceased to be an obstacle. She might have been poisoned, but for Charles this was not an insurmountable problem. Cold and calculating as he was, the end in view was what concerned him; he had few scruples himself about these expeditious methods. As for Mary, he agreed provisionally to require only that she should have honourable treatment and be married if possible to a husband of her own rank, provided he were chosen from outside England – perhaps the Infant Dom Luis of Portugal, the emperor's brother-in-law. This, he said, should suit even the concubine – his term for the queen – because it would remove Mary far from English soil. He would also give the princess to understand that she must appear less stubborn. He even added that if the concubine objected to the legitimacy of Elizabeth coming up for discussion this need not lead to the negotiations being broken off.

Anne learnt of these unexpected marks of his friendly regard from the ambassador Chapuis, whom the emperor had instructed to read, to all the interested parties, those passages in the letter which concerned them. We discussed them afterwards between ourselves, for she did not seem wildly delighted by them. (Actually, as I found out later from what followed, this goodwill was for show only. All that Charles wanted was to divide and rule, to drive a wedge between France and England so as to put him in a position to impose his will, first on one, then on the other.) "Your Majesty," I said to the queen, "seems not to notice that in fact the emperor is supporting her against Princess Mary."

"No, no," she said. "He supports me against a third wife. Chapuis has told him that I am no longer able to conceive, whereas a third wife could produce a male heir; and that would put a stop to the rights of his cousin, as it would to Elizabeth's.

If on the contrary Henry gives up the idea of renouncing me, at his death the kingdom will have only the choice between Elizabeth and Mary, and the kingdom prefers Mary."

"Even so," I insisted, "for the moment the emperor is an outright opponent of a third marriage."

"No-one, not even the emperor, will ever make Henry give up what he wants. And what he wants is Jane Seymour."

I had to recognise that on that side of things the situation was worsening from day to day, as the young woman increased her hold over the king. Edward Seymour, her brother, had just been recalled from Vienna to become, as George Boleyn had once been, a Gentleman of the King's Chamber. It was a favour there could be no mistaking. And Chapuis did not mistake it, for he at once paid court to the young man. The precise resemblance between Jane's rise and that of Anne several years earlier justified the worst fears.

Recently, too, Henry had sent a purse full of gold to his lady-friend. She had sent it back with the messenger, telling him to say to the king that she came from a family of repute; that the riches in which a young girl took pride consisted not in worldly wealth but in her honour and her virtue; and that she would never accept money from one who was not her husband.

Anne had to recognise there the kind of shrewdness that had served her so well. And since she believed that her rival was too stupid to have thought of it on her own, she traced it to the elder ladies of the court who were giving Jane lessons on how to conduct herself with the king. Henry responded as he had before, admiring the girl's modesty and promising, in guarantee of his own honourable intentions, never to address a word to so sage a person in the presence of her family.

In order to have speech with her every day he installed Edward Seymour and his wife in a room in the palace presently occupied by Cromwell, whom with his usual brutality he sent to find a bed elsewhere. The consequence was that Jane, her brother and Lady Seymour had endless opportunities of representing to the king how the whole kingdom detested his marriage with Anne and considered it illegal.

For several months Cromwell had been speaking in the same sense; to win the emperor to his side he had gone back to giving his support to Princess Mary. Often he could be seen, as he passed her in church, doffing his hat to her with ceremony: something he had not done for years. People even joked with him that he unbonneted at the mere mention of Mary's name. When Catherine died the cross of gold destined for her daughter was confiscated and assigned to the royal Treasury; Cromwell had it given back to Mary. Further, he persuaded the king, in his reply to the members of the League, to suppress the clause the queen had made him put in, stipulating that the princes should have to follow, in the matter of the divorce, the favourable opinion entertained by Melanchthon and the theologians; in which Anne, it must be admitted, had rather forced the truth since at the time bishops and Lutherans had still to meet to agree on the answer to be made. It had been a mistake, it had put the Lutherans in a delicate position from the start, and disposed them against Henry, Anne and the divorce as responsible for having set Protestantism on the defensive. Was Cromwell, in profiting from this mistake to have the clause suppressed, nursing in secret the idea of a more serious reversal of policy? Did his new line involve bringing Henry closer to the Church of Rome, if not a return to it altogether? Which would mean not only abandoning the queen but setting himself openly against her and her whole policy. Indeed, he spoke ill of the queen sometimes to the point of offending the king, still concerned that the royal consort should be treated with respect so long as he had not repudiated her.

Nothing of all this distracted Henry from his new matrimonial project. When in the course of conversation Chapuis asked Cromwell – for the emperor's information – what he really knew about such intentions, the chancellor replied that all he could say to reassure Charles was that Henry would not be going to look for a third wife in France.

This discretion and this vagueness were an embarrassment to Chapuis. If these new projects were serious, if a third wife threatened to damage Mary's interests through the birth of a Prince of Wales, ought he still to take the lead in the conspiracy against the concubine? He referred this to the emperor who, for precisely the reasons that Anne had explained to me replied that he was not sure whether the repudiation of Anne was still a thing to be wished. He instructed Chapuis accordingly to inquire from the princess herself: which would Mary prefer – the certainty of her own accession one day to the crown or to see her father drive out the usurper? In her reply Mary – and she had her letter read out to Lady Shelton so that Henry and Anne should be informed of her feelings – let Chapuis know that her own interest came after that of her father: her first care was that her father should save his soul by breaking off from a life of damnation; if he did that, she would forgive him all the harm he had done to her mother and to her.

This reply did not extricate Chapuis from his cruel state of uncertainty. At first he reverted to his original impulse and made contact again with the conspirators, involving Cromwell, who followed his line readily enough. Whereupon a message came from the king, desiring the ambassador to be pleased to kiss the queen's hand, since the emperor was at last acknowledging her as such. Curse it! Was the marriage project then abandoned? In that case better for his career to forget about the plot and show himself as a good courtier. But if the rumours were true, if Henry's intention really was to marry again, surely it would be best not to get mixed up with the queen. What should he do to avoid becoming compromised? He got out of the difficulty by sending word in answer to the king that he thought it preferable to await the conclusion of the discussions just opened on the propositions that the emperor had made in reply to Cromwell's.

But this side-stepping gave no satisfaction to Henry at all. He took it as a flouting of his own sweet will, and Chapuis found himself all at once in a situation that made him tremble. On his way to Mass the monarch took the ambassador with him to the chapel where the queen was about to enter from her side. A meeting with Anne was unavoidable and Chapuis would have to pay her his homage. The courtiers were as puzzled about it as he was himself. Did this mean that the queen was coming back into favour? However that might be, Rochford stood the ambassador beside the door by which his sister was due to enter and soon Anne made her appearance. So Chapuis had to make a respectful bow. She returned his salutation with a smile and went and sat down beside the king. On the faces of all present I noticed a tremor of surprise. What did Anne think of it herself? I did not know how to answer my own question, not having seen her for several days. Was this a new caprice of the king's, intended to mystify us all? Or a genuine return of his friendly disposition towards her?

In the course of the dinner that followed I was again able to lull myself with certain hopes. To begin with, the dinner took place in the queen's apartments. Secondly, all the ambassadors and most of the courtiers were present. But Anne did not have as neighbour the emperor's representative and I thought that not a good sign. She seemed to me to have the same feeling herself but still played her part in the game of reconciliation. Speaking to Chapuis across the table, she blamed the King of France for his conduct in Bresse and Savoy and his pretensions over Milan. If, by expressing sentiments that were not her own, she thought to please the king, the unpredictable Henry gave us a surprise. Was this yet another caprice? At all events, far from echoing her words and accusing Francis, he complained instead to Chapuis of not being treated by the emperor in a manner appropriate to England's greatness, power and munificence. It was one more display of blustering with words and I saw Anne turn pale and Cromwell shift uneasily on his seat, while the ambassador turned crimson. When Henry went on to insist that if the emperor wanted his friendship he should begin by getting the Pope's sentence annulled, I thought like all the rest that this signified an open rupture. Cromwell in particular must have believed it so because after dinner he took the king aside to a window where everyone could see that he was having a vehement dispute with him. Then he broke off and, saying that he was thirsty, abruptly walked away from the king in a burst of uncontrollable anger. As for Chapuis, he departed soon after and although the king showed great courtesy in seeing him out their parting was nonetheless icy.

As I left with the queen I thought she looked terribly shaken. "What does the king want? What does the king want?" she kept repeating. "Is it a change of policy? Or is it not simply that he wished to contradict me? To show that he can no longer bear, even at the risk of destroying everything, to have me meddling in politics? The folly of this man will send me crazy."

"Perhaps he does sincerely want a friendly relationship with France?"

"Do you know, then, how he sets about it? His way of speaking to Castelnau, who has taken the place here of my nice du Bellay? He railed violently against Francis, accusing him of ingratitude. He claimed – not that Castelnau nor anyone else will believe it for a moment after this outburst at dinner against Charles – that the emperor is making all sorts of approaches to him; that he is asking him to intervene on behalf of the Duke of Savoy; that he is seeking his help in the event of an attack on Milan; that he claims him as an ally against the Turks; and that he proposes to him a general treaty of alliance and invites Henry to be at his side on the day he enters Rome. Castelnau can only laugh at these extravagances."

She was wrong. Perhaps Castelnau did at first lend an incredulous ear to Henry. But when the king went on to tell him that to all Charles's propositions he had returned a blunt refusal; that he had declined to intervene on behalf of the Duke of Savoy; rejected any alliance which could turn against the King of France; and put in a plea for the duchy of Milan to revert to the Duke of Orleans, he was a little shaken. None of all this was true, of course, as any rational person must have realised. But when Henry said that he had been informed of substantial forces assembled by the emperor in Piedmont, and declared himself sincerely anxious to help Francis make good his positions in Bresse and Savoy before he risked such an adventure,

Castelnau must without doubt have taken seriously language so restrained and so obliging. For he made a favourable report to his king, assuring him that in his cousin of England he had a faithful and dependable ally. In a jovial letter du Bellay made haste to pass this on to his friend the queen.

Anne was much less happy about it than he expected. She was even – up to a point – rather appalled. Henry was rejecting the emperor's offers just when – or because – they might have influenced him in favour of keeping Anne as his royal consort. She knew Henry too well not to have a premonition that his change of policy, as sudden as it was paradoxical, owed nothing to any grand designs for England but served merely his mean, if not contemptible, designs for a new marriage. By protecting the queen – even if it meant in the long run protecting Mary – the emperor was working against Henry's passionate desire to marry Jane Seymour. To indulge this passion Henry would have to put off the reconciliation with Charles for a while and take it up again only after he had got rid of Anne. It followed that this encumbrance of a queen must be made to quit the scene as soon as possible.

# XV
## (1536)

# *The Trap Set*

After his altercation with the king, following the dinner at which henry had spoken insultingly about the emperor, Cromwell found himself so overwhelmed by suppressed anger, so distraught by the fear of perhaps seeing his policy wrecked, that he fell ill to the point of having to keep to his bed.

Norfolk had taken advantage of it to become the man in charge. He had profited substantially from the parcelling-out of lands confiscated when the abbeys were dissolved and had watched with a jealous eye Cromwell's attempts at closer relations with Charles, Pope Paul and thus with the Church of Rome, generally because this could lead to lands and other confiscated property being taken from him and restored to the monasteries. Had Cromwell come round already to opposing his former policy to which he now gave the name of sacrilege? The Duke accordingly had strongly supported the king in rebuffing the emperor (and, by the same token, Cromwell). Hence the propositions subsequently put to the French ambassador.

Yet hardly had Castelnau embarked at Dover than Henry, with his customary indecision, took fright. He feared that Francis, aware of Henry's diatribe against Charles and feeling his own position strengthened by this rift, would take advantage of it to become more exacting himself. Might it not be better to make some new approach to the emperor and by this means keep Francis in check? It was in this state of irresolution that Cromwell, now well again, found Henry. It encouraged him to hope that he could persuade the king to support the Cromwell policy once more. But first he had to regain the sovereign's ear and Norfolk was now firmly established in the seat of power. To challenge him directly would involve too great a risk. So having looked at the problem in all its aspects Cromwell decided that he must step out of the political arena for the moment and first give Henry satisfaction in some other interest that he had at heart; this was neither the French king, nor the emperor, but his novel passion for Jane Seymour.

In order to assuage this passion the king would have to marry the young girl just as he had had to marry Anne; which meant that he must repudiate Anne as he had repudiated Catherine. The hindrance to his doing so was his inveterate cowardice in the face of any irrevocable decision; in particular he feared the effect on public opinion of a second divorce. If the king were now to separate from the queen with no better excuse than a new love affair, who could any longer believe that in annulling the first "incestuous" union he had not resorted to a brazen pretext and thus exposed to ridicule the sacred ties of marriage?

These two difficulties, seemingly insurmountable, could prove a trump in Cromwell's hands. Let him find the solution, let him – Cromwell – achieve what Henry would recoil from putting his own hand to and – lo and behold! – he would be restored in full to the king's favour.

For several good reasons, however, this trump could be a weak one. First, if he played it he would be without an ally; he had tried to obtain the Bishop of London's opinion on a similar problem and the prelate had replied that "he would discuss such a matter only with the king and even then only if he could be sure that the king would not later change his mind, for he much regretted having formerly supported Henry against Catherine". Cromwell would also have the whole Boleyn interest against him. Besides, even supposing that he got the divorce, Anne would still be Marquis of Pembroke; with a substantial fortune to back her she would carry influence as Catherine had, repudiated though she was: Anne in her search for vengeance against Cromwell could prove an enemy as implacable as she had been for Wolsey. Finally, Norfolk or

Cranmer or some other churchman might in advance of Cromwell ferret out some biblical text which could be interpreted as being in support of a divorce and so establish a claim to the king's gratitude, thereby dispatching Cromwell into outer darkness.

For all these reasons he had to strike fast and hard; the faster and the harder because this was the right moment: the iron seemed hot and it must be struck before it cooled. For the second time Henry was showing an inclination – but would it last? – to edge away from all the Boleyns. The first sign had been the recent affair of the Garter. One of the Knights had died and Rochford, Anne's brother, had felt sure of being awarded the vacant ribbon. His rival, Sir Nicholas Carew, was an enemy of Anne. A few weeks earlier and the king would have accorded it to George; now it was Nicholas who won it. The whole court interpreted the rebuff as signalling the imminent disgrace of the Boleyns, whose detractors, given this encouragement, were promptly joined by those who hitherto had been hesitant. Straightaway the Princess Mary found herself inundated with letters professing allegiance and congratulating her on the revival of her own hopes.

So it was the right moment; and Cromwell was set to seize it. But how? A divorce, even if grounds for one could be cleverly made out, would again take much too long, and be unsure and dangerous. It followed that what had to be got rid of was the person of Anne Boleyn herself, without attacking her status as wife or queen. Rather than cast about any longer for ways to repudiate her, better to have her prosecuted, judged and condemned – whether to exile, imprisonment or death would not matter so long as the marriage became void.

I do not know how Anne came to be aware of Cromwell's fell designs. By his embarrassed manner perhaps when they found themselves together. No man is so harsh or so inflexible that he can – without letting up for an instant – avoid every look, every false smile, every twitching of his muscles that would let a victim who is on her guard perceive that there is a plot to ruin her. Hard, downright, stubborn, insensitive as

Cromwell's face might be, Anne knew it too well not to register its most fleeting intimations.

"What this traitor is plotting against me," she said, "I do not know, but it is something sinister and I dread it."

"Do we not know? It is the divorce – to please the king."

"No, that would take too long. Better if they could invent some ground of complaint against me that would put me outside the law."

"He would not dare. Besides, that would not set the king free. Remember: Catherine, banished from his bed and exiled to the country, nonetheless remained his wife."

"It's true. He must be pondering, then, some villainy of another kind."

It occurred to me, though I did not mention it, that Cromwell might be thinking of giving it out that she was mad. But Joanna the Mad, Queen of Spain, had not been deposed for that and when her husband Philip died the old King Henry had even thought of marrying her, thus making her Queen of England as well. This led me to fear an attempt at poisoning and I warned Anne.

"It's possible," she said, "but not likely. The days of the Borgias when you could poison without risk have gone by and Catherine's death, still unexplained, has compromised the king overmuch already."

"May Your Majesty nonetheless be on her guard!"

"You may be sure of it," she said, kissing me. "I have no longing whatsoever to die."

I did not want to be too confident but I thought that once on the watch Anne with her natural shrewdness would find ways in the weeks ahead to discover the particular danger in which she stood.

But if Anne was shrewd, Cromwell was diabolic. It was not till much too late that she realised the truly satanic manoeuvre he had embarked upon. He began by putting on an air in the king's presence of having something on his mind until Henry asked him what it was. He said he had suspicions of a plot that was being weaved. There were always plots, one after the other, so at first Henry saw nothing in this to take notice of. But when, shortly after, Cromwell spoke of his fears that this plot was being hatched within the king's own circle, Henry lent an ear. And when finally Cromwell said he was almost certain that the mainspring of the plot would be found among the Boleyns – a presumption made plausible by the fact of their disgrace – Henry was quick to believe it, for he saw that this could give him a godsent opportunity to be rid of Anne.

Without any shilly-shallying therefore he gave Cromwell full powers to conduct an inquiry into any form of treason and to carry it through to its conclusion, no matter what might be the rank or quality of the persons found to be implicated.

So armed, it seemed to Cromwell that he had attained his object. But changeable as the king might be, he was no less astute – nor in consequence less wary. Since Cromwell was obviously inventing a plot with all the pieces in place he might well go on later to invent other combinations. There could for example be no certainty that, having once set up and won this cases on the basis of false testimonies or forged evidence, he might not then threaten to reveal its baseness and illegality so as to have a hold on the king and effectively become sole master of the kingdom.

To avoid this risk the accusation must not come from Cromwell but rest on a commission of men of note either honest, or reputed to be such, and so render the Crown clear of all suspicion. This would pre-empt any attempt at blackmail and likewise any subsequent rumour.

Accordingly Henry ordered Cromwell to set up a commission which, to make it appear more impartial, would include a minority of partisans of Anne Boleyn. Indeed one of the first to be nominated was her father, the Earl of Wiltshire.

From him Anne learnt of the inquiry and that it would be presided over by her uncle Norfolk, now her enemy; she understood thereby that her fate was sealed. Like the hapless Wolsey in his time she knew that where an action is brought by the Crown a plea of "not guilty" becomes, under the law, a crime of high treason. We were dumbfounded.

Sometimes when calamity is at hand one misfortune is closely followed by another of infinitely less importance, but which nevertheless hurts cruelly. Anne had always been fond of dogs. She had several, including Urien, a superb greyhound from Italy and Little Purkoy, her favourite, a spaniel of exquisite beauty. And it was at this very moment that her beloved spaniel died. It was a sinister omen for Anne. She no longer had any doubt of the fate in store for her.

She said so to her father. Wiltshire would have none of it, persuaded that since he was of the commission there would be no case brought against any Boleyn. It was only when he was told to keep the inquiry a strict secret that he began to worry. Then, when the commission, instead of sitting in plenary session, appointed four of its members to take the business further, when, so far from himself being one of the four, he saw the nobles most embittered against the queen – with Cromwell and Norfolk at their head – nominated to preside, his anxiety gave way to panic. He realised that he had been duped, that his daughter had been condemned in advance, and that his own downfall would follow. Whereupon he lost no time in turning against his daughter, in ranging himself among her accusers and in so informing the king.

All Cromwell now had to do was to draw together the heads of the indictment against Anne. The most effective would be to charge her with having poisoned Catherine. But this would not be without danger for the king and in consequence for himself. Better to keep it as a last reserve. And since there were no means, however far-fetched, of convicting her of attempts against the king, there was nothing for it but to fall back on her private life, in other words to charge her with adultery.


On this head witnesses would not be lacking. Anne Boleyn's relations in time past with Henry Percy, and later with her cousin Wyatt, were matters of public knowledge. If there was nothing to prove that she had accorded them her favours there was nothing to prove the contrary. But if they were cited, quite certainly Percy and Wyatt would make vigorous denials which would unsettle public opinion. Besides, even if they confessed it, this would involve Anne in disrepute but not in adultery, since out of marriage this could not arise. But to prove it within marriage, one would come up against a major obstacle: the king would never allow the legitimacy of his daughter Elizabeth to be called in question and any incriminating testimony on this score would involve the crime of high treason. It would be very difficult therefore to persuade any, even the most devoted, to expose himself to proceedings that would be fatal if he dared to attribute misconduct on the part of the mother, before the princess was born. In short, the past must be written off. There remained the present or rather the future; there was the possibility that the queen could do today or tomorrow what she could not be proved to have done already; merely to give grounds for such belief would be sufficient.

Cromwell accordingly set on her tracks a whole army of spies, one of whom at least would surely have the luck to be witness of an indiscretion or of something that could be given the appearance of such and from which the desired conclusion could later be drawn. That the queen could not avoid compromising herself Cromwell had no doubt. Her small personal court contained enough high-spirited gentlemen and the least mark of intimacy between herself and another, surprised no matter where – in the garden, in a passage, between two doors – would more than do the trick. And since Anne, deserted by all, would be in such bitter need of her few faithful that increasingly she must seek out their company, let her be found alone with one of them just a moment and she would fall into the trap they had set for her.

At this point in our story I am concerned not to pass over anything in silence. The least concealment would lead to the false idea that there was something to hide. In fact no-one was better placed than myself to have known and be able to state positively that in this domain the life of Anne Boleyn was transparent.

People have said that the queen was vain, that she was a

coquette. They have said that she liked to make herself adored, that to wind your way into her good graces you needed only to show yourself an admirer. I will not deny that during these critical weeks she let herself be drawn into situations that could be misconstrued. When you lose all your friends, one after another, what means will you employ to hold on to those who remain? Will you not bind them to yourself by force of sentiment? Then you must go on to keep this affection alive. For a young courtier the temptation to sail with the wind is powerful – not only for ambition's sake but so as not to perish with those who perished. And those who still held out for the love of Anne, how could she not have clung to them, as the shipwrecked sailor to the spars that have not gone down with the ship? Cling she did, but I can attest that her conduct never passed the bounds of virtue. Besides, it was in her interest: a lover once satisfied slips away more easily than one who hopes; Henry was the proof of it. But neither must you be too aloof, to the point of destroying all hope. It would be this that gave play to the unworthy rumours circulating at court, to the charges in the indictment and, at the inquiry itself, to the allegations made by Cromwell's spies.

A stag at bay is lost; and Anne was at bay. From now on she had a pack unleashed against her. If in those conditions she had, as we say, "sinned" she would have had much excuse. She did not, for the reasons I have given and for another which I shall now mention: Anne had never entirely got over a certain repugnance she felt about physical love. Moreover, a queen cannot take a single step, open or shut a door, but that the whole court will know it. In a palace crammed with domestics night and day, where ladies and gentlemen are for ever on the move, nothing can remain secret or even unobtrusive. Everything becomes known at once. Indeed, Cromwell could have done without his spies to give evidence were it not that their master's protection meant that they ran no risk whatever of being prosecuted for high treason. But the evidence they gave would surprise no-one who had witnessed the same doings.

Of the brilliant little court, now more and more reduced,

which revolved around Queen Anne there remained only a handful of gentlemen, but those still ready to die for her. One is famous to this day: her cousin Thomas Wyatt, but there was no malicious gossip about the poet – as much because his poems were loved as for the fear of getting into his bad books. The queen's relations with other favourites might have seemed less chaste (though here too one would have accused her wrongly).

On one of them she counted much; he was called Mark Smeaton. Well-read, sensitive, very musical, an artist to the finger-tips (but I had always suspected him of a certain weakness of character), he came of a family of modest fortune. Assuredly he loved the queen with a tender affection but I can guarantee that she gave him nothing in return but the same tenderness, founded on the passionate taste they shared for things of beauty. Now for some little time I had watched with anxiety Anne clinging on to this man, when it was all too evident that he was edging increasingly away from her each day. "The rat deserts the sinking ship," I told myself in alarm. All the same I hesitated to upset Anne by making known to her what I thought; besides, I was convinced that she must see in him what I saw. But, as I've said already, what drowning man will not clutch on to a plank, though it be rotten?

One day at a reception given by the queen – there were spies in every corner – the gallant was observed to be standing alone on a balcony, with a grumpy look on his face which he made no attempt to hide. Anne could not resist joining him there to ask the reason for this moodiness.

"That's my business," he replied in an off-hand manner. The queen was deeply offended.

"And that's an impertinence," she told him, "as low as your own origins. Do not imagine that I will ever again say a word more to you than you deserve."

"There's no need," he said. "I can read it all in your looks." Whereupon he left her standing there and with great strides crossed the balcony, passed through the drawing-room, descended the grand staircase and the outer steps and disappeared by the court of honour.

As it happened, I was under the balcony at the time and had overheard these few words, spoken low though they were. I was not the only one. One of Cromwell's spies must have reported them to him, for next day Smeaton, riding back to London, was stopped on the road. Subjected in the Red Chamber to a savage interrogation he confirmed my impression of him by avowing all that they wanted, except on one point: his personal relations with the queen, he said, had been no more than friendly. But the first turn of the screw made him declare that the queen had lovers; at the second he gave quite readily the name of Francis Weston; at the third that of Henry Norris; at the fourth, all in one go, those of Richard Page, Edward Bryerton and Thomas Wyatt. At the fifth he admitted without being asked that Anne had had incestuous relations with her brother George. At the sixth turn of the screw he said no more, having by then lost consciousness.

I was naturally not to know of these absurd "confessions" of Smeaton until the case came on. When one after the other this covey of gentlemen were arrested I believed like everyone else that they were suspected of a plot. The implications of this would be no less terrifying, since the queen would be involved. As it turned out I was not far wrong: the bill of indictment would refer both to adultery and to conspiracy. But it was only after it was all over that I came to understand how the six young men, but in particular Smeaton, Weston and Norris, had contributed to their own fate by their behaviour.


All three, at the period of Anne's coronation, were Gentlemen of the King's Chamber. Quite soon she had attached them to her service as her escort; with, it is true, many other young men, all, like them, full of wit and gaiety. For a long time this little court around the queen had rung with their laughter and bright sayings. But since the death of Catherine and the rise of Jane Seymour the sparkle had disappeared and the atmosphere had turned heavy. Witty they might be, these young courtiers, but they were light-weight and their ranks had thinned. Of them all only those three and three others remained loyal – even so, Bryerton was so discreet that I was hardly conscious of his presence and Page almost as unobtrusive.

If the first of the three, Mark Smeaton, could not stand up to the torture – a man of subtle wit, he was also a coward, a fact of which he was perhaps unaware himself – the second, Francis Weston, showed more spirit. He was the son of Sir Richard Weston, vice-treasurer of the Exchequer. He had been page to the king for a long time before becoming Gentleman of the Chamber and a Knight of the Order of the Bath; altogether he had been resident at court for close on ten years. A year before Anne's coronation he had married the daughter of the late Christopher Pickering, which had brought him other large properties in addition to his already splendid fortune in lands, rents and pensions. Less of an artist than Smeaton, he was better read and above all of a much stronger character; the queen's disgrace had in no way shaken his fidelity. Anne had a great liking for him; as for myself, his death was more of a shock to me I can tell you.

He was said, although a married man, to be in love with the queen. I have good reason to think that Margaret Shelton attracted him yet more. He paid assiduous court to her and, as I know from a reliable source, she was by no means unresponsive.

If Francis and Maggie were lovers in the dark it was because the king, when he had grown tired of her, had betrothed her to the other compromised gentleman, Henry Norris. Long a favourite of the king and keeper of the privy purse, Norris had been one of the architects of Wolsey's fall and had then attached himself to the Boleyns and to the queen especially. As a fiancé for Margaret he was by no means gallant. For his heart was elsewhere, and this "elsewhere" was very highly placed. But his intentions were so well concealed that only the queen and Margaret Shelton – and I – had any suspicion of where they pointed.

Anne sailed very close in these crossed intrigues, rebuking Norris for having his thoughts more on another than on his betrothed and wanting Francis to be more attentive to his wife instead of paying court to Maggie. She told him so and perhaps the answer that he gave was meant to baffle this justified suspicion. He said that there was only one person in his heart but she was beyond his reach. These last words, pronounced as he pronounced them, could leave Anne in no doubt of the identity of the "person". She did not believe it, but all the same she made no protest. In her helpless plight she wanted, we may be sure, to believe that neither in Weston nor in Norris was there smoke without fire; that by putting up with the smoke of their words she was fanning the flame of their hearts; and that without such encouragement she would have run great risk of the flame going out.

Anne was incapable, however, of hiding anything and she opened her heart to me. We both loved dearly her cousin Margaret, whose heart if she had known what Francis had said might have been broken. I told Anne that Maggie would surely be touched if the queen were to speak to her openly but that for the sake of Her Majesty's happiness she would certainly withdraw. Anne smiled, kissed me and said that she had given her heart to no-one; that the pretended love of Francis was aimed above all at preserving Maggie's reputation; and that Norris's love was no more than the ambition to be well placed to marry the widow if the king by any chance should happen to pass on. Despite our sad plight we had a good laugh about it together. Then she admitted that she needed their support too much to put them back in their place and see herself abandoned.

Neither of us at that moment could foresee that these young men's devoted friendship, far from supporting Anne, was to prove fatal to her.

# Thomas Cranmer

Often at sea the most violent gale is preceded by a strange period of calm. Just so, although the climax was close at hand, the life at Greenwich went quietly on. No-one unless he had special knowledge could have believed that anything out of the ordinary was in store. On the first of May a tournament was held at Deptford near Greenwich. To see Anne and the king in their gallery draped in velvet and gold, both of them clad sumptuously in gala outfits, no-one could have guessed how matters stood between them. No more than to see Rochford, the queen's brother, superb on his palfrey with the Boleyn arms, break lances with Weston and Norris to the sound of applause, the king clapping his hands as readily as any. He made the victors come forward to receive his congratulations, leaving the queen the honour of handing to them their cups and trophies.

When the tournament was over, Henry climbed heavily on to his horse; he had grown older and stouter and his leg hurt him; he had lost the spring of former times. He called Norris to him, and while riding beside him, he asked him what he thought of the queen's chaplain. Rather surprised, the young man said that he had talked with him only once; the man had seemed very pious and had given Norris wise advice. Then why had Norris sworn to him that the queen's morals were above reproach? Taken aback, Norris stammered out that the chaplain had questioned him rather sharply on the subject. The king then said that if Norris would admit to having had adulterous relations with her he promised him forgiveness and even some advancement, but that he should be merciless if Norris would not confess it. Norris replied that to do so would be perjury. He knew, while he said this, that he was digging his own grave; and perhaps he did love the queen sincerely, for he swore again that she was the purest of women. Whereupon Henry in a fury rode off at full tilt, leaving Norris where he was. And it was no great surprise to the young man, coming up a little after, to find himself surrounded by six archers and led off under escort to the Tower of London.

The patrol was commanded by Sir William Fitzwilliam who in his turn urged Norris to make the avowal but with no better success. Half in anger, half jeering, he left him, saying that he was going straight back to Greenwich where the commissioners would be interrogating the queen in his presence and she would confess everything.

It was only a threat – all this became known later through Norris's chaplain – but the reality was not much more encouraging. When at bed-time Anne learnt that Smeaton, closely followed by Norris, had been taken to the Tower – before even being informed of the circumstances of their arrest – she called for me and told me that her hour had come. I tried to reassure her but she felt certain that under torture both would confess to anything. On my advice she had herself conducted in the morning to Whitehall to see the king, but he had fled; though he hated her, this braggart was still afraid of her and of the ascendancy which in spite of her disgrace she maintained over him; and abandoning Whitehall he had gone for refuge to Westminster. In the evening she took the road again to Greenwich, followed in the shadows by two armed figures who kept close to her carriage. Realising that she was in the hands of Cromwell and his minions, at midnight she considered fleeing. At that hour the whole palace was asleep and with care it would be easy to make a discreet exit, passing through the attic and going out by the gardens. While the queen was putting together some necessary items I went off to make sure that the way was clear, then to the stable to saddle two mares to carry us to the waterside. But when I returned she had given up the idea, saying: "I cannot abandon Elizabeth."

"But if harm comes to Your Majesty the princess will be abandoned just the same."

"There is a big difference. To run away would be to confess that I am an adulteress and would leave my daughter to be declared a bastard. In Cromwell's hands, in Henry's, perhaps in Mary's, she would be banished or worse. If I am not to turn my back on everything that I have done, her legitimacy takes first place. She must be queen."

Anne added that supposing one could elude the sentinels we would find the customs officers at the port and *they* would not be asleep. How could we hope to get on board without the alarm being given? I offered to go ahead and, although there was a moon, make use of the night to slip into a small boat so as to pick her up at some place along the coast which would not be watched. Once on board a fishing-boat it would be a simple matter with the help of a little gold to get through to Ostend or Boulogne. When she shook her head I made the further suggestion that she should take Elizabeth with her. "Impossible," she said; "I can neither take her with me nor fly without her. And what's more, if I *were* to fly, neither Charles nor Francis would want to give me a welcome. Even if they didn't hand me over to Henry, at least they would have me put back on board ship. And where should I find refuge? In Denmark, in Norway? I have no friends there and would be flying from port to port. No, no, Maggie dear, let us think of it no more and as in all things resign ourselves to God."

It was resigning herself rather to the devil. Next morning she was summoned to appear. She obeyed and was conducted to Westminster, still closely followed all the way by two officials. She presented herself at the Council where she learnt from the king's commissioners what powers they had been given. Immediately they began pressing her to acknowledge her adulterous relations with Smeaton and with Norris, assuring her that both had confessed to them. When she cried out indignantly and got up to go, one of the officers brutally threw her back into her seat. Another, placing both his hands on her shoulders, forced her to stay where she was. She wanted to protest that this was not fit treatment for a royal personage but she saw that apart from the Marquis of Winchester no-one was listening to her. Norfolk was looking up at the ceiling; Fitzwilliam filing his finger-nails. She lost hope and said no more. For three hours then they pestered her with questions. They could get nothing out of her, but finally her exhausted nerves gave way and she burst into tears. They must have pushed her hard and savagely to reduce her to that, since even when things were at their worst I had never seen her weep. Now when she passed me, as they led her away to the royal apartments, I could see she was in tears.

Next day she was brought back to Greenwich. I was not able to see her there, for she was kept out of sight. I knew at once when Norfolk appointed four ladies to accompany her that she would be shut up in the Tower of London. He did not want to seem to surround her with spies but rather to appear impartial, so he had contrived a subtle mixture: myself first, whose love for the queen was common knowledge; then Lady Boleyn, wife to Uncle James but – to put it mildly – little attached to her niece by marriage; a Mistress Stonor, nice, insignificant but entirely opportunist; finally a Mrs Coffin, a stout woman whose friendly-looking face seemed to belie her rather sinister name but who filled me straightaway with insurmountable mistrust.

I hoped we should be allowed to meet Anne again in her apartments but we were told to stay where we were. It was only at the moment of leaving – it had to be at flood tide so as to travel upstream more easily – that we were summoned to follow her.

While I was fretting during what seemed an interminable wait I did not know that at that very hour Viscount Rochford was being arrested. Was it for fear that he might stir up his sister's friends or did they want to accuse him along with her of incestuous adultery? Probably both, on the word of his wife Lady Rochford. She had been on bad terms with her husband for a long time. She was a jealous and envious woman who hated the queen and had always resented George's brotherly affection for Anne. Their mutual understanding, often full of banter and mockery, profoundly irritated her slow intelligence. Before the commissioners she admitted, with her eyes modestly lowered, that suspicious meetings between the two had often convinced her that they felt for one another a criminal passion. This was accepted as prime evidence. But when they then wished to call Thomas Boleyn they found he had made himself scarce. And it was from a distant province that he wrote to Cromwell to dissociate himself from an unworthy daughter whose conduct, so he said, he had always condemned.

I did not yet of course know anything of all this when at last the wait at Greenwich came to an end. A little before mid-day we embarked with Anne and four soldiers fully armed, preceded by another vessel in which were Cromwell, Norfolk, three lords and an escort of guards. In the sunshine a number of small boats were plying on the River Thames, some on fishing or transport business, the rest rounded up by the queen's enemies for the pleasure of witnessing her dethronement. My heart was wrung to think that our passage would be marked by hoots and gibes but this at least we were spared. It may be that, still queen, Anne imposed the respect due to her title; or perhaps her royal bearing, so noble and dignified, caused her enemies' insults to die upon their lips. In the same funereal silence as on the day of her coronation and under the same blue sky Anne found herself for the second time making the three-hour journey on the Thames up to the Tower.

Norfolk, Cromwell and the other lords landed first so as to await her with Kingston, the constable of the Tower, at the Traitors' Gate. Chapuis was there also, to be able to report to the emperor how by the judgement and punishment of God the concubine had sunk at last into the depths of vilest ignominy. Which was not true. Never for an instant that day did Anne carry herself as other than a queen.

She knew, and so did I, that Sir William Kingston had always remained loyal to Catherine and Mary. The fear had struck me that she would be thrown – with her four attendants – into some dark and damp dungeon but fortunately I was wrong. Whether the queen in her fallen state still inspired her due deference in her gaoler, or whether the king, if not out of remorse then as a last tribute of respect, had given the order – at all events it was in the same royal apartment where she had awaited the coronation that the three ladies of honour and I found ourselves with her once again. Lady Kingston, the governor's wife, even came to offer what she could to lessen the severity of the sad days that lay ahead. The first service that Anne requested was that she should fix up in the little chamber adjoining our room a chapel where she could pray to God for her soul's salvation if mercy were not to be granted her. The governor's wife frowned but Anne once more declared herself innocent of the adulteries of which she was accused. When a little later Lady Kingston passed this on to her husband his response was to order her to leave the premises at the first word that the prisoner might again speak in her defence.

Did Cromwell know that while his aim was to limit the legal proceedings to Anne and her "accomplices" he was in fact letting loose a tremendous hurly-burly? The news had spread in London with the speed of the wind, a wind at once of excitement and of terror. All the "gentry", whether at court or not, were caught up in the ferment. There was a rash of denunciations. Anne's enemies had other enemies of their own whom they saw a chance to ruin – and acquire their property at the same time. Fortune lay ahead for whoever could find new suspects, new guilty men. The commissioners noted all this down and kept calling for incriminating evidence. From one day to the next the multiplication of proofs and of accomplices was prodigious. The thing acquired dizzy proportions. None of those few people who were heart-broken by Anne's calamity, nor of the friends of the three young men arrested along with her and her brother, dared to raise a finger on their behalf. One who nonetheless made the venture paid dearly for it: the knight Roland Buckley, Chamberlain of North Wales and an intimate friend of Henry Norris. He had a brother, Richard, who was well placed at Court, and wrote him a letter begging him to intercede. But he must have been watched, for the bearer of the envelope was arrested on his way, searched and imprisoned. The envelope was handed to the Bishop of Lichfield who forwarded it to Cromwell. Roland was interned in the town gaol. This served as a public warning to everyone not to interfere in what was not their business.

There was one casualty of a higher rank, the Archbishop Thomas Cranmer. For a long time now his credit had fallen, together with the queen's, and one hardly ever heard him spoken of. He spent most of his time at Canterbury and was there when a letter from Cromwell reached him, telling him of the arrests and forbidding him to reappear at court. Cranmer saw his last hour come. Hoping however that Henry still had the Church of England at heart, he began to address a petition to him to the effect that if he struck at the queen who had helped to found that Church, he was disavowing those who had worked with her, of whom Henry himself was the first. But he had scarcely taken pen in hand before an official brought him an order to repair to Lambeth, the London residence of the archbishop, and there await the king's good pleasure. Two days later he received a summons to cross the Thames and appear before the council at Westminster. There he again tried to take up the argument that he had wanted to put before the king but the four councillors interrupted him. They informed him of the "proofs" that they had against the queen and ordered him to declare himself either for or against her. Trembling all over, the archbishop broke down, saying hurriedly that he was convinced of her guilt and swearing that he would never again acquaint the king with what he had in mind. He was then allowed to go. To make his position still more secure he wrote at once to Henry, this time protesting his horror at the odious crimes of Anne Boleyn. Even so, he was sent back to his diocese with instructions not to leave it.

Meanwhile at the Tower the ladies of honour and I were allowed to serve the queen but forbidden to have speech with her except in the presence of Kingston or his wife, so that no confessions she might make should be lost. I was never at any moment able to be alone with her and so I had no opportunity to ask her why she had spoken to Lady Kingston as she did. Mrs Coffin, while giving the impression of being harmless and obliging, nevertheless put to her a great many insidious questions which – to my amazement and alarm – Anne answered quite openly. It was in this way that I learnt, at the same time as Lady Kingston, all that I have mentioned earlier of her relations with Smeaton, Weston and especially Norris. I made desperate signs to her, feeling sure that all that she was saying, instead of proving her innocence as she seemed to think, would be repeated to Cromwell who would interpret it in his own way and use it to strengthen his case. But she either did not see me or did not want to see me. At the time I shuddered to think that she was losing her nerve and giving way to an irrepressible desire to speak out. But it would have been out of character, and I have since become convinced that her motive was indirectly to put me wise to all that I did not know so that later, possessed of the whole truth, I would be able to restore her good name for posterity – which is the sacred task I am engaged on.

It was only in listening to her, by the way, that I learnt at all of the existence of Bryerton; in answer to an underhand question from Mrs Coffin Anne said she met him only rarely. I knew nothing of his origins myself. But in his turn he was seized and put in prison. In the days that followed came the arrest of two others whom Anne knew well – or rather, had once known well: Richard Page and Thomas Wyatt. Not to mention a good number of gentlemen who were called before the council and there threatened, hustled and bustled into putting a sinister interpretation on everything that had occurred in the queen's circle and then set free: free but so terrorised that not one would ever have dared to go back on the evidence drawn out of them by these means.

Thus abandoned by all, the eight prisoners were finally summoned to appear. But Wyatt had become famous and a popular hero. Cromwell decided that to bring a charge against him would be too dangerous and so, while keeping the poet in the Tower, he refrained from any further action against him. Fitzwilliam obtained a pardon for Richard Page, his cousin whom he loved dearly. Both, however, while still in prison were told that when they were released later they must disappear for a while into the far-off provinces of the north.

Finally, the grand jury at Westminster was given the verdict of the inquiry. Anne was convicted of having had culpable relations – incestuous with her brother George; adulterous with Smeaton, Weston, Norris and many others – of being, in fact, a genuine Messalina. She had accorded them her favours in order to drag them into a plot against their Sovereign. She had admitted to having hated her royal husband and so as to be able to marry one of her numerous lovers had thought of poisoning Henry as she had poisoned Catherine. Finally, by her abominable conduct and the mockeries she showered on the talents of His Majesty she had exposed her gracious Sovereign to ridicule and public contempt. All this by plunging the unhappy king into the deepest distress had so affected his health as to bring him near to the gates of death.

Even supposing that Anne Boleyn had not been the irreproachable queen and rare woman whom I knew; nay, suppose even that she had shared in the debauches to which the whole court – except herself – gave way; who could honestly lend credence to this ridiculous list, to the gross stupidity of the indictment? And yet this is what has happened. Everyone has believed it; everyone still does. This image of a spiteful, vulgar, ambitious and perverted queen is the one which more than twenty years after her death still holds sway.

Have I known how to set this odious portrait right? How to show you Anne Boleyn as she really was in her days of power? Or must a distorted picture of her prevail into all future time? I would like in my old age to be sure that these inexpert pages will triumph over the lie. But has one ever seen, in the course of centuries, the truth about a king or a queen get the better of their legend?

*

During this period of deep distress Henry celebrated the imprisonment of Anne just as he had recently the death of Catherine, piling on the banquets, balls and masquerades – and that with so joyous an ardour that even the court took offence. I have reason indeed to ask myself whether this exaggeration of rejoicings was not meant as a way to drown his private thoughts. To the Duke of Richmond, the bastard whom he had by his first favourite, Bessie Blount, Henry had given a glimpse not of course of regret or remorse but, in between insulting remarks about Anne, something very like terror. As though Anne's absence appeared to the king like an abyss; as though on one side of him land had disappeared. Ever since he had married her – and even earlier – had she not been his brain and his will-power? What should he do from now on, left alone to take all the decisions? Even when he most hated Anne, most wearied of her, it was she whom he still consulted at the first serious difficulty. This sudden solitude in the face of perils without and within forced him to take a good look at himself and what he saw he did not like. He now saw in the mirror, beneath the powerful, well-set frame, both feet firmly on the ground, only the poor hesitant man that he was; beneath his brutality, tyranny, cruelty only the cowardice which had given rise to them; beneath the culture and the education he had received only the dangerous lack of thought or inspiration. Anne's intelligence, the vigour and liveliness of her mind had been the remedy for all that. But now?

This is perhaps why, for fear of having to take note of this void within himself, he went beyond the bounds of decency, dancing, guzzling food and drink, making carousal as though his joy wanted the court and the whole kingdom to be its witness. Far from hiding his orgies within the walls of the palace he prolonged them out of doors. Drunken dancing at night with shouts, laughter and trumpetings disturbed the indignant sleepers on either bank of the Thames and the fishermen watching by their nets. These saturnalia lasted on into the small hours. While Queen Anne, even suppose she had been an adulteress, was stagnating in a prison, gilded though

264

it might be, this provocative merry-making sounded very wrong in people's ears. Without being moved to sympathy for Anne Boleyn, they were seized with a strong antipathy against this king who was trumpeting his joy at the graveside. And carrying his impudence so far as to read aloud to the whole court and in presence of bishops and ambassadors a spiteful tragedy which he had written, so he told them, about Anne Boleyn and which ended on the scaffold. This avowal of what he was intending to do was thought by all to be in the most shocking taste. Chapuis and the Bishop of Carlisle complained to one another about it, as reflecting far worse on the king's own reputation than on that of a woman of whom admittedly they disapproved.

Often when a child has done something wrong, instead of putting it right he will aggravate the error by trying to make out that he was justified. In the same way Henry expended much energy in intervening personally in the perverse procedure which he had hitherto been astute enough to entrust to others. He thought up new complaints against Anne with a clumsiness so stupid that it gave the lie to the proofs the commissioners had been so laboriously constructing.

Unfortunately, where matters now stood, no blundering could bring help to the unhappy prisoners. There was no longer any need even to hand-pick the jury in the law-court so as to be sure of their goodwill. They were there only for the show. The session had become such a formality that none of the accusers took the trouble to attend, neither Cromwell nor a single one of the commissioners. And the accused were dispatched to Westminster Hall, there to be judged and condemned.

It was on a fine morning in May that the session of the king's tribunal opened in the Star Chamber at Westminster, which served for meetings of the king's council and for tribunals of the Crown. The windows opened on the orchards and you could see the apple and cherry trees in blossom; in the sky you could hear the twittering of swallows. This time, all the commissioners were present; they sat as judges under the presidency of Sir Thomas Audley (afterwards a baron and chancellor). Even Thomas Boleyn had come back to take his seat so as to let the king see how wholly devoted he was.

The jury was made up of men who were no more impartial: its members were twelve officials of the king. One, a cousin of the Boleyns, openly declared himself their enemy; another had the profitable post of tax collector; a third was an official of the Exchequer; a fourth was expecting to be nominated to the House of Lords; another had signed a bill for £10,000 to Cromwell's order, payable at any moment; two jurymen were receiving pensions from the Crown; of the five others, one was son-in-law to the late Thomas More; another, bailiff of Wakefield; a third, captain of the castle of Bewcastle, while the two remaining were wardens, one of Plumpton Park and the other of the castle of Sandale. They in turn had to make a show of taking the oath, binding themselves to judge according to their soul and conscience. Then the prisoners were called in.

Kingston introduced them in order: Smeaton, Norris, Weston and Bryerton. Smeaton appeared dazed. The three others listened in a haughty silence to the bill of indictment. By the way, it was not until they were thus read aloud in court that the defendants became aware of the charges being brought against them. They were expecting to be charged with adultery, since it was to extract from them just such a confession that they had been (without result) put to the torture; the charge of conspiracy dumbfounded them. They knew they were condemned in advance, but supposing they had been in the mood to justify themselves they would, by being kept in ignorance, have had neither time nor means to prepare their defence.

Smeaton was the first to be interrogated. Not daring – because of lèse-majesté – plead "Not guilty", but in the vain hope of obtaining a judgement of mercy, he made haste to admit that he had kept to himself his knowledge of the crimes of which the queen and his fellow-prisoners were accused; then, strong in this avowal, he protested his innocence on all the rest. This piece of meanness did him no good; it merely deprived him of the little honour remaining to him without saving his life.

Weston, Norris and Bryerton were braver and also more clear-sighted. In defiance of the law and the judges they declared in turn their plea of "Not guilty". The most dire warnings did not make them shift their ground. What they were attempting, because they knew that their own fate was sealed, was at least to save the queen. They denied it all – adultery, con-spiracy – and declared themselves resolutely loyal to the king whose zealous servants they were. Then they listened without emotion to the supplementary charge of lèse-majesté, to the closing speech for the Crown and to their condemnation to death by unanimous decision of the jury.

But their denials remained embarrassing. To follow them by convicting the queen for adultery was enough to make more than one of those present raise their eyebrows, giving ground for suspecting the judges of mere obedience and want of in-tegrity. A suspension of the sitting at least was essential. The hearing was accordingly adjourned for two weeks: a delay that allowed Cromwell to take counsel with Norfolk on how to counter the effect that these denials were having on public opinion. They concluded that they must invest the proceedings against the queen with a peculiar solemnity. Anne should be judged not by a jury whose bias was plain to all, but by twice as many archbishops and peers of the realm, of whom some at least might be made to look as though they were honest.


Henry in any case needed this delay for reasons relating to the succession to the Crown. Failing a male progeny and with no certainty that Jane Seymour, if he married her, would give him a son, he had fallen back on his bastard the Duke of Rich-mond. But Parliament would allow this line of succession only if the daughter of Queen Anne were declared illegitimate. Now if there was one thing Henry did *not* want, it was to let it be thought that he was not the father of Elizabeth. She must therefore be the product of a marriage duly consummated but declared null and void just as his marriage with Catherine had been.

It remained to consider how. There were several ways. The first was to acknowledge that by marrying in Catherine's lifetime Henry had committed bigamy. But that would be to acknowledge also his bad faith in the matter of the divorce and to re-establish Mary in her legitimate rights.

Another way seemed possible. According to certain articles of canon law it appeared that to have taken for his mistress, before the marriage, the sister of his future bride – in this case, Mary Boleyn – established between Anne and Henry a degree of relationship which made their marriage an incest. One could then deduce the nullity of this union. But it would be too like the procedure employed for Catherine and the use of dubous means to get rid of Henry's *second* wife would revive the earlier scandal still very much in people's minds; it was not the moment for the king to expose himself to such comparisons.

What might have a better chance of succeeding would be to recall the former liaison of the queen with Percy, now Earl of Northumberland. The sentiments of the man once so devoted had changed and he had agreed to be one of the jury to condemn Anne. Henry therefore thought he would have no problem in persuading Percy to go back on his former oath and admit that between Anne and himself a promise of marriage had been exchanged. That Anne had concealed such a promise would convict her of perjury and so invalidate her union with the king.

One of Percy's best friends was sent to persuade him but the new earl was afraid that there might be some catch in what he was being asked to do and he held to his original declaration without altering a word.

As a last resort it remained to extract the same avowal out of Anne herself. The king summoned Cranmer, whose cleverness in time past had made possible the king's second marriage. He held out to the archbishop the prospect of a return to favour if he obtained from the prisoner an admission that she had concealed this promise of marriage and so had married Henry by trickery. As the price of this confession her life would be saved and she could take refuge with her daughter at Antwerp.

Pressed by Cranmer, Anne asked for time to think it over. The three ladies of honour and I begged her to consent. I soaked her hands with my tears but she would not make up her mind. When Kingston came to the rescue she asked him: "Is it possible that I could die unjustly?" To which he answered that "even the poorest subject of the king obtains justice". This drew from Anne a laugh which it hurt me to hear but her decision had been taken and no entreaty could persuade her to change it: "To leave English soil with Elizabeth upon such a confession would be," she repeated, "to deprive her of her rights." Then when I pointed out to her what small chance the child had of one day mounting the throne: "There are more chances than you think," she said. "And she alone, brought up by you, will be able to will what I have willed. If on the contrary I yield the place to Mary, you know as well as I do that she and Cromwell will bring England back into the bosom of the Church of Rome. I do not want to save my life at the cost of that."

When next day Cranmer came for her answer Anne met him with an obstinate refusal, which the archbishop in fear and trembling had to carry back to Henry. But he swore upon his honour – or his dishonour – that he would make it his business to annul the marriage in the same way as he had sealed it.

Next day Cranmer called together at his Lambeth residence six representatives of the Crown including the Duke of Suffolk and two so-called representatives of the queen – men whom she did not know. Then before this commission which had legal powers vested in it, Cranmer repeated, this time to Anne's detriment, the procedure by which three years earlier he had caused the marriage with Catherine to be annulled. Honest advocates would have discovered in this dubious process the opportunity for a bargain and staked the annulment against the life of Anne Boleyn. But if these "defenders" of the queen were to dare so to plead they must have been neither employers of the king nor men whose life depended on it. So they breathed not a word and thus Cranmer, to his eternal shame and without the need to make any equivalent concession, could solemnly declare null and void this marriage between Anne and Henry which he himself had consecrated.

Now that all obstacles to Henry's desires had been disposed of there was no need to hold up any longer the judgement and condemnation of the ex-queen Anne Boleyn. Even so, the king was afraid that if Anne were made to pass all the way through the city up to Westminster Hall she might excite in the course of the journey a wave of compassion for herself and of hostility to him. And it was the great hall in the Tower of London that he had fitted up for the tribunal.

# The Execution

What I have now to relate was like a nightmare to live through and it is as a nightmare that I remember it. Everyone has had, at least once in their lives, this painful sense of unreality. As though between outward things and yourself, between yourself and other people there were a sheet of glass that you can neither touch nor pass through. One is told that, in that same way, after death your soul can see the world going on without you. One is there and yet not there. Words, deeds, gestures are unrolled before your eyes as if they had no meaning.

What at this moment I was examining with the same far-distant eye was, at the end of a very large room, longer than it was broad, a platform hastily put up for the occasion where the judges sat behind a long table. Lit by thousands of candles, the room was as bright as daylight.

Norfolk, as Grand Seneschal, presided. At the foot of the dais a group of well-known people were bustling about; these I recognised without any sense of knowing them. Seated, getting up, walking about, coming back, sitting down again: the Lord Mayor of London was there, with aldermen and the heads of corporations around him. Behind their bench was the entire court, squashed together, sitting on other benches but no less restless. Finally, at the back, standing behind a barrier, a crowd of inquisitive folk of every description who had been queueing throughout the night.

The hall, while awaiting the spectacle, buzzed noisily. I had difficulty, I might add, in distinguishing this medley of chatterboxes from the mad rush of blood in my ears. I felt like a dog which, lying as still as a statue before a door, stares at it fixedly; time that seems never to move is a present that flows on and on. And when, breaking at last into this time that never moved, a door at the far end opened and Sir William Kingston appeared, preceded by an officer and followed by the queen, I did not know how long I had been waiting – for one minute or for eternity.

The queen was followed by her mother, by Lady Kingston, and by the executioner holding the iron of his axe symbolically turned away from her because she had not yet been judged. An armchair had been prepared for her but she preferred to remain standing. A deathly silence had fallen on the hall which sounded to me louder than the uproar that in an instant it had quelled; the beating of my blood was like hammer on anvil.

As to what happened after that I shall give you only its dry outline for in the state I was in I could make little sense of it at the time, and it was not till the session was over and I had recovered my spirits that I could put together in my mind – after a fashion – the incidents and the order in which they occurred.

The bill of indictment was first read out to the queen. In listening to it she did not shudder for even a moment. There followed two speeches for the prosecution; the first in the name of the kingdom by Christopher Hales, the second in the name of the king by Cromwell in person. The two vied with one another in taking up again the heads of the indictment, developing them in detail and matching them with irrefutable proofs.

The proof that she had committed incest with her brother was that often they would talk together by themselves in the same room.

The proof that she had committed adultery with Francis Weston was that on several occasions she had given him money, and the same for Smeaton and Norris.

The proof that she had poisoned Catherine of Aragon and contemplated a similar murder of Princess Mary was that Norris had received in addition lockets of gold for that purpose.

The proof that she had plotted against the Crown with Rochford, Weston, Norris, Smeaton and Bryerton was that she hated the king since she had been heard laughing with them about some of his doublets, his music or his poems.

After they had gone on to develop these proofs in detail the two prosecutors sat down and it was the queen's turn to speak. Despite the imminence of the danger threatening her, she refuted these "proofs" point by point with her habitual calm.

Certainly she had discussed political matters with her brother when there were no witnesses present; as she had likewise with Wolsey, Cromwell or Thomas Cranmer. Was anybody suspecting them?

Certainly, Francis Weston had received grants of money from her on several occasions, but no more and no less than the other gentlemen of her suite; or than the Bishops of Worcester and Salisbury or the Archbishop of Canterbury. Just as these worthy churchmen, with other gentlemen, had received the same from the king himself, without their being all for that reason suspected of ill conduct.

No doubt she had given Norris lockets of gold for a thousand services rendered. But had he ever had access to Catherine? And since when had people been poisoned with gold?

No doubt she had happened to laugh *in the presence* of the king but never *against* him; and she defied anyone to have been able to detect in her the slightest mockery of the king. The love and respect she entertained for the sovereign could not be refuted for an hour or a single minute.

All this was spoken in a voice so calm and eloquent that the members of the jury seemed perturbed. Hope revived in me, my spirits rose and I was mad enough to believe that the judges would allow themselves to be convinced, as certainly any honest man would have been. But alas! for those men it could never be a matter simply of being convinced. They were not there to decide whether Anne was guilty or not, nor upon what charges. They were there to condemn the queen to death, to suit the will of a ferocious king. After withdrawing to deliberate they came back promptly with the verdict he required. Immediately the executioner reversed the iron of his axe, with the cutting edge now towards the queen. Then Norfolk pronounced the sentence, that the one called Anne Boleyn, deposed from the throne, be either burnt alive or beheaded as the king in his benevolence might decide.

Anne was so fully expecting this sentence that she let no hint of fright escape her. She asked only for permission to say a few words: "The king gave me my royal title. He has taken it back. His will be done." She repeated several times that she was innocent and that, being so, she would meet death with serenity. The only deaths that saddened her were the ones which were to strike the four young men of high quality who were as innocent as she. She asked that prayers should be said on their behalf, adding that the king, as much as they, was in need of prayers for his salvation. Then with a sign that she had finished she let herself be taken back to her apartments in the Tower.

She had hardly gone out when ghastly cries were heard from where the judges were sitting. It was Henry Percy of Northumberland who was rolling on the floor, convulsed. I could not make out the wild words that came from him in a dreadful voice but I knew it would be his own shame that was sticking in his throat. He had to be carried out. But in my own desolation I could feel not the least pity for him.


To complete its task, all that remained for the tribunal was to condemn George Boleyn, Viscount Rochford. But the hearing had to be suspended for an hour since the terrible uncle Norfolk, perhaps like Percy overcome by a distracted conscience, had burst into tears. It took him a long time to calm down.

He was pale as he read out to his nephew the three charges against him in a husky voice: conspiracy, incest and a third which would be raised later. When the charges had been detailed, the accused was given leave to speak.

George was as certain as Anne had been of the inevitable outcome and he allowed himself the pleasure of being insolent. Conspiracy? Because with the queen he made fun of the king? No, he had never done that – but he might well have done it, considering the view he personally took of His Majesty's talents.

Incest? Because he had been many times closeted with his sister "with a guilty intention"? But, like her, he had been still more often closeted with Cranmer, Cromwell and even with the king, his relative; the jury must decide what intention there had been in that.

Since his first reply murmurs and stifled laughter had run through the audience, while those on the platform were showing signs of some alarm. After his second reply the laughter was less restrained and Cromwell in a voice of thunder had to call for silence. He proceeded to say that the third item of the bill of indictment could not be given in public. So it would be passed in a sealed envelope to George, who was forbidden to read it aloud. He likewise should give his answer in writing.

But at the pitch to which he had worked himself up George took not the least account of the ban and it was in a clear and distinct voice that he read out the lines accusing him of having publicly doubted that Elizabeth was the king's child, for the reason that His Majesty hardly seemed any longer in a condition to beget. It was what had been for years the murmur at Court and it put this terrible braggart in a rage. George made it quite clear that he disapproved such talk, whose effect would have been to cast doubt on the legitimacy of his niece; but the mere fact of his having dared to read out aloud any such accusation sent his audience almost into a panic. One expected lightning to strike, the ceiling to collapse. As for the jury, they got up hurriedly to withdraw and deliberate.

They were away for what seemed a long time. So much so that one could begin to wonder whether Rochford, having cleared himself on all the points of the indictment, might not finally be acquitted. While we waited, much money was bet on it. The fact is that these tortuous proceedings, these "proofs" which were no proofs, were coming to seem to public opinion more and more shady. Shadier still appeared the distress of a king who, with Anne only one step from death, was holding high festival on the Thames and making no secret of his joy.

This reprobation by the common people caused the lords and bishops grave embarrassment; they had to take note of it, which no doubt explains their long debates and hesitations. While there could have been no question, even for a moment, of their not condemning Anne to death without drawing on themselves the king's vengeance, they might have been tempted to show their impartiality by releasing Rochford and thus go some way to conciliating public opinion – and because the king was known to fear that opinion, earn his gratitude. But when Cromwell showed them a letter from Lady Rochford heaping charges on her husband, the last waverers had to strike their colours. So the jury came back with a verdict declaring Rochford guilty on all counts. Whereupon Norfolk, breaking his staff in two, got up and went out. It was the Marquis of Exeter who had to pronounce the sentence condemning George, like his sister, to be burnt alive or beheaded, according to the king's good pleasure. What's more, he should be thankful that in consideration of his rank he was spared being first disembowelled and drawn by four horses.

Before being taken back to his cell the condemned man asked to be allowed a final word to express a wish that his fortune, confiscated by the judgement for the profit of the Crown, should by the king's mercy go to pay his debts. The hearing then broke up.


On the morrow of the judgements of Anne Boleyn and her brother, the four gentlemen, Smeaton, Weston, Norris and Bryerton, were warned to hold themselves ready for their execution. I passed these horrible twenty-four hours in trying at least to save Francis Weston, whose rich family did everything they could to help me. I persuaded some foreign embassies to intervene but it was too late for any change. Weston, like his fellow-prisoners, was not even allowed to receive his mother nor anyone who loved him. He spent his last day in writing letters, begging Maggie to forget him, his wife to forgive him, his father to pay his debts and all to pray for him; the three others

276

wrote similar letters. After that they slept peacefully – all except Smeaton who, it seems, spent the night in his cell weeping and begging for mercy. In the morning, attended by a priest, they were conducted to the scaffold, one erected on Tower Green within the precincts of the fortress.

First to go up was George, Viscount Rochford. A massive crowd had gathered on Tower Hill from where, with a view over the wall, people could feast themselves on the spectacle. He was allowed to address them in a few words (on condition they were written out in advance, delivered to the governor and deposited in the archives). The condemned man knew only too well that he could not question the judgement nor proclaim to the crowd that he was innocent. Such an unwillingness to die according to the rules would no doubt have delivered him from the scaffold but would have handed him over instead to the horrific tortures from which the judges in their mercy had spared him. Not to mention that Henry had it in his power to avenge himself on all the other Boleyns, his mother, his sister Mary and a pretty cousin of whom George was fond. So he asked pardon for his crimes, cried out "God save the king" and then, simply requesting those present to pray for him, knelt down. In an instant his neck was cut through by the axe and his head rolled on the straw. It was the same with the four young men who followed him. But Smeaton struggled a little and force had to be used to make him kneel.

All this was told to me later. For I felt quite unable to be present at the executions. I was weeping bitterly in my room. I had besides to summon what little calmness remained to me so as to help in her last hours my unhappy friend whose memory was soon to become my one reason for staying alive.

I was with her when Kingston came to tell her that the execution would take place the next morning, the 17th of May. He assured her that she would suffer nothing: "It happens so quickly."

"I would like to see you in my place, Governor," she flung at him with a mocking smile. The governor was astonished by

277

this unexpected laugh, and I no less. Anne added that in fact the executioner would not need to strike hard: "I have so slender a nape," she said, still laughing, while she put her hands around it. More seriously, she went on to say that she would have preferred to die on the same scaffold as her brother so that she could have gone to Heaven with him. Affected more than he wished it to be seen, Kingston withdrew, leaving us for the first time, the queen, the ladies and myself, without surveillance. She could then take me aside and she spent part of the day talking to me about Elizabeth and my sacred task with her. With a solemnity that engraved the lesson on my heart, she charged me to keep repeating to Elizabeth (as Anne had done to me) that she must watch with the utmost care that nothing should under any pretext impair the independence of the Church of England, because the independence and power of our dear Albion were directly bound up with it; furthermore that neither the one nor the other would have the means to become strong and permanent except behind this rampart: command of the seas. Such was her testament.

Whereupon she fell to prayer and went on praying until far into the night. At dawn she had her gaoler, Kingston, summoned. With the authority of a queen she commanded him to be present when she received the sacraments. Her chaplain, Matthew Parker, brought them to her and before being given extreme unction she swore upon her soul's salvation and called God to witness that she had never keen unfaithful to the king; that her daughter Elizabeth was thus truly of the blood of the Tudors; and that it would be a wicked sacrilege for anyone to seek to call her illegitimate. She told Sir William Kingston that he would be a traitor to his own conscience if he did not bear witness to this that she was affirming upon her salvation, a witness of which the priest present would be the sacramental guarantor.

After that, she expected to be taken immediately to the scaffold. But the hours passed and no-one came to fetch her. I confess that I bore these infernal hours of waiting much less serenely than the condemned woman. She spent them, as on the evening before, talking cheerfully of various things, interrupted from time to time by prayers.

Towards the end of the day, Kingston came to tell her the reason for this delay: in a last mark of respect for the queen his wife, and Elizabeth's mother, the king had decided that she should be beheaded not by an axe – a humiliation and too often a butchery besides – (with one rather powerful neck the executioner once had to set about it six times!) – but more nobly and more surely by a sword. Now for this, a fairly heavy sword was required which the executioner neither possessed nor knew how to handle. So they had ordered from Calais an executioner from Picardy who had the necessary experience.

What Kingston did not say was that he also had been largely to blame. He could run his prison in an orderly way but he had a disorderly mind. He had forgotten to procure the black cloth for draping the scaffold; to have the coffin made to the queen's measurements, a coffin which ought to have been ready in the chapel of St Peter of the Fetters; and finally to draw up the list of those who would be present, limited to thirty, in such a way that no-one would be offended at not being invited. But of all these omissions which he had to put right in great haste during these extra twenty-four hours Kingston naturally said nothing, contenting himself with talking about the axe and the sword.

I should add that during these explanations Anne had never ceased smiling out of the corners of her mouth. Then with a suave irony she asked him if there had not been at that hour a crowd of people assembled for nothing on Tower Hill. Certainly, Kingston admitted, but they had been told to come back. "On what day and at what hour?" He replied that he himself would only be informed at the last moment. "That's it," she said; "so I shall not have any great number at my execution." And realising that the king was afraid of a reaction of the crowd in her favour she broke out again in ironic laughter. And to Kingston's further astonishment she joked in the gentlest way about those wonderfully ingenious persons who invent nicknames for anyone of importance and would have no problem about finding one for her – "Anne, the headless queen".

"No doubt," she added, "because they found that I had too much of a head for a woman."

Then, more seriously, she said again that she regretted the harshness of the treatment to which Princess Mary had been subjected; for inevitably Anne had felt compassion for this princess descended from so many royal kings. She begged Lady Kingston to pass on her regrets and to ask Mary's forgiveness. Later, when we were alone, she spoke to me again at length about Elizabeth and finally at nightfall she asked us to leave her with her chaplain. We withdrew into our rooms and she passed a part of the night in talk and prayer with him, snatching a little sleep from time to time. As much, that is to say, as the sound of carpenters' hammering would allow her (and us); for to stop the crowd on Tower Hill – supposing there were a crowd – from seeing the scaffold, one was being erected that was barely a foot high. Hence the appalling noise all night.

At sunrise Kingston came to warn us to get ready. Soon after, we joined the queen at the head of the spiral staircase, with Kingston and the chaplain leading the way. Anne was wearing a dress of grey wool, with a low neckline beneath her hair which had been gathered up into a chignon to make the decapitation easier. But she had not allowed her head-dress in the shape of a crescent moon to be removed: a head-dress that from her youth up I had seen her wear always, except on the day of her coronation.

She began to go down, ourselves following her. My companions had to hold me up all the way to the court of honour. There we found the scaffold, so low that you could not really see anything of it from Tower Hill. Inside the precincts the attendance was confined to Cromwell, Norfolk, Suffolk and a half-dozen of the king's counsellors, the Lord Mayor of London and a group of aldermen. A small number of courtiers – no foreigner among them – had been authorised to come through the gateway, which served as a barrier to keep the others out.

At the moment of crossing the threshold Anne stopped; whether she was agitated at seeing the executioner – all in red – beside the block on the scaffold and leaning on his heavy

280

sword I do not know, for she never showed it. The chaplain turned round to her and I saw her leaning forward to kiss – so they tell me, for she had her back to me – the little crucifix that was hanging on the priest's chest. They stayed like that for a moment; then with a firm step she went forward to the scaffold. Two assistant executioners helped her to mount it. Turning back, I noticed the white face of Thomas Wyatt at one of the Tower windows, his hands gripping the bars. It was a shattering sight and I scarcely heard Kingston tell the queen that she could address a few words to the spectators. She said she had not come there to preach but to die; she asked for prayers for the king, that excellent man who had treated her in the best possible way; she accused no-one of her death, not the judges nor the jury nor anyone else, since she had been condemned according to the laws of the kingdom. I understood that in saying this she wanted, like George before her, to protect her family, perhaps me and certainly Elizabeth. She asked finally that prayers should be said not so much for her as for her daughter, on whose behalf she implored the solicitude of all. Then turning to the executioner, she gave him the handful of crowns with which she had been supplied, as was customary, so that she should be reckoned as having paid him herself for his good offices. She asked him to do his work with firmness. He must have been much moved by this young queen and her calm courage, for he mumbled something that sounded like an apology.

Now Anne took off her half-moon head-dress and handed it to me with a smile. I burst into tears but turned round to hide them so as to remain worthy of her. One lady of honour blind-folded her eyes and we all four fell on our knees to pray. Among the spectators the men remained standing but all the ladies present knelt as we did. Then Anne knelt also; I hid my face in my hands; and all at once I heard the impact, dry and ghastly, of the heavy sword upon the block.

*

When the cannon-shot roused me from the fainting fit, which had lasted no more than a moment, Anne's pretty face was lying there close to me where it had rolled. Her eyes were open and she still had a smile on her lips. I seized this beloved head and pressed it so hard against my bosom that they had trouble in snatching it from me in order to show it to those present. And I was barely conscious as I helped the three others to join the head and the body together on a white sheet before wrapping them up. Four men brought a black coffin without handles or coat of arms, or ornament of any kind. The queen was laid there to rest and the lid nailed down with a hammer. The sound of the blows never ceased to reverberate in my ears.

Then the four men took the coffin away. No-one except Cromwell and Norfolk was allowed to follow it into the chapel. Under the stone slabs, then, in a corner apart, the Queen of England was buried in the most perfect anonymity; so that thereafter neither I nor anyone should know– in order that we might kneel and address our prayers to her – where Anne Boleyn was to lie to all eternity.

# After . . .

*It is true that they have stopped disputing about grace efficacious and sufficient and concomitant. But it is this very freedom of thought that has given birth among the English to so many first-rate books; it is because their minds have been enlightened that they have been daring; it is because they have been daring that their corn has traversed the seas; it is this liberty which has caused all the arts to flourish and has covered the ocean with ships.*

Voltaire

# Elizabeth

I am old now – past sixty – and perhaps I ought to have left you with that sinister image of a black coffin carried by those men in black: a coffin that two cruel enemies hid away in the darkness of a chapel so as to blot out any knowledge that this unhappy queen ever lived upon earth.

But that would be to betray this great figure to whom England owes so much. It would be to fail in my task if I were to bear witness only to her life, her honour, her unjust death: if I did not assign to her her due in the fine posthumous harvests of what she sowed during her reign but which the malice of men denies to her memory.

Here am I, the widow for many years of a good man of the nobility, whom Bloody Mary beheaded as she did so many others. It was a marriage of convenience, to which I resigned myself because after the death of Francis Weston and my long sorrow there was nothing left for me to live for, except my duties towards the young Elizabeth. Now, as it happened, my future husband was in a high position at Court and so my being there at his side would give me a better opportunity to watch over the princess. And thus to discharge to its full extent the solemn promise that I had made to Anne at the hour of her death.

I would rather say no more of the abominable Henry who, the moment the cannon-shot had announced his wife's death, went off at full gallop to the castle of Wolf Hall to throw himself at the feet of Jane Seymour. They were engaged the same day and a week later the marriage was celebrated – in the same chapel, without either shame or modesty, where the king had married Anne three years earlier.

But it is now twenty-five years since Anne died, and the king was to survive her for eleven, having had – as we know – four other wives after her: Jane Seymour, who gave him a son, Edward, and who died not long after the birth; Anne of Cleves, whom he disowned before the marriage was consummated; Catherine Howard, a niece of Norfolk – whom (after one year of union) he also caused to be put to death; finally, Catherine Parr, his sixth wife, who survived him but not without having come close to death a dozen times after fierce arguments arising out of her zeal for Luther's doctrines that went beyond what the king could tolerate.

But, to be honest, there were other matters on which I ought to do Henry justice: I ought to allow that Anne and I had underrated what, left to himself, he would do in the way of good – or ill – for England.

For, unlike the four queens who followed her, Anne's influence had been so strong on this undecided, malleable character that once engaged on the path that she had traced out Henry could pursue no other route. In supposing that as soon as the queen was dead he would cut the credits of the naval shipyards to squander them once more on his tastes for ceremonial and sumptuous festivities I was wrong. The happy results of a less skeleton-like fleet had come to be appreciated little by little – in commerce with Spain, Flanders, the Hanse, the Scandinavian countries, as also in dealings with France and the Empire – to such an extent that one so changeable as Henry could not fail to take note of the advantages it brought him. Despite several serious lapses – campaigns too costly or ill-prepared – he knew how to keep within the limits, and this time with perseverance, of the path Anne had traced out. When he died of an infected leg he left England more prosperous, enlarged by the inclusion of Wales and respected at sea. Albion was becoming the island Anne had wished for.

But after Henry's death I had to witness, with grief and anger, this dearly won independence catastrophically called into question under Mary, Catherine's daughter.

Remember first that Henry had disregarded Queen Anne's

oath at the time of her death, testifying to her innocence and fidelity to the king. Despite the chaplain's and Kingston's witness of that oath he lost no time in declaring his child Elizabeth illegitimate, so as to conjure away her rights in favour of his bastard the Duke of Richmond. Then after Jane Seymour had given the king a male heir, Edward, the question of the succession passed through ten years of troubles. When Edward came to the throne he was ten and his health precarious. The regency reverted to his uncle Seymour, Jane's brother, the Duke of Somerset, who was soon ousted and put to death by Lord Dudley, Earl of Warwick. Warwick's son had married Jane Grey, great-granddaughter (by the female line in each generation) of the old Henry* and he managed to persuade the young Edward to nominate her as heir to the throne.

The child-king died at the age of sixteen and although Elizabeth meantime had been re-established in her rights Mary had become re-established in hers too and with more support behind her was preferred above Elizabeth. She became queen and reigned for five years (1553–58). Bloody Mary was the name she quickly acquired. Her first care was to have the nine-day queen, Jane Grey, beheaded, and together with her the Dudleys, father and son; then, having quashed any challenge to her right to the Crown, she made haste, as Anne had feared, to bring England back into the bosom of the Church of Rome. She had numerous Protestants beheaded, or burnt at the stake, including – besides my poor husband – the unfortunate Cranmer. (Cromwell, sixteen years earlier, had been beheaded for having brought about Henry's marriage to Anne of Cleves, whom the king found ugly.)

But in marrying Philip II of Spain, Mary committed the fault of lining England up under the suzerainty of the emperor; then of letting her become involved in a ruinous war against France, in the course of which the last English territory on the Continent was lost ("If you open me at my death you will find *Calais* engraved on my heart"). This ranged against Mary the whole of public opinion, even that of her supporters.

* Henry VII.

286

Public sympathy reverted to Elizabeth, at that time in her early twenties. I had faithfully brought her up in the spirit of her mother's views, greatly helped by the lamented Thomas Wyatt, who had reared his son Thomas in the same ideas. That is why the young man, shocked by all the various doings of Bloody Mary, got together a band of gentlemen to overthrow her and put Elizabeth in her place. The revolt very nearly succeeded but it was put down in a torrent of blood. Wyatt and all his friends were beheaded, while Elizabeth, although she had not been personally involved, found herself back in the Tower of London. She would be there still if Mary had not died, to the relief and joy of all, leaving the crown at last to her half-sister.

She has been queen now for three years. She whom I think of as my ward has taken up the interrupted task again with a firm hand, as her mother had so intensely hoped; and she displays the same vigour, the same tenacity at governing.

But what set me off to write this book was that on one point I was at first cruelly disappointed. For I became aware to my extreme surprise of a strange silence in the daughter about the mother. From the start of her reign not once at Court, before her ministers or with diplomats, has Elizabeth pronounced the name of the one who brought her into the world. Not once paid homage to what she did, to what she and England owe her. As if Anne had never existed. Or as if, despite all that I had told her about her mother in the course of her childhood and adolescence, Elizabeth was ashamed of her. I felt no embarrassment at letting her know my mind and reproaching her for an unjust ingratitude. She kissed me and clasped me in her arms as one does an old nanny.

"You loved my mother," she said, "whom I hardly knew; make no doubt that I respect, that I admire her memory. I am not ungrateful But consider a little my origin, who I still am, and all the tribulations I have had to suffer. I am queen at last; but in the minds of many, of many lords, I remain the bastard of the concubine. Consider how insecure my rights still are: You have taught me my mother's great precept: 'Albion first,

287

gratitude and affection come after'. For the sake of England's greatness I must follow through the task my mother entrusted to me. I can do it only if I am solidly established on the throne. And for that, I must have the doubts about my birth forgotten. What better way than by silence? My mother would agree with me."

"For the greatness of Albion," I said sadly, "must the grandeur of Anne Boleyn go down in history as its opposite?"

"Re-establish it yourself," she told me with a kind of tender authority. "*You* are not held to the same discretion and if you will, you can – you *ought* – to make the noble truth known for the sake of posterity. But take care! I have many enemies. Your book might fall into their hands while I am still alive; they could allege that I had inspired you to write it. Say nothing, then, about yourself. Hide your identity."

At the hour when I finish this book – I took her word of caution as above all an encouragement to proceed – Elizabeth is already forcefully engaged on the work that her mother set in hand. And this is – come to think of it – filial love at its best. Like her mother, she has understood why the schism with Rome had to be and has re-established the spiritual supremacy of the sovereign throughout the land, putting an end to Bloody Mary's fanatic labours. Like her mother – who gave the Church of England vigour by nominating bishops at home in the new style: Latimer to Worcester, Barlow to St Asaph, Fox to Hereford, Saxton to Salisbury – she has understood the need for such elevations and devotion to a cherished memory inclines her to make Matthew Parker, Anne's loyal chaplain, Archbishop of Canterbury. Like her mother, she has understood how vital it has become to England's destiny to make of it an *English* island and to that end to impose the English language everywhere – at Court, in letters, at the theatre, in diplomacy. Like her mother, she has understood that nothing will be achieved without an indestructible independence of which the sole guarantee, whether by land or at sea, must be a formidable fleet. Within the means at her disposal she is already enlarging the number of her shipyards.

I am no seer and I cannot foretell the future. There are sure to be conspiracies whose outcome no-one can predict but they will have no easy ride. If they had little success against an uncertain, irresolute king I wager that under this hand of iron they will be doomed. Already here and there people are beginning to apply to Elizabeth the epithet "Great". That it is a sign there is no mistaking. And I like to imagine that from the place where she now is, my dear Anne Boleyn is overjoyed by what she sees.